An American Cakewalk

An American Cakewalk

Ten Syncopators of the Modern World

Zeese Papanikolas

Stanford University Press
Stanford, California

Stanford University Press
Stanford, California

"Cakewalk into Town" by Taj Mahal, copyright 1972 EMI Blackwood Music
Inc. & Big Toots Tunes. Reprinted with permission.

"Cake Walking Babies From Home" with lyrics by Clarence Williams,
C. Smith and H. Troy, as recorded in New York, January, 1925 by Clarence
Williams' Blue Five. Reprinted with permission.

Printed in the United States of America on acid-free, archival-quality paper

Library of Congress Cataloging-in-Publication Data

Papanikolas, Zeese, author.

 An American cakewalk: ten syncopators of the modern world / Zeese
Papanikolas.

 pages cm

 Includes bibliographical references and index.

 ISBN 978-0-8047-9199-1 (cloth : alk. paper)

 1. United States—Intellectual life—19th century. 2. United States—
Intellectual life—20th century. 3. Authors, American—Biography.
4. Artists—United States—Biography. 5. Intellectuals—United States—
Biography. 6. United States—Biography. I. Title.

 E169.1.P214 2015

 973.5—dc23

 2014041548

 ISBN 978-0-8047-9539-5 (electronic)

Typeset by Bruce Lundquist in 10/14 Janson Text

For Ruth

I had the Blues so bad one time
It put my face in a permanent frown
Now I'm feelin' so much better
I could cakewalk into town.

—Taj Mahal

Contents

An American Cakewalk

Introduction

This book was stimulated by my reading, many years ago, in the pages of *Esquire*, an offhand comment from the ever-fertile James Baldwin that black style was often (or did he say always?) a parody of white style. In the one example I remember, Baldwin noted, in those days of cool, that if a white man was wearing a coat with three buttons, a hip black man was sure to be wearing a coat with four. Something about that struck me, and this book is in large part an attempt to understand the reason for that kind of style. What aesthetic forms did it create? What did it try to speak to and what was the message? For in a country as new and various as the United States, at any given moment the cultural nucleus might be far less sharply defined than the numberless particles circling in sparks around it. So I began to extend my thinking to a range of American artists and philosophers whose work might from one point of view or another be seen to make its way by glancing off the predominant culture, or who themselves seemed to exist in some kind of space between worlds, like Native American shamans restlessly inhabiting the territory between the living and the dead, between the old world and the new, figures whose very poignancy and strength lay in their failure to be fully one thing or another.

In 1787 Thomas Jefferson envisioned an America whose democratic values were in the particular keeping of its independent tillers of the soil.

> Those who labour in the earth are the chosen people of God, if ever he had a chosen people, whose breasts he has made his peculiar deposit for substantial and genuine virtue. It is the focus in which he keeps alive that sacred fire, which otherwise might escape from the face of the earth.

"While we have land to labour then," he wrote, "let us never wish to see our citizens occupied at a work-bench, or twirling a distaff."[1] One hundred years later, in the years of violence and wrenching change that began with the Civil War, cities Jefferson had not even dreamed of were filled with workbenches and spinning distaffs powered by steam. The Indians to whom he styled himself a father were crowded into bleak reservations; the descendants of the slaves who had worked his fields and waited on him at his table—some of whom bore his blood—were now embarked on an uncertain freedom; and women, many of whom were much like his daughters, were beginning to demand the equality called up by the "self-evident truths" of the Declaration of Independence he had penned. The old verities America had lived by, its Enlightenment and transcendental values, its religious faith, seemed to have little place in this new world of factories and railroads and streets swarming with the polyglot mob which Jefferson had feared as democracy's greatest threat.

Women, Indians and African Americans, immigrants and expatriates, the marginalized and disaffected, what country had they? For they, the ex-slaves and the Indians, the cloistered women, the Europeanized expatriates and the impoverished immigrants—that shadowy side of America's imagination, the unexpressed doubts or nightmares that might have lain under its old assertions—they were Jefferson's children too. The forms they might adopt to live among their fellow Americans in this new era, the dodges and evasions they might practice in order to carve out a space of identity and freedom, are the subject of this book.

All great creators in some sense lie athwart their culture's values. In the period I begin with there was already an American vanguard of writers who stood out by their direct challenge to the prevailing currents: Whitman, of course, in his style and often subject, if not his politics; Hawthorne, who as Melville famously claimed cried no in thunder to his culture; Melville himself, perhaps the most complicated and complete naysayer; that most hardheaded of nature lovers, Henry David Thoreau, and that strange, poisonous little hothouse *fleur du mal*, Edgar Allan Poe. But the artists and thinkers I've selected to write about expressed their opposition more indirectly. They neither collided head on with their culture nor surrendered to it—rather they slipped aside from it as it brushed by, lived in their art and works and persons a glancing life. Like the sequestered New England woman we shall soon come to, they told their truths but told them slant.

For Mikhail Bakhtin, the profound Russian critic, the novel was a literary form unlike any others, for it spoke not in one voice but in many, the voices of classes and castes, of regions and dialects, all creating, by what he called their "dialogic" relation, a constant interaction. Bakhtin's novel was a work that was not a static piece of art, frozen in time, but a reflection of the complex workings of culture itself, a social mirror of a living world that was always in and of history.[2] But well before Bakhtin (and before the Structuralists, and the Post-structuralists, and the Frankfurt School) an American we will come upon in the fourth chapter of this book was developing ways of understanding the symbolic nature of our world and its workings. Charles Sanders Peirce, mathematician, philosopher, and many things else, had worked out an ingenious tripartite theory of the cultural transmission of symbols that grounded itself in the living experience of the process itself. Thirty years later, but still in advance of most of his European counterparts, another American Singular, Thorstein Veblen, was showing these symbols at work in the signs and rituals of social stratification. Genius knows no country, of course, but in a nation as new, as culturally, politically, and ethnically diverse as the United States, a country moreover so recently riven by a brutal civil war that had exposed so many of these divisions, there is a particular sharpness, an aptness, to such investigations. For—to return to Bakhtin—the country itself might be seen as a living and breathing novel, a many-tongued, many-sided work in progress.

The figures I write about here are a heterogeneous lot. What links them is their particular sensitivity to and quite conscious exploitation of the cultural symbols that they were inheritors of and the social nature of their position between two worlds. Working in isolation, or among a small group of their fellows, they created ways of being and expression that were neither crushed in open conflict with this new world of accumulation and sensual strangulation they found themselves in nor forced to surrender to it, but used their manipulation of its presumptions to create an alternative aesthetic and intellectual space. If they chafed against a culture they had fled, they were failures in becoming part of any other, and made of this failure their particular art. Like the New England woman writing poems that mostly lay in a drawer unread by anyone, or the philosopher freezing in an unfinished mansion that only parodied the mansion of ideas he was constructing in his mind, they were eccentrics in the deepest and most beautiful sense of the word, turning in orbits that sometimes intersected but never quite coincided with those of their peers. They were composers and dancers, poets and thinkers, yet had in common a singular ability to register their cultural moment. They were discoverers of the symbols and codes that animated and constrained their intellectual and social worlds, and they learned how to name them and how to use them for other surprising and sometimes subversive ends. They were survivors of the nineteenth century and its contradictions, and hailed and created the twentieth century and our own. Decentered, wily, marginal, wedged between the clamor of Triumph and the cry of Tragedy, they carved out a space neither tragic nor comedic, but something of both. Heads cocked to one side, they neither joined the triumphal march of a dominant culture nor threw themselves headlong against it.

.   .   .

The forms and the theaters of this resistance might be emblematized by the rise of a strangely ritualized performance by African Americans that Mark Twain saw—or imagined he saw—sometime in the 1890s.

It was, as Twain described it, a competition in elegant deportment in which, in a hired hall, elaborately dressed couples marched back and forth down the length of the room before a jury and perhaps five hundred spectators.

> All that the competitor knows of fine airs and graces he throws into his carriage, all that he knows of seductive expression he throws into his countenance.

Here follows in Twain's account a catalogue of empty grace notes: "watch-chain to twirl with his fingers, cane to do graceful things with, snowy handkerchief to flourish and get artful effects out of, shiny new stovepipe hat to assist in his courtly bows." The "colored lady" also has her accoutrements, perhaps a fan "to work up *her* effects with, and smile over and blush behind." The parade of individual couples ends and a review of all the contestants in procession commences, "with all the airs and graces and all the bowings and smirkings on exhibition at once." It has been a contest of surfaces, of pretenses, an elaborate playacting. The final review enables the panel of experts to make their comparisons and deliver their decision and the prize, "with an abundance of applause and envy along with it." "The negroes," Twain concludes, "have a name for this grave deportment tournament; a name taken from the prize contended for. They call it a Cake-Walk"[3] [fig. 1].

We see them, these cakewalkers, in old photogravures and engravings, grossly caricatured sometimes but also with their pride and elegance made emphatic, the men with their shoulders back, the leader raising his beribboned cane like the staff of a laughing hierophant, silk hats tilted to one side, the women lovely and saucy—some have appropriated their partner's hat and cane and parade them with a fine wit (a satire within a satire?). Prancing to a new music whose syncopations had just now begun to spread beyond the confines of African American life, the cakewalkers are full of the ebullience of life. Better than almost anyone else in white America at the turn of the last century, the author of *Pudd'nhead Wilson* knew that race was a fiction built on a bad joke. Yet for Mark Twain, employing it in a send-up of the affectations of bad Victorian prose, the cakewalk was a vacuous parade of social inanities. An empty vessel. For the cakewalkers, the vessel was overflowing. Strutting and fluttering, they had come to a truth lying slantwise to white America, a truth that created a breathing room in the suffocations of the narrow space that a racialized society had made for them, a kind of aristocracy of the spirit in a democracy, for those outside it, that offered only opprobrium or silence.

Figure 1. H. M. Pettit, "Close Competition at the Cake-Walk. A Popular Diversion of the Colored People in Which Many White Persons Manifest Great Interest," *Leslie's Weekly*, January 5, 1899.

Some of the denizens of this book were connoisseurs of cakewalks, some wrote music to accompany them, or like Twain simply observed them. Still others wouldn't have even known what a cakewalk was, but all of them, in their own way, responded to this nation of contending castes and classes, races and ideologies, by treading a subtle and symbolically laden dance. Like the shaman, they were experts in the manipulation of signs and languages, dancers between two worlds. Bowing and doffing, flirting and fluttering behind fans and ribbon-decked canes, the cakewalkers marched and strutted and once were joined, quite surprisingly, by a quasi-American who descended from his lofty perch to join the dance. We will come to Henry James in due course. But we might remember, as a kind of motto for this book, his words to a friend. "It is by style," he wrote, "we are saved."[4]

Chapter 1
Ghost Dance

The curing of a sick soul is a complicated and dangerous process. Often the shaman, the great doctor, must die a kind of spiritual death himself, must go on his own dark journey to bring back the soul that has lost its way. In 1870, about the time of his twenty-eighth birthday, William James suffered his own dark night of the soul. He had been in a state of general depression and philosophic pessimism. Then one evening, he went into a dressing room to retrieve some item.

> Suddenly there fell upon me without any warning, just as if it came out of the darkness, a horrible fear of my own existence. Simultaneously there arose in my mind the image of an epileptic patient whom I had seen in the asylum, a black-haired youth with greenish skin, entirely idiotic, who used to sit all day on one of the benches, or rather shelves against the wall, with his knees drawn up against his chin, and the coarse gray undershirt, which was his only garment, drawn over them inclosing his entire figure. He sat there like a sort of sculptured Egyptian cat or Peruvian mummy, moving nothing but his black eyes and looking absolutely non-human.

The image and James's own fear "entered into a species of combination with each other." The thought was horrible. Nothing James possessed, not his intellect, not his training, not his social position, could defend him against such a fate should the hour for it strike as it had struck the idiot boy. Under everything, he thought, *"that shape am I."*[1]

The vision gradually faded. Yet while its effects lasted James wondered how other people could live, how he himself had ever lived, so unconscious of the pit beneath the surface of life.

William James, who had experienced the terrifying vision of his own potential nullity, was responding not only to his own crisis of vocation, but to a world whose religious foundations and intellectual assumptions had been shattered by steam and capital, by the end of a culture built on villages and age-old rural traditions, shattered by Darwin and by violence and mass migration. Cultures in states of anxiety, finding their old systems of meaning challenged beyond their capacities to incorporate new historical and social situations, either create new mythologies or invest the old ones with new meanings. New messiahs arrive, bearing in their teachings, in their histories if not in their very bodies, the solutions to these contradictions, the language that will speak these new mythologies.

As in the curing of the sick soul, the curing of the soul of a culture involves the translation of reality into a set of symbols, a narrative which the patient, the doctor, the community of souls themselves all accept, a tacitly and often unconscious agreed-upon fiction of representation.[2] Like William James, the intellectuals of post–Civil War white America keenly felt the contradictions of their society, felt themselves increasingly marginalized in an age of money and power. They were the shamans who were entrusted with the burden of creating the new mythology or the saving rejuvenation of the old symbols.

The power of science alone could offer little comfort to those caught up in the spiritual crisis of the age. Indeed, it offered only its own terrors. "Fed on recent cosmological speculations," James wrote, "mankind is in a position similar to that of a set of people living on a frozen lake,

> surrounded by cliffs over which there is no escape, yet knowing that little by little the ice is melting, and the inevitable day drawing near when the last film of it will disappear, and to be drowned ignominiously will be the human creature's portion. The merrier the skating, the warmer and more sparkling the sun by day, and the ruddier the bonfires at night, the more poignant the sadness with which one must take in the meaning of the total situation.[3]

Twenty-some years after William James's horrible vision, in an isolated valley of the Great Basin among villages of reeds and sagebrush, in a world that was crumbling more profoundly and for many of the same reasons as that of James, another man was undergoing such a crisis of the spirit.

The Prophet

On New Year's Day in 1889, in the midst of an eclipse of the sun, a Paiute Indian, named Wovoka—Woodcutter—lay dying. As a young man Wovoka lived with a white rancher and learned the hymns and prayers of a Presbyterian house. But Wovoka's father had been a shaman, an unassimilated Paiute, and Wovoka, like many Indians in those days, lived in two worlds. As he lay sick with fever, and near death, he heard a great noise. He imagined he had gone to heaven, to the green place beyond the Dusty Path that white men called the Milky Way. God took him by the hand and showed him the people of heaven, white and red both, and they were all young, for when they died God had made them young again. There the people stayed, in that place where the meadows were always green, dancing, gambling, playing ball and the other old Indian games, among all the different kinds of animals that were good to hunt and beside rivers that were full of fish. Wovoka saw his own mother there, and many others that he had known on earth. Then God told Wovoka that he would give him great power and the authority to cause it to rain or snow and to do many other things. And God gave Wovoka dances and told him that on his return to earth he must teach these dances to his people and that they must meet often and dance five nights in succession. And God said that he must tell all the people that they must not fight, that there must be peace all over the world, and that the people must not steal from one another, but be good to each other, for they were all brothers.[4]

Thirty years before that dream, the Indians of that far-western basin suffered their last defeat at the hands of the whites. Now, traveling through the sparsely peopled desert land, a person would see in isolated spots at the edge of the few lakes or along the streams, or huddled beyond the hayfields of the ranches, or at the edges of the railroad and mining towns, or on bleak reservations, the Indians' tule lodges and brush windbreaks or the shacks made of scavenged boards and stained canvas and flattened tin cans. These were the homes of Paiute, Shoshone, Bannock. By the 1870s the Indians had become workers in the fields and houses of the white invaders, laundering, cooking, irrigating the fields, making hay, herding cattle and sheep. The streams they lived along had been poisoned by the effluents of the mines and mills, diverted to irrigate fields of wheat and alfalfa in valleys where once they had harvested seeds and crickets and held huge rabbit drives. The salmon no longer came upstream to spawn, the piñon forests whose nuts they gathered in the fall had been cut down to fuel the charcoal kilns of the silver mines. In late summer the Indians gathered to do the old harvest dance and to ride boxcars over the mountains to Oregon and California to pick hops. They spent the money they earned on white men's clothing—rough denim pants and canvas jackets, broad-brimmed hats, shapeless cotton dresses and colored bandanas. Many still slept on the bare dirt floors of their rush houses. These were the people out of whom Wovoka sprang and to whom he gave his vision and the dances he learned in the spirit land.

Years before Wovoka, when the whites first came to the desert valleys, there had been another dreamer, a shaman named Wodziwob, whom the whites called Fish Lake Joe. He too had dreamed such a dream, and had instituted such a dance. When he was old, Wodziwob decided to travel back to the land he had seen in his dream one last time. He sent his mind to the Land of the Dead, but he discovered there only a shadow world, not a green land of abundance. There were no flowers, no game, no dead ancestors restored to their strength and youth. He called out to the shadows but there was no answer. Then Owl responded, blinked his blank stare, and turned away. Wodziwob lived on, but he no longer believed in his dream.[5]

These were years of great trial for all Indian peoples in the West. The Apache, the Nez Perce, the Cheyenne, the Sioux had all suffered final defeats and were now on reservations. The Homestead Act of 1862 opened their lands to settlement. Those vast tracts of prairie and desert range on which bands of hunters and women with gathering baskets and digging sticks once roamed with the seasons, white men in Washington now deemed "surplus" and offered for sale to other white men—farmers and ranchers and speculators. The passage of the Dawes Act in 1887 was the final defeat of a way of life: henceforth Indians were to hold their land in individual allotments like white men, farming them like white men. In the white men's plans the tribes were to dwindle away, become mere legal fictions, and Indian children would learn to sit in school like white boys and girls and to sing Christian hymns in churches.

On the Sioux reservations of the Dakotas conditions were particularly bad. Many of the Sioux—the Lakota, as they called themselves—had only lately come down from Canada to surrender themselves to reservation life. They still smarted under their defeat and tried to defy the breaking up of their land or raised futile obstacles. Drought had ruined their poor crops and the government reduced their beef ration—two million pounds at Rosebud, a million at Pine Ridge, less elsewhere. In the rough wood cabins and stained canvas teepees along the Grand and the Missouri, along Cedar

Creek and the Cannonball and the White River and on the Rosebud, it was a starving time.

A Cheyenne named Wooden Leg remembered how fourteen years before, on a stream the Indians called the Greasy Grass and the whites the Little Bighorn, he had gone among the dead soldiers of George Armstrong Custer's command and found in the pockets of the corpses wads of green paper. He had not known what they were until another Indian explained it was money, and that you could take it to the traders and buy things with it. Other Indians had found ticking pocket watches and compasses whose arrows pointed always to the north. They thought these must have been the soldiers' medicines. Now in bleak military forts and on starving reservations these same Indians heard the tolling of bells in churches and schoolhouses and the brass calls of trumpets that jumped to the white men's clocks. They knew what money was, and the women made fancy beaded pouches to hold ration tickets, pouches of the sort a man might once have worn to keep a charm for love or gambling or war. The old medicine bundles had become lost, their contents dispersed from disuse. The children were taken, sometimes by force, to the Indian schools and the Indians sat in mission chapels. The Lakota had become a sedentary people.

The great hunts were over. The buffalo herds had been systematically exterminated by railroad builders and soldiers. Now the people's meat was given to them by the government and on ration day braves on horseback whooped and hollered as they chased some cow or steer cut loose from the chute at the agency. There was no sun dance. The young men, those who were not hardened against the whites, aspired to wear the tunics and buttons of the agency police.

In the winter of 1889 a group of Lakota went out from their reservation to find out the truth about the Indian prophet they heard had risen up beyond the Rocky Mountains. Not much is known of their trip, but a year later, in the winter of 1889–1890, a second Lakota delegation went west. They traveled by train on their Indian passes to Mason Valley, in western Nevada, where they found other Indians gathered to hear the Prophet. There they saw the man the Indians called Wovoka, or Woodcutter, and the whites, Jack Wilson. He was a tall man, an imposing man, and he had done much magic. Once, they heard tell, he made ice come out of the sky on a clear summer day; another time, on a rabbit hunt, an Indian had shot at him and the bullet had fallen from his clothing harmlessly onto the ground. He was a weather prophet, a visionary who had had a great dream with glad tidings for all the Indian people.

The Prophet gave the Lakotas paints and green grass and told them that he had gone to the white people, but they had killed him—you could see the marks of the wounds on his feet and hand and back. Then he had gone to the Indians. He told the Lakotas that there would be a new land coming. It would slide over the old land and any Indian who sided with the whites would be covered by it. In the spring, when the grass became green, the dead would return, for the Indians would have heeded the Prophet's call.

That winter the dances began. The Arapaho were the first to dance for the ghosts to return as the Prophet had taught them. Now many Lakota were dancing too. The men and women held hands and shuffled in a great circle, singing as they danced. Dust rose from the dancing grounds and they sang the Ghost Dance songs.

> Father, have pity on me.
> Father, have pity on me.
> I am crying for thirst.
> I am crying for thirst.
> All is gone—I have nothing to eat.
> All is gone—I have nothing to eat.

They danced for hours, until they dropped with exhaustion, their skins slick with perspiration. Some foamed at the mouth. They said they had died, and in the trance of death they saw visions. They saw the new green earth and the eagle that was coming to carry them away to where the Prophet was with the ghosts.

> The spirit host is advancing, they say.
> The spirit host is advancing, they say.
> They are coming with the buffalo, they say.
> They are coming with the buffalo, they say.

They sang:

> We shall live again.

With the arrival of the dance and the promise of the coming spring, the old ways began to revive. Medicine bundles long out of use came out of their storage places and the magic paraphernalia—the feathers and sacred paint and stones, the bone whistles—were gathered and restored. As if in a foretaste of the Prophet's promise of paradise, the old games revived too, and once more the Pawnee were gambling, playing the hand game, now to gain not wealth but spiritual strength, to determine who would be saved. In their log shacks and canvas teepees, the women made shirts and dresses of white muslin for the dance and painted them with pictures of the sacred eagle and other images from their visions. Some of the shirts were peppered with holes to indicate the marks of the bullets that could not penetrate them. The shirts made the wearers invulnerable.

On the reservations the Indian agents grew alarmed at the dancing. They called for troops and ordered the dance suppressed. Frederic Remington, the artist friend of Theodore Roosevelt and Owen Wister, was a great believer in the Indians—as picturesque savages. At Pine Ridge on the morning of the nineteenth of November there were three troops: one hundred seventy men of the Ninth Cavalry—the black cavalry men the Indians called the "Buffalo Soldiers"—and two hundred infantrymen with a Hotchkiss cannon and a Gatling gun. At Rosebud there were one hundred ten Buffalo Soldiers and one hundred twenty infantrymen with a Hotchkiss gun. More troops were yet to come, four companies of the Second Infantry, another troop of the Ninth Cavalry, and the entire Seventh Cavalry, Custer's old regiment, accompanied by Light Battery E of the First Artillery, with more soldiers on the way.

On December fifteenth, Indian police tried to arrest Sitting Bull at his cabin on the north bank of the Grand River. Once he had been a warrior, a shaman, and a political leader of such exceptional skills that for a few years he had forged a great federation of tribes that had never known any but the most temporary and local leadership. But now this man, Tatanka-Iyotanka—Sitting Bull—had become a farmer on the Standing Rock Reservation around Fort Yates. When he heard of the Prophet's words, Tatanka-Iyotanka established a dance circle on his land, with a ring of brush shelters and a sacred prayer tree. One day he went out to the prairie to tend to his horses. He heard a meadowlark calling him. The meadowlark spoke his own language. "Lakotas will kill you," the meadowlark said.

In the fight to apprehend him four of the police were killed outright and two more would soon die of their wounds. Eight of Sitting Bull's followers were killed, including his teenaged son, and over Sitting Bull himself, dead of a bullet in the chest, his wives raised a great howl of rage and woe. The body of the great chief was taken to the agency, thrown into a hole, and covered in quicklime.

Wounded Knee

> Not that the Red Indian will ever possess the broad lands of America.
> At least I presume not. But his ghost will.
>
> —D. H. Lawrence

After the battle was over, a photographer came out to Wounded Knee Creek and set up his tripod. In the three days since the massacre, a blizzard had driven across the prairie. Where there had stood the rows of the white and brown tents of the army and the grimy canvas teepees of the Miniconjou, now there were only bent willow frames and shattered poles. The corpses of the dead Indians lay under the mounds of snow like wheat raked into windrows. In the center of the field four men lay together. One of them had fallen face down. The photographer turned him over. The dead man's arms were frozen stiff, the fists clenched. Someone laid a rifle next to the corpse for the sake of the picture. Later on, when he touched up the plate for sale, the photographer would paint over the exposed genitals of the dead man.

Down in the ravine, where fleeing Miniconjous had been trapped, there were more bodies—men, women, children—shot to pieces by the cavalry's Springfields and the Hotchkiss cannons. The agency doctor found an old woman, blind, helpless, under a wagon. He came across a four-month-old girl lying beside her dead mother under a hummock of snow. The girl was still alive, barely frostbitten. On her head was a cap beaded with the American flag. Chief Big Foot lay where he had died, his head wrapped in a scarf, his arms pushed back as if by the blows of the bullets that had killed him. When the fighting started he had already been dying, wracked with pneumonia. The photographer framed the dead chief in the midst of the snowy field, opened the shutter of the camera, and moved on. His partner, the agency barber, went among the corpses, stripping the dead of moccasins, beaded ornaments, the painted ghost shirts the Indians believed would protect them from the soldiers' bullets. At the edge of a mass pit that had been dynamited in the frozen ground, the corpses lay heaped up, their limbs stiff and contorted. It was here that the photographer posed the burial crew. His shadow fell across the steep side of the grave.[6]

The battle of Wounded Knee Creek had lasted an hour. For another hour along the creek shooting had continued here and there. Then the last great resistance against the whites was finished.

The revolt of the Ghost Dancers ended where all Indian revolts ended—where the Wampanoag's and the Shawnee Prophet's and the Nez Perce's and the Apache's had—in utter defeat. The last great uprising of what was old and powerful and primitive, of what stood in the way of the great engine of American progress, had been snuffed out. In the Great Basin, isolated bands of Indians strove to continue their old communal life and migratory patterns until, in 1911, the last of them was shot to pieces by a Nevada posse.[7] The Indian pueblos of New Mexico, their own history of failed revolt against the Spaniards long past, and situated in desert land no one else much wanted, simply did their best to ignore the white world that surrounded them and to continue their intense ritual life. But on the Great Plains the resistance only appeared to be finished. It had simply taken other forms. It had moved from the battlefields in canyons and snowy plains to the realms of the mind. Henceforth, it would be played out in the Indian imagination. For this is the remarkable thing: the Ghost Dance songs continued to be sung in the meetings of the Indians. They entered the realm of the purely symbolic. The songs were still there, and the ghosts were there too.

Jack Wilson lived on long after Wounded Knee. He lived through the first flight of an airplane, and Picasso's *Demoiselles d'Avignon*. He lived through the Great War and the Treaty of Versailles. He lived through Prohibition, and women's suffrage. He lived into the heart of the Great Depression when Okies crossed the great desert in Model T Fords on the way to an imaginary California. He lived on, in Nevada. He continued as a healer and shaman and sent packets of red pigment and the feathers of eagles and magpies and even his broad-brimmed Stetsons as magical artifacts to Indians who wrote him from all over the West. Sometimes he charged five dollars, sometimes twenty. It was his living. In the movie theater at Yerington he saw a lantern slide of his face projected on the screen before the show; it was a kind of white man's joke on a local celebrity and in the darkness he watched the black-and-white horses gallop across the screen. But what was this white man's cleverness to someone who had died and gone to heaven and seen the ghosts of his ancestors? And in fact, when the limousine that had brought him across the state line to watch Tim McCoy filming some horse opera was about to take him home, he told the cowboy star, "I will never die." For many years after that, and perhaps even now, he has not really died. The songs he inspired are still sung, because they had never been so much about what would come as about the human imagination's capacity to reorder the world.

Amidst the despair and privation of the end of the old life the Indians themselves refused to surrender to the role of victimhood, to be fabrications of white guilt or white sentimentality as they refused to be fabricated savages. For scholar and novelist Gerald Vizenor, the term *Indian* itself (always spelled in his work with a lowercase *i*) is a white simulation, the sign of an absence. "The *indian*" says Vizenor, "has no native ancestors." For all that remains and that remains to be created by the native peoples of this continent he is forced to coin a new term: not *survival* but—and like all neologisms it clangs on the unaccustomed ear—*survivance*, an "active repudiation of dominance, tragedy, and victimry."[8] The motive force of this repudiation is found deep in what makes us human, the art of play.

For the shaman who takes upon himself the dangerous journey to the other world to bring back souls besotted by death is not only a soul-catcher, but a trickster as well. Fated to suffer the loneliness of exile from the daily world, he is a sideways person, an artist of the world of possibilities. Dancing on the borders of society, he is the hunchback, the crazy man, the sacred transvestite, drunk with sex or celibacy, a visionary and jester, a quack and a magician. Just so the shaman dances on the borders of the spirit world as well. He walks among the shadows of the dead, but he teaches us how to live. If he dances alone, he has following in his train an invisible community, for he leads us to the places between the world we find and the world we desire, where we can live and dance.

The Year 1890

In the years after the trauma of the Civil War that collection of cultural assumptions and their symbolic representations which the anthropologist Dan Sperber calls a "community of interest" was, in the United States, falling apart. The Civil War had been in part an expression of a process of economic rationalization, an industrial war fought for railheads and steamboat landings on inland waterways and ports along the coast. It was a war of material production and the vast and careless use of men in bloody carnage. When it concluded, the great moral sore in America, the slave system of the South, had been expunged; but the country had not been healed by that, nor by that other war which had been raging since the third or fourth decade of the nineteenth century, that industrial war of attrition which had eaten up village by village and farm by farm the old Jeffersonian vision of a pastoral and independent America.

Twenty-three years after the end of the Civil War, in 1888, in the holy city of Concord, Massachusetts, Amos Bronson Alcott, friend of Emerson and Thoreau, of Brownson and Ripley and Margaret Fuller, and more uneasily of the elder Henry James, died the death of the flesh. The New England of Alcott's youth was dying too. Concord was a museum, Walden an accident; more typical were the factories on Fall River, with their whirling spindles and their time clocks and the constraints and disciplines that were molding the new America, an America no longer of small towns and farms, but of metropolises that pulled American lives together in great webs of economic complicity. Against the cannons of Gettysburg and the clamor of the industrial world, against the awful specter of class warfare in cities and mines and factories and the growing control of economic life in this country by increasingly remote and ruthless corporations, the spiritual language of transcendentalism, the language of Hegel and Kant as it passed through Emerson and Channing, had turned into a kind of dim gibberish; nor had the language of science, the language of Darwin and Lyell, provided any acceptable substitute, any cure for the doubt and anxiety and fear that seemed to lie just under the strident optimism of the Gilded Age and its myth of Progress.

The year 1890, which saw the publication of William James's *Principles of Psychology*, and which ended with the massacre of the Ghost Dancers at Wounded Knee, contained in itself enough of the emblematic events of the Gilded Age to stand for all that era's contradictions. The Civil War's end led to the linking of the steel rails that were the very emblem of the Soul Journey linking East to West which concluded the long pilgrimage back to primal Eden that Walt Whitman had embarked upon in his imagination so many times. Those same rails led to the termination of a kind of mental frontier in the mind of white America. In 1890, the supervisor of the federal census looking over his reports, found that there were no more major tracts of land available for white settlement and declared the frontier finally closed. Now that that imaginary territory of virgin land no longer existed, the transcendent purpose white America imagined as its vocation would turn in upon itself and find expression in towering cities and the violence of foreign and industrial war.[9]

That same year brought into the Union the frontier territories of Idaho and Wyoming—this last a state, it should be noted, where women had the vote. In that year New York City saw its first moving picture and Chicago the first entirely steel-framed building. William Dean Howells published *A Hazard of New Fortunes*, whose title tells much of its purview, and Ignatius L. Donnelly his disturbing novel of an oligarchic dystopia, *Caesar's Column*. The records of the United States Immigration Service show that in 1890 9,249,547 immigrants entered the United States. In 1890 Jacob Riis published his shocking book of photographs of urban poverty, *How the Other Half Lives*. In those same tenements another immigrant, a Jewish anarchist from Vilnius named Abraham Cahan, was looking more deeply into the lives Riis photographed and found not only despair and endless toil, but possibilities of self-realization and the human material that would create artists and scholars, great businesses and the unions that would contend with them. In the South the hopes of black men and women for a share in their land had received a lasting wound fourteen years earlier with the removal of federal troops, and white supremacists had carried on their war against their fellow citizens with poll taxes, hoods and the noose, and a sharecropping economy that condemned both poor whites and emancipated blacks to lives of grinding poverty. 1890 saw eighty-five lynchings of African Americans in the country, an off year, it appears: the next year would bring one hundred thirteen, a number more typical for the last decade of the nineteenth century, including the lynching of a black man in the town of Port Jervis, New York, that the brother of an aspiring novelist named Stephen Crane tried to prevent. At Harvard one of William James's students, a young African American who would look deep into the soul of both black and white made his debut in white America with a commencement address to his graduating class, a coolly dismissive appraisal of Jefferson Davis. And in 1890 a newspaperman and novelist from New Orleans named George Washington Cable published a book called *The Negro Question* that would put him further at odds with fellow white Southerners; while in the Faubourg Marigny another New Orleans denizen, a Creole named Ferdinand Joseph LaMothe, who would become Jelly Roll Morton, was born. The war between labor and capital would continue: 1890 saw the founding of two of the most militant of American labor unions, the United Mine Workers of America and Eugene V. Debs's American Railway Union. In New York, newly organized Jewish garment workers won a major victory after a seven-month strike. 1890 would also see the passage of the Sherman Antitrust Act. Yet as both conservative and radical thinkers agreed, the great trusts were an inevitable consequence of economic evolution and the real use of the Sherman Act, as it came to be seen, was not to break up corporations, but like the Hotchkiss cannons that had raked the Ghost Dancers on the Dakota plains, to break up collective acts of defiance in the form of strikes, boycotts, picket lines.

In the end, America abandoned its prophets. In 1890 Henry Adams was in Tahiti, a puritan among the pagans, trying to assuage the ache of a private tragedy, the suicide of his wife five years earlier, and his embittered sense that he had no place in the new age. The first volumes of his history of the United States in the Jefferson and Madison Administrations were coming out, and the famous questions he had asked about the future of the American character in the year 1817 with which he ended his volumes were being answered, but the answers were not the optimistic ones his history suggested. Adams had set it down that in the United States the laws of history developed not from the rivalries of European nationalities, but from "the economical evolution of a great democracy." Yet that evolution had led, increasingly, to violence and finally to economic chaos.

The book, he would write his admired Elizabeth Cameron, belonged "to the *me* of 1870; a strangely different being than the *me* of 1890."[10] American intellectuals produced no Wovoka, whose marvelous dream held out a promise of renewed spiritual life; their nostalgia for the older, pastoral America and its vision, for the transcendental certitudes of their fathers, for the faith in a rationalized science, produced in many of them only a profound bitterness or ineffable sense of loss, and it is significant that in 1890, in Camden, New Jersey, the last great poetic optimist, Walt Whitman, the Great Literatus, shaman, and death-singer, signed a contract for the building of his tomb. That awful solitude that Tocqueville saw at the heart of American character, the price of a new land and of democracy itself, had created a terrible gulf between one citizen and the next of which the America of the post–Civil War period was just becoming acutely aware. Still, the language of corporate America proved elastic enough to contain within itself both its own contradictions and the contradiction of its society, and it was able to absorb or to undermine or to subtly change the idealism that once defied it on the part of intellectuals and artists on the one hand and laboring masses on the other. That language, essentially the language of science, of rationalized capital, of imperialist expansion carried on under the cloak of democratic altruism, held the American rostrum, largely smothering the voices of its detractors in its din. In a remarkable kind of symbolic legerdemain the democratic virtues had expanded to take in not only Jefferson's fictive yeoman farmers but the very bankers and masters of the railroad trusts and corporations who exploited them and the thousands on thousands of workers who labored at factory workbenches and tended steam-powered distaffs for the benefit of "the fittest" of this new world of the Social Darwinian dispensation.

But there were other Americans who could not so easily fit into the optimism and triumphalism of Social Darwinian America. One of these was the son of an immigrant farmer, an outsider who had seen firsthand what had come of that agrarian dream and whose clear eye saw beyond the false fronts of the local village emporium and bank and into the moral pretensions and parade of conspicuous wealth of the larger swindle. I have already introduced the eminent and often troubled scientist and philosopher William James. Yet one more of these outsiders was a many-sided prodigy, a man of science, a philosopher, and a friend of William James's named Charles Sanders Peirce, who in 1890 was living on an isolated farm in Pennsylvania, near the site of the Port Jervis lynching of the following year. Having quarreled with everyone and scandalized polite academia, Peirce was rebuilding a farmhouse into a grandiose kind of intellectual hotel while developing a philosophical master plan in which the world could understand itself as a system of signs, a system that with his customary hubris he saw as complete in its architecture as Aristotle's. The American writer with whom I will couple him, a clergyman's son named Stephen Crane, who saw life as an artist does, was in 1890 miserably misplaced in a course of mining engineering at a Pennsylvania college, but was principally devoting his time to fraternity hijinks and baseball. And in England, an expatriate American writer, the younger brother of Peirce's friend William James, a novelist and short story writer who took as one of his major themes the complex interplay of two worlds, Old Europe and the young United States, and who himself was of both and neither, had finished a novel about politics, the theater, and the irreconcilability of art and the active life called *The Tragic Muse*. Another outsider, and the figure we shall take up next, was a New England recluse whose posthumous volume came out in 1890, and who happened to be a poetic genius. Like the other writers and artists we will look at, she was of her age yet beyond it, an uncanny practitioner of a new kind of art that would not so much break with the conventions of her own time as reconfigure them from the inside and in so doing give birth to a poetry of profound and disturbing beauty.

Chapter 2
Valentines

Palaces

It was an enchanting scene. All along the shore, its slopes covered by lawns and trees in bloom right down to the water, were a multitude of country houses, "big as boxes of candy," but showing careful workmanship. There was nothing like these little marble palaces in France—one or two were even in the classical style—and Alexis de Tocqueville, sailing toward Manhattan along the shore of the East River in the spring of 1831 thought he might even send home a sketch or plan of one or two of the prettiest.[1] The next day, when he went out to inspect more closely one of those little palaces that had particularly caught his eye, he found that its walls were of whitewashed brick and its columns of painted wood.

The candy-box palaces came to be a symbol, for Tocqueville, of the very type of the arts of this new democratic land, a land that lent itself to the practical, the immediate, the material, and whose democratic genius might root up trees for ten miles around the magnificent palace it had built for the Congress in Washington, D.C., with its pompous name, the Capitol, lest they interfere with the comings and goings of the citizens of an imaginary metropolis; but a symbol whose grasp of art itself was on its face doomed to failure. Only the aristocratic societies, Tocqueville thought, could be the mothers of the arts and of disinterested science. Placed above the multitude, the aristocratic society naturally conceived a lofty idea of itself and of man. It loved to invent for him "noble pleasures, to carve out special objects for his ambition." But in democratic America, the true aristocrat was the dollar.

This all-abiding pursuit of wealth was why Tocqueville proposed that for all their vaunted independence and individualism, Americans ceded their political life to the middle ground—a tropism toward a safe consensus that seemed, if you extended Tocqueville's analysis, even to the arts. We were destined to be an ersatz Europe, with a fat bank book and with a façade of secondhand culture slapped over a denuded wilderness.

But surely this democratic land of cash and mediocrity would produce something original. What, imagined Tocqueville, would it be?

> Style will frequently be fantastic, incorrect, overburdened, and loose, almost always vehement and bold. . . . Small productions will be more common than bulky books; there will be more wit than erudition, more imagination than profundity; and literary performances will bear marks of an untutored and rude vigor of thought. . . . The object of authors will be to astonish rather than to please, and to stir the passions more than to charm the taste.[2]

Only five or six years after Tocqueville made his way up the East River to his rendezvous with Democracy, Emerson was calling for a literature suited to a new land, a literature not of the aristocratic few, but of democratic man with a direct pipeline to the Divine Soul. "We have listened too long to the courtly muses of Europe," he proclaimed. "The spirit of the American freeman is already suspected to be timid, imitative, tame. Public and private avarice make the air we breathe thick and fat. . . . The mind of this country, taught to aim at low objects, eats upon itself. There is no work for any but the decorous and complaisant."[3] The literature Emerson had in mind for his country would not be "the great, the remote, the romantic," that imitation Europe of the painted brick and wooden column. It would be something new and utterly grounded in the everyday reality of the United States.

> I explore and sit at the feet of the familiar, the low. Give me insight into today, and you may have the antique and future worlds. What would we really know the meaning of? The meal in the firkin; the milk in the pan; the ballad in the street; the news of the boat; the glance of the eye; the form and the gait of the body.

"Let me see every trifle bristling with the polarity that ranges it instantly on an eternal law;" Emerson cried, "and the shop, the plough, and the ledger, referred to the like cause by which light undulates and poets sing;—and the world lies no longer a dull miscellany and lumber-room, but has form and order."[4]

Walt Whitman, a newspaperman and ex-schoolteacher, took up the challenge. Like Emerson he called for a national poet, a Great American Literatus who would embody this miscellany of the ordinary. He was, of course, calling for himself, and he created a poetic language out of interminable lists of the ordinary forms and occupations of American life as he knew them, out of vignettes of American moments that sometimes seemed taken off the pages of a newssheet, out of the "blab of the pave, tires of carts, sluff of boot soles," that "barbaric yawp" that he imagined himself sounding over the rooftops of the world; created it out of the stars and the weeds that grew around ponds and grandiloquent jets of semen and out of the aroma of arm-pits (his own armpits) that combined in a sort of American pantheism. You might say this democratic monster had been incipient in the self-evident truths of Thomas Jefferson's Declaration of Independence, a kind of every-man of industry and accomplishment (and for a self-proclaimed loafer, how much Whitman wrote, rewrote, and rewrote again), that very "rough" in shirtsleeves and slouch hat which Whitman, the former Broadway Dandy, impersonated on the title page engraving of *Leaves of Grass*.

But let us return to Tocqueville. Could he have probed the future of American letters, he would have seen taking form out of the mists, in a quiet corner apart from the Melvilles and the Hawthornes and the Poes striding head-on into battle with their country, or Whitman, who for all his yawp would hitch a ride in his work clothes on the railroad train of Manifest Destiny, a small woman stitching together her unread poems in her room in Amherst, Massachusetts. The New England woman had not read Walt Whitman, but she heard he was disgraceful; of Poe and his lurid poems she knew "too little to think." But wasn't her work, which Tocqueville's com-ments on style seem hauntingly to prefigure—though one must argue his point on profundity—finally the greater scandal?[5]

Valentines

> Awake ye muses nine, sing me a strain divine,
> unwind the solemn twine, and tie my Valentine!

First there were valentines. Chains of jaunty couplets full of the sheer zest of life linking the names of her girlfriends like blossoms sitting on a tree waiting to be plucked. "Oh the earth," she wrote at twenty, "was *made* for lovers." Then there were the couplets that a young lady or a young man, if he were poetic, might write in an album on an afternoon visit. A few spontaneous lines that would be shut up in the heavy covers, to be perused again or not. There were riddles, as well. The young woman was fond of riddles, provided they weren't too easy; was, her biographer Richard Sewall says, perhaps fond of being a riddle herself. On Sunday there were the familiar lines in the hymnbooks with their inexorable tread, sung against the wheezing organ and rising ominously from the pages of the Bible the voices of God and his prophets and his all-too fallible people. She said of her parents that they were religious, and addressed an Eclipse every morning they called their "Father." She was not. Or rather her religion was complicated and personal, divulged only in the lines of her poems and in her letters to her closest friends. Beyond the church was another town, parallel to Amherst, where the dead lay waiting for the Resurrection. On tombstones and in obituary notices there were lines for them too.

In the fields around the town were flowers to name and botanize and finally to snip out and stick in a flower press, their delicate sexual parts, stamens, anthers, pistils, flattened and dried so that only a pale version of their splendid colors remained, finally, perhaps, to be forgotten, crumpled to dust. There were sleighings and sugarings and socials. One winter she wrote of the fun to be had in Amherst. There were two hat factories in the town too, but their workers and what went on in them were of no particular interest.

New England was full of smart girls like the young Amherst woman. They went to local academies or even boarded away. Other smart girls were living in dormitories in mill towns like Lowell, tending the looms from five in the morning until seven at night. They were cheerful and high spirited enough not to be quite contented with their work—they were New England girls, imbued with pride and independence and a sense of equality, after all—but freedom from the family and the endless unpaid drudgery of the farm, the chance to earn money of their own, to engage in courtships away from village gossip, made their lot easier. Some even might write a poem or have a letter published in the *Lowell Offering*. They had to think, one of them said. The tremendous racket of the machinery they worked with made for a kind of privacy, where their only conversations were with themselves.[6] The minds of other young women might have found themselves in Abolition or with the newly vital feminists who had staged a historic meeting at Seneca Falls, New York, in 1848. Or be just destined to sit there as if they were in the vitrine on a mantelpiece with the stuffed pheasant and the sheaf of last year's wheat. The poems that such girls or a shy young woman might write were clipped out in rhythms as familiar and punctual as the clock ticking in the silent hall, waiting for some visitor, perhaps the local minister, perhaps a suitor who might never come; their subjects the predictable round of flowers, birds, thwarted love, and death—always death—their rhymes as unstartling as last year's bonnets. Mark Twain, who made a sort of specialty of satirizing the cultural pretensions of his age, had his fun with the literary remains of the death-obsessed Emmeline Grangerford in *Huckleberry Finn*, but the real thing, published in local papers, was often (and unintentionally) much funnier. And sadder.

> She has gone, we hope, to heaven, at the early age of seven
> (Funeral starts off at eleven), where she'll nevermore have pain.[7]

The poems might be mawkish, but the fact of death was ever present, and before long plaques in town squares and colleges would list the names of men, often really only boys, buried in fields outside of places called Gettysburg and Cold Harbor and Fort Wagner.

Thoreau, who lived in a town such as hers, said that most men lived lives of quiet desperation. He knew little of how most men lived, but meant to say, perhaps, that being forced to live in such a way would be for him a life of desperation and in reaction made off to a few square miles of field and forest, a woodlot and a pond, cut through with country roads and not far from the hoot of a railroad, that served him as a wilderness. For Emily Dickinson, the world was also a few square miles—of town mostly and a few fields—while the wilderness, with its strangeness and vast expanse, was solely in the mind, and in a peculiar voice that is sometimes almost a whisper, a girl's voice, quiet, diffident, or some confident boy's and still more often direct and full of anguish or ecstasy, in rhythms that halt and linger, a voice that has sometimes a sly malice under its coyness, and sometimes a destructive power that illuminates the ordinary, she created a world that like her odd rhymes lived not in village certitude and the predictable, but in doubt.

Beyond the narrow rituals of the town, the visits and churchgoing and baking and botanizing and funerals, whose precincts narrowed and finally shrank to the space of her small upstairs room, were the great booming voices of the poets and writers she read. Mr. and Mrs. Browning and John Keats, and prose writers scarcely less lyrical, Mr. Ruskin and Sir Thomas Browne and Revelation. There were others she failed to mention in this list from a letter to Thomas Wentworth Higginson. Shakespeare, above all, and George Eliot who wrote about villages such as hers, wrote about the passions of strange girls living much in themselves. There were the Brontës who wrote about what it was to give yourself to emotion. Over all, unmentioned by her, there was the spare silhouette of a former preacher and current lecturer, at once present and strangely remote, whose spirit penetrated two generations of writers and thinkers.

Perhaps Emerson was a dream that was necessary for us to have in order that we might wake up from it. F. O. Matthiessen in his classic *American Renaissance* caught the moment exactly as Emerson "turned his back on the 'pale negations' of Unitarianism, and began to utter what, after long and quiet listening to himself, he knew that he really believed." What he believed was that "life is an ecstasy." "That the moment was an almost unbelievable miracle, which he wanted, more than anything else, to catch and record."[8]

Emerson had lifted the roof of the New England meetinghouse and let in the sky. It was a sky full of light and the drifting clouds of his imagination. He had expanded American thought beyond the narrow chamber of sin, redemption, and duty, beyond the rational keys of the Enlightenment, and opened it to nature, to a larger, fresher purview of the world that would take in German idealism, Byron and Napoleon and the Bhagavad-Gita. But under those fleecy clouds was a kind of chill. He had purchased his intellectual independence at the expense of the human connection. Henry James Sr. would call him in a description that cannot be bettered, "a man without a handle." There was always something in him that withheld and withdrew, something cool and distancing that only was released in his passion for nature, but never for his fellow human beings. He taught New England new ways to think, but he could not teach it how to feel.

Emily Dickinson had gone to other tutors for that, to the Brontës and Shakespeare, and especially into her own interior world. With her constant interrogation of her inner life, with her intense focus on the question of belief, she was a child of the Puritans, but for all her spiritual questioning and its anguish, she was a Puritan without a sense of sin. A girl might stain her apron climbing over the fence to enjoy the strawberries and God might know, but she imagined if God were a boy he'd climb too—if he could. She thought the Bible was a wise and merry book,[9] and her religious poetry is full of a kind of homespun language and often prankish glee. She called herself a pagan. (At Mount Holyoke, which she attended for a time, and where the stages to salvation were ranked, she was listed among the "hopeless.") She said that she was one of the "*bad* ones," that she could not renounce the beauty and ecstasy of the world for Christ, yet the other world had a reality for her that was concrete and absolutely geographical; she had never spoken with God or visited in Heaven, but she was as sure of the unknown blue land beyond the clouds as if her tickets were already purchased and were in her hand. She was rather a Christian without a doctrine, a believer without an unbroken sense of her personal salvation. But unlike her religious forerunners, and unlike the transcendentalists, she could push doubt to the very edge—and over. Emerson recalled sitting in church as a child, amusing himself by saying over and over some common word such as "black," "white," or "board," twenty or thirty times until the words lost all meaning and he began to doubt which was the right name for the thing, when he saw that neither had any natural relation, but all were arbitrary. He thought it was a child's first lesson in idealism.[10] The woman in Amherst had a different idea: "tis a dangerous moment for anyone when the meaning goes out of things and Life stands straight—and punctual and yet no signal comes," she wrote in one of her letters. She wrote poems, some of her most famous, that leave us perched over this brink.

> Safe in their Alabaster Chambers –
> Untouched by Morning –
> And untouched by noon –
> Sleep the meek members of the Resurrection,
> Rafter of Satin and Roof of Stone –

But we see only the sleep of these meek members of the Resurrection, the grand procession of years, the great events of history falling "Soundless as Dots, / On a Disc of Snow." The speaker in perhaps her most famous poem imagines a fly buzzing at the moment of her death in that hush when "the King" be expected in the room. At the edge of death, or at the edge of resurrection, we wait suspended.

The other side of this questioning was found in that word she shared with Emerson: *Extasy*, as she would spell it for most of her life. Words were real to her. They opened her narrow chamber with a presence and reverberation that made them ring. In the vastness of reverie a single clover in her garden and one bee could make a prairie. Mermaids sang in the basement. The mouths of singers opened like the lips of Sicilian volcanoes to pour out the lava of language. The miracle, the true gift, was to be oneself and not somebody else.

A Door Ajar

> Why has not man a microscopic eye?
> For this plain reason, man is not a fly.
> Say what the use, were finer optics giv'n,
> T'inspect a mite, not comprehend the heav'n?
> Or touch, if tremblingly alive all o'er,
> To smart and agonize at ev'ry pore?
> Or quick effluvia darting through the brain,
> Die of a rose in aromatic pain?
>
> —Alexander Pope, An Essay on Man: Epistle I

If there was a body that had no cuticle of skin, for which every breeze was a crisis, or if there was an ear that could hear the silence of the fields, or a heart that trembled at a word and overflowed with emotion, that could not endure a love measured out in sips; if there could be such a body and such a person, life would be a constant ecstasy and an almost unendurable pain. It would be not out of disgust for the world, but out of a love for it of uncommon intensity that a person having such a lot might shut herself away. The ordinary run of human intercourse, with its hand-me-down sentiments and convictions and its falseness, would be an intolerable intrusion. Such a person would wonder how human beings could live without thinking. "She had to think," Emily Dickinson's sister, Vinnie, said of her. "She was the only one of us who had that to do."[11] So her seclusion, coming on gradually, did not seem strange to those closest to her, her brother and her sister. It did not seem the response to a sudden shock in love or to a death, though there were those, but indeed a part of her that had always been there, finally expressing itself. "It all seemed to her so cheap and thin & hollow as she saw it," wrote Mabel Todd, of Emily Dickinson's view of the "Dimity Convictions" of everyday Amherst (she was writing from what Austin or Vinnie or both told her of their sister), "with the solemn realities of life staring her in the face, that she wanted none of it." "I find ecstasy in living," she told Thomas Wentworth Higginson to dispel his concern about her closeted life; "—the mere sense of living is joy enough."[12]

It is curious that her sister and brother did not know that in this seclusion she had gone beyond the numerous letters that still connected her to family and to a select group of friends; that in fact she was writing poems. Sometimes perhaps two a day. Closeted in her room, she pushed Emerson's dictum of self-reliance beyond anything Emerson himself might have imagined. But what was chill and smug in Emerson was hot and passionate in Emily Dickinson. In her, without a need to be detonated by the hyperbole of the world itself. The circus parade passed outside her window with its drums and trombones and its menagerie. The music faded into the distance and left not a grain of desire in her to follow it. Once Emily Dickinson stood upstairs with her niece and closed her thumb and forefinger around the imaginary key to her room. Then she gave a quick turn of her wrist: "It's just a turn—and freedom, Matty!"

About 1858 she began stitching the poems together in little booklets, a sort of secret dowry that would never be displayed in her lifetime. With single-minded purpose she wooed herself away from fame. For all the warmth of their correspondence, she had been given no encouragement to publish by the two influential editors to whom she showed her poems. Perhaps she found that after a time it was just as well to send her poems in letters to her friends or keep them shut up in a drawer. "If fame belonged to me," she wrote, "I could not escape her—if she did not, the longest day would pass me on the chase." Then she imagined what her fate would be. "The approbation of my Dog," she said, "would forsake me." Her Barefoot Rank was better. Publication, she wrote in about 1863, is the Auction of the Mind of Man.

As she retreated more and more into the privacy that seemed the necessary condition for her work, she nevertheless would often leave a door ajar. She would listen to whatever gossip or talk her sister Vinnie was engaged in with a visitor, sometimes entering into it in her voice that was always like a question. Mabel Todd, who became her brother's lover, would sometimes come to play on the piano or sing, and Emily Dickinson would send her by way of recompense a flower, a glass of wine. And sometimes Emily herself would play on the piano—her own strange improvised compositions.

She had written flatteringly to Thomas Wentworth Higginson, how could one who was a poem need to write a poem? She was herself a self-created poem, a riddle without an answer. Her letters from an early age had started to turn themselves into literature, and close readers might even mine them for fragments of verse, lines and stanzas and even whole poems. Like her poetry her letters became more and more studded with private metaphors and ellipses that turned in upon themselves and that puzzle and tease a contemporary reader and must have puzzled and teased recipients who might have known more about their contexts.

Alongside the Victorian moralizing and sentimentalizing of Tennyson, or Whitman's shocking spermatic gushers (which Henry James shrewdly said had merely become a new platitude), this half-ajar poetry gained in intensity from its refusal to fully disclose.

We do not know if the passion and longing in her poems is religious or erotic. Perhaps it is both. The Metaphysical poets she read republished in the *Springfield Republican* had that same intensity of focus, as had Blake. We might think of the poems of Sor Juana Inés de la Cruz or Saint Teresa of Ávila and, moderns as we are, see the religious theme as only a disguised eroticism; but it may be that in ages of faith—ages that also bring with them doubt and its storms—the erotic is only an earthly metaphor for the ecstasy of religious communion. She wrote once that she wished she could be a child forever. It was a wish that perhaps anticipated her retreat from the world, but more than that, I think, to retain childhood's special apprehension of the freshness and magic—she might have called it the ecstasy—of the world. A number of her poems take on a child's persona, sometimes, surprisingly, a boy's. There is something cloying about them to this ear, something a bit self-satisfied. If she did not remain a child—and this is perhaps what is off about those poems, that they are an affectation of childhood—her solitude and sexual inexperience served to keep her in the throes of a passion of adolescent intensity, but it was passion that had neither the self-pity nor the narcissism of adolescence, and its intensity was wrung by the strength of her mind. Much speculation has been advanced on who those anonymous lovers might be to whom her passionate poems were addressed, and who the unnamed recipient was whom she addressed as "Master" in the drafts of three letters found in her papers, and which might have been unsent. It is possible that the letters themselves were expressions of a relationship that existed only in her mind, possibly not even guessed by their intended reader. But it is less important to know the name of the Master in these letters, with their abject worship, their erotic longing, and their sometimes scarcely concealed anger, than their import as glosses on her poems. She wrote to Higginson that when she says "I" in her poems it is a supposed person. It is a statement protective of herself, of her privacy, but on a more profound level it is an expression of the multiple voices and psychological complexity that she contained within herself and which she did not try to quiet, but in fact called up into expression.

"Tell all the truth," she wrote, "but tell it slant – / Success in circuit lies." To approach the truth (and truth, she said, was her country) one could only begin by creating a state of being, a state of emotion. Like the half-open door behind which the world entered and through which she spoke, privacy was the condition of truth telling.

Beardless Among the Poets

The beards of the great poets seemed to prop up their heads like eggs in a nest of straw. The beards bespoke gravity, seriousness—good things for poets to have, for making verses was a frivolous thing to do in these United States. If one had a beard one might be a railroad magnate or a banker or even a senator. Emerson had no beard, but Longfellow had, to hide his scarified lower face, and so did Tennyson.

Emily Dickinson was quite aware of both her ambition and her beardlessness. She joked about it, imagined herself among the poets and their work as the only kangaroo among the beauty. But such conscious difference includes in itself its obverse. And only with that obverse is its originality understood. Such forms as Emily Dickinson chose—the valentines, the riddles or the inside-out riddles that her apothegms really were, the "graveyard" and "death" poems, the poems of longing for belief or of imagining Christian heaven or the inability to imagine it, the lyrical "I" of the Romantics, longing or hoping or in regret—were embedded in her escapes from the expected. The startling word or image, the unexpected reversal of a platitude, the inexact rhymes—these were the elements of her assault on the poetic mean of her day. But perhaps most original, and most shocking, was her assault on the platitudes of poetic rhythm.

If Sidney Lanier's own ponderous beard pulled his verse downward by the weight of its seriousness, down to the melancholy, the nostalgic, the lugubrious, still it left his ears open. He had a musician's discrimination, was a musician himself, a flautist of some gifts, and he knew that rhythm was the first essential. He quoted Shakespeare's ass-eared Bottom: "I have a reasonable good ear in music: let's have the tongs and the bones." Rhythm might in fact be the foundation of the world.

For Lanier it was the timid poets who tried to capture the deep and universal rhythms of nature in a rigid succession of iambs, in sonorous endstopped lines that rolled with such soporific predictability that we ceased to really hear them. In searching for the power of the music of Shakespeare and the greats, Lanier went to the sources of English poetry in the practice of the people. For there the power of the great systole and diastole in nature was played off against their absence, against frustrated expectation, delayed fulfillment. It was the sense of rhythm of children and common people that gave him his clue to the power of this rhythmic license. He found this sense in nursery rhymes, in the great but "defective" English and Scottish ballads apologized for and smoothed over and rewritten by editors and collectors. He found this license in another, and quite curious place: the slaves he had seen on the plantations of his youth dancing to no other instruments than the sounds of their hands against ribs and thighs and the thud of their feet on a plank floor, "patting Juba," a music based on complex syncopations and surprising rests, a music quite literally of the body.[13] The intellectual young woman sitting in her room in Amherst had never heard a slave patting juba, had never heard the clack of the bones at a minstrel show, but she was hearing her own rhythms, creating her own surprising silences and violences and leaps as strange to the ear of her time as the African complexities of rhythm that Lanier had heard. Perhaps she found her own license in nursery rhymes or in Shakespeare. Perhaps she found them in her own body.

In Amherst a secondhand organ had long ago replaced the parish's first instrument, a double-bass viol whose lugubrious tones sawed under the familiar words of the hymnbook. Vinnie could be quite satirical about it all, giving a bravura performance once in which she imitated how the superannuated village soprano singing "Broad is the road that leads to death" had to drop off in a cracked subsidence from the key when the melody ran too high, leaving it up to the old man bullying the double bass to soldier on in harrowing discord until she rejoined the key at last, while the old man prolonged the last few notes of his instrument in grating woe.[14] Emily Dickinson might have enjoyed Vinnie's performance, had she been there. But by then she had ceased going out, even to her brother's house next door.

Her congregation was of the same tradition Vinnie had had such fun with. It was the familiar iambs of Isaac Watts, the relentless tread of the stanzas' feet under their lugubrious burdens, fours and threes, fours and fours ("Broad is the road that leads to death / And thousands walk together there"), their implacable end-stopped rhymes. Her technique was to decenter those familiar expectations. Decenter them around their expected religious conclusions, certainly, but around the expected rhythms and simple rhymes too. Wordsworth's insistence in the preface to the *Lyrical Ballads* that the "spontaneous overflow of powerful feelings" that defined the poem for him was triggered by "emotion recollected in tranquility" had long been absorbed, and so tranquil had the metrical practice of the Victorians become that in spite of such dubious adventures as Longfellow's "On the shores of Gitche Gumee" or the trite clippety-clop of "Listen, my children, and you shall hear," one could sense the rhythm train coming miles before it reached its destination with an expected final chug, punctual to the syllable and soporific as an afternoon nap. But there were moments—moments in Tennyson—where the predictable rise and fall of the syllables broke down. Something happened then. Something that we imagine the young woman in love with poetry heard with excitement and wonder, for it opened the poem to a universe of emotional possibility.

Emily Dickinson could write perfectly "correct" rhythmical stanzas if she chose, just as she could write with the expected sentiments of her age (she copied out some of the conventional verse from the *Springfield Republican* in manuscripts found after her death, and she could recommend such poems to her friends). But it was in her deviations that she most expressed her surprising originality. She wrote many poems in hymn stanzas, bending them to suit herself, but many more—and these were her most powerful—in metric schemes of her own, which she then stretched and abrogated and violated. "You think my gait 'spasmodic'—I am in danger—Sir," she wrote to Thomas Wentworth Higginson, literary correspondent of the *Atlantic Monthly*. "You think me 'uncontrolled'—I have no Tribunal."[15] For all her coyness and posing in these remarkable letters, when it came to her poetic practice she would not give an inch. For it was the rhythms that made her poems live, that made them expressions of a lived experience. Above all else, the poems were meant for the ear, were intensely present performances, because ultimately they were things of the body, of texture and the sound of vowels and sibilants against the palate, the muscular closing and opening of the vocal cords, heartbeats and pulses, and above all, of breath. She was emphatic about it. "Do my poems breathe?" she cried.

Emily Dickinson discovered something profound about the extension of the body that was the poem, something that toward the end of her life another of America's great originals hit upon: at the bottom, breath and thought, body and mind, were one and the same. "The stream of thinking," William James was to write, "is only a careless name for what, when scrutinized, reveals itself to consist chiefly of the stream of my breathing."[16]

Thus beyond its words, the meaning of a poem, its emotional core, might be found in its silences, the silences suspended between the breaths. There is a pause in a line of verse that extends itself a fraction longer than the other pauses and marks the boundary between phrases, a silence where the line gathers itself before it concludes. This rest or caesura is the fulcrum of the line, the balance point of the see and saw of its metrical scheme. Wrench this silence this way or that from the accustomed pad of the line's foot, as Emily Dickinson does, and the movement has a visceral effect, a catch of the breath, a wrenching of the emotions themselves.

> Wild nights – Wild nights!
> Were I with thee
> Wild nights should be
> Our luxury!
>
> Futile – the winds –
> To a Heart in port –
> Done with the Compass –
> Done with the Chart!

This balance point wants to weigh lines of unequal length. Cutting the first three lines exactly in half here has a kind of violence, unsettling as the proportions of an abstract painting divided perfectly down the middle. The waves buck and heave in the storm above the expected rise and fall.

Breath forced through the valves of the vocal cords was thought, but so was its absence, a hesitation in the flow, an unexpected holding of the breath. The fermata that indicates an extrametrical prolongation of a chord in music is the same sign that indicates a rest extended beyond its metrical duration. It is a swelling of emotional intensity, a thinking in the body.

> Rowing in Eden –
> Ah – the Sea!
> Might I but moor – tonight –
> In thee!

Here the dashes are not grammatical in the way that commas might be, but are indications of suspended beats, of breaths held on the brink of completed thought or of emotions, until they finally resolve and release themselves in the long rising inflection of the final "thee." Scholars note that in her manuscripts Emily Dickinson has a number of different ways of indicating these dashes, as if to spell their varying lengths of time. She would complicate her metrical schemes further by the concussions of emphasis between the dashes of her poems, by capitalizations and enjambments that seem to replicate the very halts and punctuations of a thinking and feeling being. For the poem wants to give the sense that it is happening as it unfolds itself, that it is being made on the page and in the ear of the reader as thoughts suddenly emerge, bubbling up from the silence.

"With each stanza, at times with each syllable, she presents us with a constantly changing horizon of actual and latent rhythmic possibilities," poet John Shoptaw writes in his elegant essay "Listening to Dickinson."

> Come slowly – Eden!
> Lips unused to Thee –
> Bashful – sip thy Jessamines –
> As the fainting Bee –
>
> Reaching late his flower,
> Round her chamber hums –
> Counts his nectars –
> Enters – and is lost in Balms.

"The key to seduction," Shoptaw writes, "is deferral, and we are put off from the first syllables." He continues to develop the complexities of the poem's deferrals until they finally subside in the last line, and its "last perfumed word."[17]

It wasn't Emily Dickinson's ambition to recollect in tranquility, to summon up emotion out of retrospect, but to create the very moment of the living idea or pain or ecstasy itself.

New England Light

> There's a certain Slant of light,
> Winter Afternoons –
> That oppresses, like the Heft
> Of Cathedral Tunes –

Heavenly Hurt, it gives us –
We can find no scar,
But internal difference –
Where the Meanings, are –

None may teach it – Any –
'Tis the Seal Despair –
An imperial affliction
Sent us of the Air –

When it comes, the Landscape listens –
Shadows – hold their breath –
When it goes, 'tis like the Distance
On the look of Death –

Slant, Circumference. Breath, Meaning, Truth. These are the important words
for Emily Dickinson; and, of course, *ecstasy.* Ecstasy, the moment of surrender or triumph, or perhaps both at once. But more often the world presents
its face as a kind of riddle to be read. How read? A riddle is a form of name
magic, very old, a kind of reverse spell. If you can name something, you
have it in your power. A riddle withholds that name and in it binds up all
the mystery and paradox of the world. We guess a riddle and the knot is
instantly cut; the anguish of unknowing disappears into the name, but the
riddle itself is consumed. Its fabulous unresolved pieces become simply ordinary. Sometimes in Emily Dickinson the naming itself, while it solves the
poem, supplies the syllable, the rhyme that will conclude, does not solve the
mystery, but intensifies it.

Just as a riddle has two seemingly incommensurable halves, solved only
by the saying of the magic name, so too is there a kind of sexual congress
of opposites possible in a poem. Thus it is that the poem that refuses to be
consoled presents the poet at her most powerful—alone, but for all her ab-
jectness, proud.

Words for Emily Dickinson were real, yet she knew how easily they could
lose their meaning, how inexact they could be when thrown at the ear head-
on. She wondered how the ladies of Amherst could talk so blandly of the
things of the soul, a language that made her dog ashamed. Circumference
was all, yet one could only surmise it from some place inside itself, and only
God could draw it, as Blake had shown him, compass spread. It was greater

than the Dimity Convictions of the town, greater than the squabbling
doctrines that made the churches debating societies. To tell the truth one
glanced off it at a tangent. A poem for her was like that, approaching great
truths through paradox and through tension and through, finally, silence.

The most terrible thing of all was not to feel, to walk through the world
as a kind of figment. For if breath in her might be one of the keys to the
physical immediacy of her poems, it was also in itself a sign, an indication of
a higher, more lucid life:

> I breathed enough to take the Trick –
> And now, removed from Air –
> I simulate the Breath, so well –
> That One, to be quite sure –
>
> The Lungs are stirless – must descend
> Among the cunning cells –
> And touch the Pantomime – Himself,
> How numb, the Bellows feels!

What would a poem be without a kind of spiritualized breath? A simulation of life, a poem that would be a kind of pantomime of a poem.

One knew the truth by going deep down into pain, into the pain of separation. She wrote that she would know why when Christ would explain in "the
fair schoolroom in the sky." For the present there was the drop of anguish

> That scalds me now – that scalds me now!

Like the door that was ajar to the world, that fed her solitude without
destroying it by either the totality of self-immurement and forgetting or the
flood of the world itself, the poems were ajar to full disclosure. Their tensions were in their possibilities, in the rhythms of the absences of the fully
disclosed reality, and in their presence as physical objects, with their silences
and syllables and the rhythms that play off against some unheard center. In
that amniotic fluid of pain the internal difference is where the meanings lie.

So her poems lived, most profoundly, in her willingness to express despair.
Pain itself, the sharp pain of loss especially, was where she found herself.

We can speculate but we finally do not know the cause—or causes—of
the stations of despair that no poet has more clearly marked.

> The first Day's Night had come –
> And grateful that a thing

So terrible – had been endured –
I told my Soul to sing –

She said her strings were snapt –
Her Bow – to atoms blown –
And so to mend her – gave me work
Until another Morn –

And then – a Day as huge
As Yesterdays in pairs,
Unrolled it's horror in my face –
Until it blocked my eyes –

My Brain – begun to laugh –
I mumbled – like a fool –
And tho' 'tis Years ago – that Day –
My Brain keeps giggling – still.

And Something's odd – within –
That person that I was –
And this One – do not feel the same –
Could it be Madness – this?

But what the world called madness might be a lens through which the truth appeared, "divinest sense" that ran against the Majority, that made one "dangerous, / And handled with a Chain –" So the pain must be kept protected from the Majority, a precious substance in itself. Pain was the very symbol of her "election."[18]

I cannot live with You –
It would be Life –
And Life is over there –
Behind the Shelf

The Sexton keeps the key to –

Pain was in the separation of erotic love and a self-chosen celibacy, the separation in this world from God, but it was what made for meaning, made for the keenest pang of life itself, and poetry.

So we must meet apart –
You there – I – here –
With just the Door ajar

That Oceans are – and Prayer –
And that White Sustenance –
Despair –

A Visitor

The years of the Civil War were years of personal crisis for Emily Dickinson and coincided with her most furious output and the writing of many of her most powerful poems. The crisis may have been one of faith, or of love, or fear for her eyesight, for she spent the only really prolonged time away from home in those years being treated by a Boston ophthalmologist. It might have been all of these. Yet the war itself hardly touched her. While her fellow poet the disgraceful Walt Whitman was nursing the wounded in Washington and stood witness to the appalling physical carnage, and even though she had worried about her preceptor Thomas Wentworth Higginson who had been wounded in combat and returned to lead a black regiment, of the war itself there is hardly a trace in her letters and what there is could have the appalling insouciance of a queen of the *Ancien Régime*: "I shall have no winter this year—on account of the soldiers—Since I cannot weave Blankets, or Boots—I thought it best to omit the season." And again, "A Soldier called –" she wrote in 1862, "a Morning ago, and asked for a Nosegay, to take to Battle. I suppose he thought we kept an Aquarium." (She did write in her letters a few elegies on Amherst boys lost in the war, and one poem, quoted by Richard Sewall with a solemn and restrained note, on the death of Francis Dickinson, killed in action "in Yonder Maryland."[19]) It was a strange myopia for one of so powerful an imagination as hers. Wars, volcanoes, mobs, elections were only there to provide her with metaphors for her poems. It was as if the village and her acquaintance with it was her world, her heart an Alabaster Chamber of its own where history dropped and melted remotely beyond.

Eight years after she first wrote him, Thomas Wentworth Higginson finally met the woman whose originality expressed in letters and poems he found difficult and too unpolished for publication and who had once signed a letter to him, "Your Gnome," no doubt in response to a comment of his on the gnomic quality of her expression. But Higginson, who had carefully copied down the songs and speeches of the African American men of his regiment—

one of the first literary men to understand the power of black eloquence—had an eye and an ear for Americans not cut to a conventional pattern.

"A step like a pattering child's in entry," he wrote to his wife,

> & in glided a little plain woman with two smooth bands of reddish hair . . . with no good feature – in a very plain & exquisitely clean white pique & a blue net worsted shawl.
>
> She came to me with two day lilies which she put in a sort of childlike way into my hand & said "These are my introduction" in a soft frightened breathless childlike voice – & added under her breath Forgive me if I am frightened; I never see strangers & hardly know what I say.[20]

She was forty. In spite of her shyness, there in the "cool & stiffish" parlor of her father's house, with its open piano and a few engravings and books, among them two of Higginson's own, the small plain woman talked. It was wonderful talk, continuous and deferential, thoroughly ingenuous and simple, and with many things that Higginson found wise, but which, he imagined, his wife would have found foolish.

"Women talk: men are silent," Emily Dickinson told Higginson; "that is why I dread women." She asked him how did most people live without any thoughts. "There are many people in the world (you must have noticed them in the street) How do they live. How do they get strength to put on their clothes in the morning?" And she told him how she judged a book of poetry, which tells us the standard she must have held out for her own work: "If I read a book [and] it makes my whole body so cold no fire ever can warm me I know *that* is poetry. If I feel physically as if the top of my head were taken off, I know *that* is poetry. These are the only way I know it." Then she asked Higginson, "Is there any other way." When Higginson asked her if she never felt the want of employment, in her hermitlike existence, she answered "I never thought of conceiving that I could ever have the slightest approach to such a want in all future time," and she added, "I feel that I have not expressed myself strongly enough."[21]

Higginson saw Emily Dickinson one more time before leaving Amherst and met her father, "thin dry & speechless." When he left Amherst he wrote his wife that he was never with anyone who drained his nerve power so much. He was glad he did not live near her.[22]

Gradually Emily Dickinson abandoned the meticulous copying and sewing of the little booklets of poems, the fascicles, and by the last decade of her life wrote fair copies on unbound sheets, or left them either unfinished or finished on single pieces of paper, often mere scraps written on old envelopes. Though she continued to write until her death in 1886, her production gradually slowed. After her death forty fascicles and ninety unbound sheets and seven or eight hundred individual poems or fragments were found in a drawer in her room.

The Suspended Syllable

> They shut me up in Prose –
> As when a little Girl
> They put me in the Closet –
> Because they like me "still" –
>
> Still! Could themself have peeped –
> And seen my Brain – go round –
> They might as wise have lodged a Bird
> For Treason – in the Pound –

It was a kind of awful solitude she had attained, a solitude like the Creator's itself, a blasphemy in verse that her self-imposed prison, which was for her the ultimate freedom segregated from the prose of the world, had made. The proud solitude, the difference, was her special triumph, her "White Election" to the realms of poetic greatness.

If she loved the world, she nevertheless had an absolute faith in an afterlife that was as real, more real. The moments when the poem momentarily halts, where the breath catches, is a reflection of the moment when the breath will halt in the ecstasy of a world without time. She had imagined such a world, a great exhalation of the breath.

> Great Streets of silence led away
> To Neighborhoods of Pause –
> Here was no Notice – no Dissent
> No Universe – no Laws –
>
> By Clocks, 'twas Morning, and for Night
> The Bells at Distance called –
> But Epoch had no basis here
> For Period exhaled.

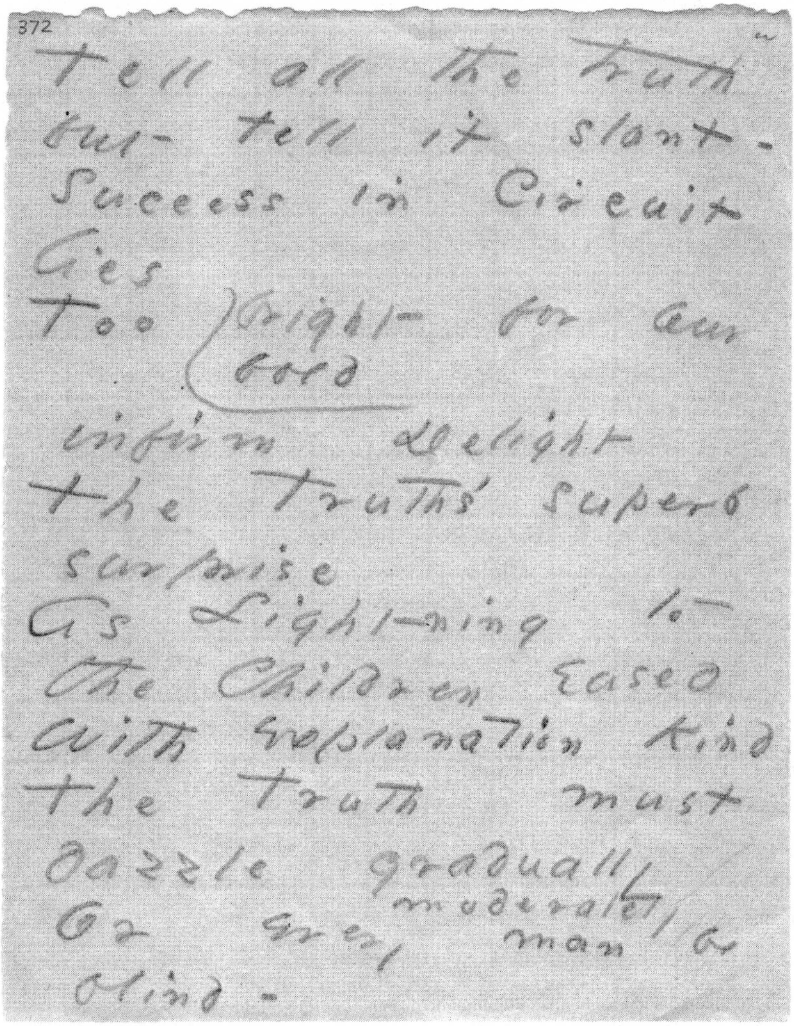
372
Tell all the truth
but tell it slant -
Success in Circuit
lies
Too bright for our
bold
infirm Delight
The Truth's superb
surprise
As Lightning to
The Children eased
With explanation kind
The Truth must
dazzle gradually
moderately
Or every man be
blind -

Figure 2. Emily Dickinson, manuscript of "Tell all the truth," the Amherst College Archives and Special Collections, the Emily Dickinson Collection, Amherst manuscript no. 372.

The dark unchanging parlor of her father's house, the alabaster chamber of the tomb, the silence of her room, finally, the silence of the suspended syllable, the moment when the breath stops in her poem to gather itself into a word, to conclude a line or a thought, were only rehearsals for those great streets of silence that her poetry finally aspired to, and toward which she was always walking, with the halting and stopping, the revision, the constant choosing of poems she sewed into packets or left loose in her drawer, the workshop of her life, and poems that were themselves still suspended, unfinished at her death.

> Eternity may imitate
> The Affluence ~~Ecstasy~~ of time
> But that suspended (arrested) syllable
> is wealthier than him

Four years after Dickinson's death in 1886, her first volume of poems was published. It quickly went through a number of editions, and there were more collections to follow. The volumes were at first lightly edited to conform to the prevailing poetic norms, but the poems themselves, often so startling in their ideas and images and abrupt transitions of emotion, had found the audience that she could not find in her lifetime and had finally scorned; for the United States was undergoing profound changes in its fundamental structure, in its population, in its spiritual foundation. The quiet chamber in the small college town had left the door ajar not only to the visitors in the parlor, to the church bells, to the noise of the parade outside the windows, but to an era as difficult and paradoxical and frightening as her poems.

Chapter 3
Cakewalk

> Voyez ce mulet là, Miché Bainjo,
> Comme il est insolent!
> Chapeau sur coté, Miché Bainjo,
> La canne à la main, Miché Bainjo,
> Bottes qui fé *crin, crin*, Miché Bainjo.
> . . .
> Voyez ce mulet là, Miché Bainjo,
> Comme il est insolent!

> Look at that darky there, Mr. Banjo,
> Doesn't he put on airs!
> Hat cocked on one side, Mr. Banjo,
> Walking-stick in hand, Mr. Banjo,
> Boots that go "crank, crank," Mr. Banjo

> *Look* at that darky there, Mr. Banjo,
> *Doesn't* he put on airs![1]

I like this Miché Bainjo, hat cocked to one side, boots that go *crin, crin*—or crank, crank, as you please. I like his walking-stick, and I like his *insolence*. George Washington Cable, who discovered this song in Ware's *Slave Songs of the United States*, found himself unable to translate the pun on *mulet*, muleteer, with its echo of mulatto, and substituted the useless "darky." But if we go looking for the origin of that phenomenon the cakewalk, which is at once a dance and a kind of music, a ritual and a contest, it is in the multiple refraction of puns, linguistic and social, that we will find it. What are you up to, Miché Bainjo (*crin, crin*), courting or simply taking the air? But above all, in this land of the all too visible invisible dark side of the New Orleans color line, being *seen*.

At the upper end of Orleans Street, as Cable reconstructed it, was the Place d'Armes, flanked by the retail quarter with its fine goods and wares. It was the place for political rallies, the haunt of lovers walking in the moonlight, the place, as he put it, for all that was best in the New Orleans of the 1820s, 1830s, and 1840s. At the opposite end of the street lay the Place Congo. No meaner name, Cable said, could be given to this place, the resort of the butcher, the raftsman, the sailor, the quadroon, the painted girl, the slave. The white man's plaza had the army and navy on its right and left, the courthouse, the council hall, and the church at its back. The black man's plaza was outside the rear gate, "the poisonous wilderness on three sides and the proud man's contumely on its front." It was here that in their brief moments of Sunday liberty the slaves gathered to sing and dance.

The instruments were African, marimba brett, four-string banjo, canebrake flutes, gourds, triangles, jew's-harps, huge wooden horns, and that "long-drawn human cry of tremendous volume, richness, and resound," to which no instrument within the slave's reach "could make the faintest approach," and always the drums, long hollow drums with goatskin heads, laid flat on the ground and bestrode by the drummers, and a smaller drum made out of a joint or two of a very large West Indian bamboo, from which came its name and that of a dance Cable was to describe with great interest, the bamboula.

But it is quite likely that Cable had never seen this or the other dances he described, the conjaille, the calinda, and those Voodoo dances and ceremonies so "revolting" and "morally hideous" that even in the West Indies the French forbade them. Tradition had it that the dances were suppressed in 1843, he said, so he filled that emptiness with his reading and his own romanticized, racialized imagining of the licentiousness of the dancing.

> For the true African dance, a dance not so much of legs and feet as of the upper half of the body, a sensual, devilish thing tolerated only by Latin-American masters, there was wanted the dark inspiration of African drums and the banjo's thump and strum. . . . No wonder the police stopped it in Congo Square.[2]

But I don't think it was the licentiousness of the slaves dancing to the drums of Congo Square, as Cable thought, that caused the dances to be suppressed (and indeed, the illustrations Kemble provides—and where did he get them?—show dancers in quite dignified poses, while the tunes themselves are pretty little things), but the threat of that multitude of slave bodies themselves, dressed in rags or impossible finery, dancing under the very walls of the prison and the fort: you could not put a thousand men and women, no matter how lewd, into the calaboose. In the minds of the white men watching the signs underwent a metaphoric shift: the libidinal freedom of the slave body called up another freedom, which could only be bought by blood. Bras Coupé, the escaped slave who is the real hero of Cable's *The Grandissimes*, was also the hero of the bamboula in Cable's mental Place Congo. It was in the body dancing to its own tune that the sign of freedom lay.

The strange thing about the color line is that while color, as an absolute of race, is imaginary, the line in the codes and traditions that enforced it is quite real. Like those lines drawn on a map that separate zones of time, or longitude and latitude, crossing that unseen line could have consequences, and in the days of Miché Bainjo those consequences could be horrific. George Washington Cable knew that as well as any white man could. His extraordinary novel, *The Grandissimes*, set in the New Orleans of the 1830s, is the story of two brothers split by the fiction of race, one of them white, the other in that strange not-white, not-black half-light of the New Orleans Creole, the f.m.c., the "free man of color." It is thus in this shadow world of the legally black, light-skinned man (or woman, in the case of Cable's sometime lecture partner Mark Twain's magnificent blonde Roxy) that the fiction of race is focused in its richest absurdity. Because as Twain, for one, well knew, the tragedy of race is that race is a comedy. And only those who understand the joke know where to look for the freedom of the unfree.

The modes of open resistance for slaves were few: the desperate one of rebellion, the equally dangerous one of running away, the ultimate one of suicide. Yet there was another kind of resistance that, within slavery itself, provided a multitude of living variations: the satiric arts.

Was there a cakewalk before the cakewalk? In eighteenth-century Virginia there was a special provocation in the way a slave might walk. Some slaves, Philip D. Morgan writes, "might have succumbed to their stereotype or perhaps parodied it, for some sauntered in a seemingly exaggerated fashion." But there were other slaves who took an opposite tack, "Strutting rather than shuffling, swaggering rather than shambling." Morgan continues,

> some slaves walked in a most unslavelike manner. A "stately" or "strutting" walk, a "proud carriage," carrying the "head high," walking "remarkable grand and strong" or "boldly" represented one small way in which slaves could resist the dehumanization inherent in their status.[3]

Fawning and flattery, even, could turn a hyperbolic bend and become mockery for the benefit of the slaves working in the kitchen or in the hall. (Cable prints a rowing song in which the slaves at the oars imagine Master returning from town in a pleasant mood and "will treat his boys all 'round.") More-open mockery was available as well. In 1772, a correspondent calling himself The Stranger, writing in the *South Carolina Gazette*, told of observing a country dance five miles out of Charleston one September night, where about sixty blacks sported in an entertainment which was opened by "the men copying (or *taking off*) the manners of their masters and the women those of their mistresses . . . to the inexpressible diversion of that company."[4] Cable remembered a song from his childhood, the call of a black peddler woman selling rice croquettes from a tray balanced on her head. At sunrise she would go from street to street, chanting a satiric calinda song about a grand ball the magistrate Miché Preval gave in his stable, charging the blacks three dollars for a ticket. The song had many stanzas, and even the white masters added their own inventions.[5] All these efforts, from the most subtle in-group satire to the most open mockery and burlesque, to simply affecting a bold and strutting walk when a slave was expected to cringe, were different modes of resistance to the expectations of the white world. The trick was in how far the black woman or man, slave or free, was able to push an imaginary line. Take care, Miché Bainjo. In 1806 the legislature of the Territory of Orleans made it illegal for slaves or free people of color to presume themselves equal to whites.[6]

Learning to Read

Frederick Douglass remembered as a boy listening to the songs of Colonel Lloyd's slaves as they tramped through the woods on the way to the Great House Farm. He was a slave then himself, and as he listened the songs revealed at once the highest joy and the deepest sadness. He thought the singers of these spontaneous songs consulted neither time nor tune. But Douglass, the boy listening to these chants, to the calls and responses, could not articulate the meaning of those songs. With their terrible sadness, but also with their joy, the joy of the salvation and rebirth or the joy of going up to the Big Farm—which could in fact have stood for Heaven or Freedom or the North or that lost African past—the sorrow songs were more articulate than the young slave knew. "I did not, when a slave," he wrote, "understand the deep meaning of those rude and apparently incoherent songs. I was myself within the circle; so that I neither saw nor heard as those without might see and hear." To be inside the circle, to be without a place to stand outside the givens of your lot, without a perspective, is for Douglass to feel, but not to understand. Yet he traced to those songs his first glimmering conception of what slavery did to men and women. He could never get rid of that conception. The songs followed him all of his life, deepening his hatred for slavery and his sympathies for his brothers and sisters still in chains.[7]

For Douglass, the great step that would take him outside that circle that limited his understanding of his life as a slave was learning, at the age of twelve, to read. His autobiographies are classic works of the Enlightenment.

Douglass's account of this process of self-knowledge is one of the great texts of psychology, and in fact, the awakening of despair, the initial abjection, clearly illustrate what William James would outline in *The Varieties of Religious Experience*, fifty-some years later, in his chapters on conversion. The conversion in Douglass wasn't to belief in an afterlife and servitude to a benevolent god, but to freedom, and with his knowledge and indomitable will, he finally found means to escape slavery. But for the men and women still in bondage, the great question was what they might make of their lot *within* their servitude.

The slaves watching the cotillion through the windows of the Big House, or through the kitchen door were learning to read the language of their masters as surely as Frederick Douglass had. Yet in order to use this vocabulary of flourishes and graces and flutterings they needed to translate it into their own terms. Those terms had their beginning in West Africa, because much of Africa's expression, its religious life and its praise and its mockery (and Africa was rich in the tradition of mockery) was carried by the linked forms of music and dance. But the mockery had a deeper meaning than mere satire. For it lay at the heart of West African mythology. Henry Louis Gates Jr., in his classic work *The Signifying Monkey*,[8] his quest for a theory of African American literary criticism, discovers in the Yoruban trickster god Esu and his West African kin the progenitors of the role of interpreters of signs, the translators of the fates laid out in the toss of the sacred palm nuts and the obscure riddles of the gods. Yet interpretation is also a form of riddling itself, of reimagining and thus an act of creation, and it is not for nothing that Esu, god of the crossroads, is imagined with penis erect. The term

Gates uses to describe this process is Signifyin(g), which contains within it the conventional meaning of signifying and the multiple African American practices of signifyin', which range from cutting verbal insults, through competitions in improvisation, to praise, but always done through indirection, always foregrounding the liberating spirit of play. Like a jazz musician riffing on a theme from some hoary show tune and taking it to a new and unimagined territory, interpretation can rewrite the language of fate.

Like all languages, that of the cotillion sprang out of a social world, and as far as the white world of the plantation went, the slaves were always metaphorically looking through the windows. Because of the poverty of the slaves, their proscribed social selves, simple imitation of the rites of the cotillion would thus be a zero, a failed language from the start. Mockery was thus the necessary vehicle for translation into a language that was true to the slaves' understanding of their lot and their desire to find some kind of freedom within it.

The Cakewalk

When he himself was very old, the actor Leigh Whipper remembered going home to South Carolina to attend his mother's funeral and talking to his old nurse. Back in the 1840s, when she was quite a young girl, and full of bounce, she was a "strut gal," a slave who received special privileges for her dancing. Like a prize racehorse, she was taken from one plantation to another to enter dancing contests, while the slave owners bet on the outcome.

> Us slaves watched white folks' parties where the guests danced a minuet and then paraded in a grand march, with the ladies and gentlemen going different ways and then meeting again, arm in arm, and marching down the center together. Then we'd do it, too, *but we used to mock 'em*, every step. Sometimes the white folks noticed it but they seemed to like it; I guess they thought we couldn't dance any better.[9]

Shep Edmonds too described these slave dances. "They did a take-off on the high manners of the white folks in the big house, but their masters, who gathered around to watch the fun, missed the point."

Or maybe not. "What exactly could the masters do about it?" ask Marshall and Jean Stearns, from whose *Jazz Dance* these examples are drawn. To admit that the slave satire was anything more than childish imitation would be an admission that when they looked at the mocking figures of the dance, they saw themselves.[10]

Seen through the lens of African tradition, the people promenading in the Big House were dead from the waist down. And, in fact, they might in some symbolic sense really *have been* dead, for in West Africa straightened knees and elbows and hips were the signs of the corpse: it was the loose, the limber, the bent knee that was the emblem of life.[11] Africa dances close to the ground, torso bent, knees bent, the body one whole lively coil of vitality and movement. Sometimes the limbs have lives of their own, move independently of the rhythms of the trunk, but the dance is always sensual, always alive.[12] So the rigid backs and the military strut of the cotillion might be laughable in themselves, but become exquisitely exploitable by black caricature: in that old plantation contest for Mistress's cake, the spine is not merely straight but thrust backward at an unbelievable angle; the hips and legs are not only reminiscences of the military march and the fencing school from which they are derived, but are impossible contortions, legs thrust straight out in front, arms bent at the elbows ridiculously high, chins tipped skyward under the straps of imaginary busbies. Flipped upside down, the cane of sobriety and dodderhood becomes a drum major's baton, a portable maypole, a magic phallus sprouting ribbons and rosettes in this dance of life.

Brooke Baldwin, in her essay "The Cakewalk: A Study in Stereotype and Reality," cites instances of representations of the cakewalk in the white press as early as 1863. It appeared increasingly in blackface minstrelsy as a grand Walk Around, the final tambourine-rattling procession that might have been some travestied version of the Ring Shout, that Afro-American revenant of the old African religion. In his celebrated *Blues People*, Amiri Baraka lingered for a moment to enjoy the multiple ironies caroming off this complex signifying:

> If the cakewalk is a Negro dance caricaturing certain white customs, what is that dance when, say, a white theater company attempts to satirize it as a Negro dance? I find the idea of white minstrels in blackface satirizing a dance satirizing themselves a remarkable kind of irony—which, I suppose, is the whole point of minstrel shows.[13]

After the Civil War the "peregrination for the pastry" would find its way increasingly into white representations of black life, whether grotesquely caricatured or presumably realistic, and became more and more a part of the white imagination. "Postbellum white caricaturists substituted denial and denigration of black culture for their race's lost license to control it," Baldwin pointedly observes.[14]

What was to be made of the rubble of the cotillion? The leftover bows and feathers and top hats of the potlatch? In the post–Civil War South the cotillion was a vestigial remnant of a caste that had lost its place. But the cakewalk, that mocking parasite, survived and grew. With its syncopated gestures and elaborate relations with a white society that despised or condescended to African Americans, it was the bearer of a complex truth beyond parody. For parody, like imitation, is sterile. Parody can mock, but it cannot create; it can caper in the castoff finery of pretension and pride, yet when the ladder is kicked out from under it, it discovers it doesn't even own its own laughter. But what if beyond the rituals of mockery there is something else being born? Just as Emily Dickinson played her idiosyncratic rhythms off against the familiar expectations of the hymnbook to create something powerful and new, for a few years history and opportunity and the tropes of black and white America came together in an elegant dance, a competition of style. A style that might represent a race's own aspiration to a place in American life.[15]

By the 1890s the cakewalk had acquired all its elements of satiric resistance, hope, comedy, and grace. When Abraham Cahan—and we will come to him—attended a cakewalk in New York, he found the categories of the contestants set as Straight, Fancy, and Burlesque. Indeed, flickering through the 1903 American Mutoscope and Biograph Company's one-minute films in the Library of Congress (easily found on YouTube) are all three possibilities. If the cakewalk still could be danced with minstrel show buffoonery, it could also be danced with elegance and grace. Professionals like George and Aida Overton Walker, Charlie Johnson, and Dora Dean, who danced to a strobe light in formal attire and white gloves, had made the dance a thing of real beauty.[16]

No one knows what music the first cakewalks were danced to—probably the same jigs and marches that black fiddlers played for their white masters' dancing parties. But the cakewalk had long needed a music of its own, a music that was as hybrid as itself, one that had embedded in its very form a witty tension between two histories and two social worlds, but that was capable too, beyond its satire, of the most subtle refinements, of an elegance to match its wit. Well before the time of the first annual cakewalk championship held in Madison Square Garden in 1892, it found it.

Syncopation Rules This Nation

Syncopation [ad. med. L. *syncopatio - onem*, n. of action f. *syncopare*: see SYNCOPATE.]

3. *Mus.* The action of beginning a note on a normally unaccented part of the bar and sustaining it into the normally accented part, so as to produce the effect of shifting back or anticipating the accent; the shifting of accent so produced.

—*Oxford English Dictionary*

The syncopation of jazz is no more than an idiomatic corruption, a flattened-out mutation of what was once the true polyrhythmic character of African music.

—Gunther Schuller, *Early Jazz*

Since the 1840s in all the best parlors of America matrons squeezed into whalebone corsets, and wearing enough silk to tent a small army, and gentlemen in starched shirtfronts had listened as girls and sensitive young men dripped their tears over the keys of Chickering pianos while poets kept expiring, dear old mothers kept going to their final rest, and spotless virgins synchronized their last gasps to the tremolos that accompanied them to the other world. It was an age of sentimentality, and sentimentality ran through the popular music like an ineradicable spore. Racially proscribed though he might have been, there were even available gentle voices to call to Old Black Joe. Stephen Foster had caught perfectly the pitch of a land in mourning for an imaginary pastoral. A northerner, he set this innocent lost world in the antebellum American South and you could hear, under the clacking of the bones and the tambourines in his jolliest songs, that pastoral crumbling all the doo-dah day, before a world become increasingly in thrall to steam power and gun powder and Empire.

Of course there were other songs as well in this post–Civil War America, the satiric songs of the vaudeville stage, some a bit risqué and some that even mocked the same Victorian sentimentality. But in the retrospect we are allowed, something essential is needed to lift the music above the quivering of the parlor pianos and the brass band crassness of the vaudeville tunes. What that something was had already been hinted at for a white audience in crude imitation in the minstrel show; and it had been heard in the bravura performances of America's first piano virtuoso, that flower of rare breed,

Louis Moreau Gottschalk—his mother a New Orleans Creole, his father a London Jew—who had been turning fragments of slave music represented by a banjo tune or the bamboula into concert hall showpieces since 1848. Yet these incursions hardly touched the essential sentimentality or the consciousnesses of white America except as novelties, and Gottschalk was as apt to maunder through the corridors of his endless salon music or tug the Victorian heartstrings with something like "Morte!" as he was to try to capture the sexual zest of the rumba or the calinda.

What was missing was what Sidney Lanier heard in that complex slap of hands and feet the slaves called Juba. It was an element central to African American music and without which much of it would be unimaginable: syncopation. The term itself is a tricky one, for it relates to a variation of European rhythmic practice, and had itself been a part of European music; but just as there were no such things as blue notes in African music, which was not diatonic,[17] so to African ears there was no syncopation of set rhythms, since Africa was polyrhythmic to begin with. Slaves were heard singing rowing songs described as a bit late in the beat, but the writers who noted this rhythmic anomaly were white.[18] The "lateness" was the Western ear trying to absorb the habitual African accent on the offbeat.

To catch syncopation making its way into American music we will return to those first songs and dances of white minstrels like Dan Emmett or Daddy Rice or the famous black minstrel William Henry Lane—Master Juba—and hear in the clack of the bones and the thumping of tambourines the ghosts of the rhythmic languages of Africa in sometimes strange compromises with Irish jigs and Anglo-American marches, a process that began when black slaves and the Irish and Scottish laborers and indentured servants who were scarcely above them in status in eighteenth-century Tidewater Virginia and Maryland danced to each other's fiddle tunes.[19]

In the "Doctor Hekok Jig," which may in fact have been a slave tune, we hear an early model of this kind of syncopation [fig. 3]. The stutters and starts that obtrude on the smoothness of the melody are the spasms of a strange dance coming out of Africa and the conventions of the Irish jig.[20]

The first tunes whose syncopations would be familiar to contemporary ears were rags, which were mired in their association with the Coon Songs, those racial travesties that African Americans, like the greatly talented Ernest Hogan, who took a ditty he heard in a saloon called "All Pimps Look Alike to Me" and recast it as the wildly popular "All Coons Look Alike

Figure 3. "Doctor Hekok Jig," in Hans Nathan, *Dan Emmett and the Rise of Early Negro Minstrelsy* (Norman, University of Oklahoma Press, 1962), p. 203.

to Me," and equally talented white men like Ben Harney ("Mr. Johnson Turn Me Loose"), churned out. The songs, with their razors, knives, shooting, and libidinous rage, were taken up enthusiastically by both black and white. Yet it was the melodies, those strange, jaunty, syncopated struts that lingered in the ear, and remained to be made something better of by a handful of piano players, mostly black, a few white, that would lift the rag into something very close to art.

Rag. Yes, this new music was a *ragged* music. It was built on a rhythm a white audience, especially, might experience as made up of shreds and patches. Like the cakewalk, this jaunty music had something inherently satiric and liberating within it. You could rag "Stars and Stripes Forever" and give it an insouciant bounce; open up the rhythm a little, let it swing, and you could syncopate "La Paloma" and the "Anvil Chorus" and the "*Tannhäuser* Overture" and a theme from *Il Trovatore*.[21] This might be seen as wit or sacrilege; like everything else, it depended on how you looked at it. Take the minstrel show patrols, those travesties of African American military companies, which may have contributed their mite to the origins of the cakewalk and which, for some reason, kept post–Civil War white America in stitches: flip the mirror around and you might wonder just what is being satirized after all, as anyone who has ever had the pleasure of watching the drum major of a black ROTC drill team jiving a cadence can tell you.

For ragtime syncopations *play upon* the expected, upon the regular pulse of a European bass line. Against this beat are posed the silvery syncopations of the treble clef, cascades of melody that skip across and tease the oompah, oompah of the European march.

You start up something like this in the left hand:

Figure 4.

Add this, over the top of it, with the right hand:

Figure 5.

And you end up with

MAPLE LEAF RAG.

BY SCOTT JOPLIN.

Figure 6.

Copyright 1899 by John Stark & Son.

By the 1890s the cakewalk, that irrepressible dance, would be performed to the music of rags played and sung in the dangerous realm of the saloons and bordellos of the dark side of town.

Dangerous Cakewalking

In the railroad center of Sedalia, Missouri, in the last decade of the nineteenth century, the tensions in African American life were expressed in spatial terms, a poignant irony for men and women who were defined in the white world spatially as well—defined by the seats they could not sit in, the railroad cars they could not ride in, the voting booths and schools they could not be present in. At one end of the black district were the churches, and the Negro college where the young Scott Joplin was taking classes in harmony. At the other were the social clubs, the saloons, and whorehouses. The social clubs aspired to respectability, but they could be dangerous, sometimes scenes of ugly fights and killings. Lounging through this environment was the pimp, index fingers pointed out, "shooting the agate," as Jelly Roll Morton would describe it, in a lavish display of conspicuous wealth and leisure.

The end of Reconstruction left the shell of the Old South an unconscious parody of itself. Huey P. Long Jr. and William Faulkner's Flem Snopes replaced the Lees and the Jefferson Davises as the arbiters of the white South's economy, politics, and social world.[22] For the freed slaves the truth of this post-Reconstruction South was the hood and the rope and the sharecrop system. But the cakewalk was destined to outlive its plantation origins. There was a new economy in the United States after the Civil War, and it was not based on family farms and cotton fields, but on unprecedented industrial expansion, on new cities covered by the plumes of smoke from the mills and factories that were springing up throughout the Northeast and Midwest especially, and on the rail lines that served them. African Americans were riding those rail lines too, crowding the Jim Crow cars for the promise of a better life. Between 1890 and 1910 a quarter of a million of them had migrated to the North alone. But once again those black bodies, working in mines and steel mills and in hotels and private homes and on the railroads that carried them out of a historyless slavery, moving now to a new music on the dark side of town, were seen as a threat.

The social clubs of Sedalia were dangerous to white and black propriety too, for the racial mixing that went on in them. There was a stand at one end of the Black 400 Club in Sedalia where whites were given seats of honor to watch the cakewalking; but they were sites of less genteel mingling too, as white sports might try to dance with a black girl, take her home for the night. The ragtime music played in the clubs and saloons could never outlive its origins.[23] Scott Joplin himself was a representative of its contradictions. He had moved up from rural Texarkana, Texas, to travel the border South trying to make his way as a musician, organizing quartets and bands and playing what was then called "jig piano." If he was trying to create something elegant and fresh with his rags, what his publisher John Stark would call "Classical," he was nevertheless earning his bread playing in saloons and social clubs like Sedalia's Maple Leaf and behind the red lights of Lottie Wright's and Nellie Hall's.

By the turn of the century Joplin had moved to Saint Louis's Chestnut Valley that with its violence and seductive vice was the sporting world of Sedalia writ large. Cecil Brown has brought the District to life through his studies of a couple of killings that gave birth to two of America's most enduring ballads, the murder of Billy Lyons, so the song says, for his brandnew Stetson hat by the ward heeler and pimp Lee Shelton on Christmas night, 1895, and the 1899 shooting by the twenty-two-year-old prostitute Frankie Baker of her two-timing mack, Al Britt. So came Stagolee, so came Frankie and Albert—aka Frankie and Johnny.[24] The connections between the ragtime musicians and the District were deep. Al Britt got caught with Frankie's rival coming home from playing piano for a cakewalk competition. Scott Joplin found beautiful half-Indian Louis Chauvin, dying of opium addiction and TB in a Chicago whorehouse, plucking out the theme of what would be one of the most beautiful of ragtime pieces, "Heliotrope Bouquet," on the parlor piano.[25] But the melancholy strain that appears in "Heliotrope Bouquet" and a number of rag's finest pieces comes more from a fin de siècle *tristesse* that it shared with the popular music of the day, such as "After the Ball Is Over" and the music of the European salon, than from this rough and racialized world, which expressed its melancholy more fully in the blues and what Du Bois called "the Sorrow Songs," the spirituals of the black church. For ragtime, with its underpinning of cakewalk satire, and what Joplin called its "weird and intoxicating effects," is essentially a music of elegance, joy, and wit.

The rags were irresistible. "It was music that demanded physical response, patting of the feet, drumming of the fingers, or nodding of the head in time with the beat," as James Weldon Johnson describes it.

> The barbaric harmonies, the audacious resolutions, often consisting of an abrupt jump from one key to another, the intricate rhythms in which the accents fell in the most unexpected places, but in which the beat was never lost, produced a most curious effect. . . . Anyone who doubts that there is a peculiar heel-tickling, smile-provoking, joy-awakening charm in ragtime needs only to hear a skillful performer play the genuine article to be convinced.[26]

Joplin never published a piece having anything like the popularity of the "Maple Leaf Rag" in his lifetime, though the success of "Maple Leaf" was eclipsed after Hollywood got hold of "The Entertainer" in the early 1970s. But he was only one of a host of ragtime composers, black and white, good, great, mediocre, and awful, in Chicago and California and Texas and up and down the East Coast.

The keepers of America's morality saw ragtime as a plague. Nothing but bad could come from it to America's youth, in rebellion because of the "unwholesome" black influences coming through the morning-glory horns of crank-up Victrolas. Ragtime was "syncopation gone mad," and its victims, like rabid dogs, were best treated with a dose of lead. The counters of the music stores were loaded with "this virulent poison which, in the form of a malarious epidemic," was finding its way into the homes and brains of the young. Its "restless rhythm and suggestive words" came from the brothels and its music was regularly found in "the dens of vice and in the vilest of cabarets" along with "sporting papers and salacious novels." In short, America was falling prey "to the collective soul of the negro"[27]—thoughts that sound familiar to white Americans of a certain age who remember dancing to Fats Domino and Little Richard and whose suburban grandchildren are now chasing the runaway cabooses of hip hop and rap. Edward A. Berlin's invaluable history of ragtime, from which these examples are drawn, captures the feel of the outraged reaction of proper (and usually white) society.

But ragtime had its respectable defenders, musicians and critics, as well. Charles Ives, himself the composer of some lovely ragtime dances, dismissed ragtime's critics as "old ladies of both sexes."[28] With its "hide-and-seek accent," its dangerous formula of "two thrills a beat," ragtime was undoubt-

Figure 7. Scott Joplin and Scott Hayden, "Something Doing," 1903. Val A. Reis Music Company, St. Louis, Missouri.

edly the "folk-music of the American City," as Hiram Moderwell had it. There was in ragtime's sound the very "jerk and rattle" of this American city,

> a personality different from that of any European capital. . . . No European music can or possibly could express this American personality. Ragtime I believe does express it. It is to-day the one true American music.[29]

Whether it was a plague or manna in the desert, the ragging of America, like the subsequent jazzing of America, depicted so brilliantly as the "Jes Grew Phenomenon" in Ishmael Reed's now classic *Mumbo Jumbo*, was unstoppable. And if there were ragtime marches and ragtime waltzes and ragtime tangos, there were also endless ragtime cakewalks.

On the cover of Scott Joplin and Scott Hayden's cakewalk "Something Doing" of 1903 we see these cakewalkers observed by a white audience, much as Mark Twain might have looked on a decade or so before [fig. 7].[30] The members of the audience are peering through lorgnettes and spectacles and opera glasses at a pair of resplendent black cakewalkers, she in picture hat and ribbons, he decked out in frock coat and spats, his beribboned cane held upside down à la mode, in his eye a twinkling monocle. The audience views the cakewalkers with a sort of condescending mirth, as if watching a children's dress-up parade. The cakewalkers are cartoon figures, yes, but not caricatures. The belle glances over the shoulder of her beau, he smiles and winks through his unglassed eye, and perhaps—it is a question the artist consciously or unconsciously asks—they know something their white audience doesn't. But these cartoon figures are not looking at the white audience looking at them. They are looking at some unseen audience watching the watchers and at the same time watching them: for there is a witness off the page, a third possibility, beyond the bonds of the reciprocity of parody and the parodied. They are looking into something not yet created, rich with possibilities of meaning and style. They are looking into a future that is both in them and in us.

A Ragtime of the Mind

> But there is also an American Negro tradition which teaches one
> to deflect racial provocation and to master and contain pain. It is a
> tradition which abhors as obscene any trading of one's own anguish
> for gain or sympathy; which springs not from a desire to deny the

harshness of existence but from a will to deal with it as men at their best
have always done. It takes fortitude to be a man and no less to be an
artist. Perhaps it takes even more if the black man would be an artist.
                                  —Ralph Ellison, "The World in a Jug"

Joplin aspired to lift ragtime from its birthplace in the minstrel show, the
whorehouse, and the saloon and dreamed of creating a music beyond the
local professor in the dime-store window butchering the "Maple Leaf Rag"
at finger-cracking speed, of freeing ragtime from the music stand of the
parlor piano where "Sugar Cane" sat next to "Silver Threads Among the
Gold." The lyrics of the Coon Songs embarrassed him. He wanted a music
that expressed the life of the African American world, its aspirations and
ideals. He dreamed of a ragtime opera, a work that would move his beautiful
music into a real theater. A music of dignity, elegance, and joy.[31] There is an
early, lost opera by Joplin called *The Guest of Honor*, and scholars imagine
that that guest was Booker T. Washington, whom Theodore Roosevelt had
invited to dine in the White House, the first African American so distin-
guished. If this is true, the theme of the opera would be one that pervaded
black life in America, the theme of education as a way toward equality in
an unequal world. This is the theme of the Joplin opera that has survived.
Treemonisha is a mélange, part sentimental operetta, part lively ragtime, a
compendium of hoedowns and spirituals and cakewalks and quartets with
a concluding slow drag that can bring tears to your eyes with its loveliness.

The rhymes in *Treemonisha* are forced, the characters undeveloped—
imagine what Mozart's librettist Da Ponte would have done with Parson
Alltalk or with Zodzetrick, who with his factitious elegance anticipates
Sportin' Life of *Porgy and Bess*. But it is with the story itself I want to deal,
for the story tells us much about the world Joplin grew up in, a world he
transformed into a simple fairy tale.

It is a dreamworld where the whites exist only outside the margins of the
text, absentee owners of the plantation, whose nonpresence only reinforces
the vulnerability and dependence of its newly freed slaves. Treemonisha, the
eighteen-year-old heroine, comes to the plantation from the world outside
as well, a changeling, and therefore a child of destiny. The text makes it clear
that she is "light-skinned" and this hint of a shameful liaison will be transformed by the opera into a triumphant blending of African American aspiration and the opportunities that only the white world in those first years of

emancipation could provide; for Treemonisha will come to be educated by the white folks, an education that no one in her community has yet obtained.

It is significant that Joplin in some sense cast himself as this changeling girl, for like Treemonisha he saw himself as bringing light into a world where he found so much ignorance and brutality. The lynch mob and the color line lie beyond the borders of the opera, but the violence and ignorance of the black world itself that Joplin found in Chestnut Valley were transformed in the opera into the woods haunted by the conjure men, tricksters who prey on the poor farmers with their good luck charms and their spells and by the dangerous powdered dreams supplied by Zodzetrick, the goofer dust man.

Treemonisha, for all its fairy-tale simplicity, is like *The Magic Flute* and like Frederick Douglass's autobiography, a work of the Enlightenment, of light and purity shining into darkness. The farmers drive the conjurers and the goofer dust man from the woods, tricking them with their own superstitious terrors. Seven years before the passage of the Nineteenth Amendment, Joplin had Treemonisha voted the leader of this community of illiterate farmers.

The last song, danced to the slow drag, is for that reason heartbreaking in its wish, the wish of a whole generation of black men and women—

Marching onward, marching onward
Marching to that lovely tune

But Joplin was dying and there would be only one hurried performance of *Treemonisha* on a bare stage in a rented Harlem theater, without lights or costumes or orchestra, without its many dances. Its lilting and joyful and touching songs strung upon a plot that was no more hackneyed than many in the Grand Opera repertoire would not be heard except in individual pieces for sixty years. The building in which Joplin had written his opera of the triumph of love, reason, and racial pride had become a house of assignation. He died of the effects of terminal syphilis in 1917 in Manhattan State Hospital on the East River, almost to the end feverishly scratching out themes on scraps of paper.[32] For all his aspirations, he could neither bring his music to the opera stage nor outrun its origins in the whorehouses and sporting clubs of Sedalia and St. Louis. Those origins killed him. By the time Joplin died, the elegant and poignant music of which he was one of the greatest creators had largely been swamped by Tin Pan Alley productions such as "Alexander's Ragtime Band," which if ragtime means syncopation, wasn't ragtime at all, and inane novelties such as "A Coon Band Contest," at the same time that it had entered the respectable precincts of composers such as Ives, Stravinsky, and Debussy.

Years before, the white audience on the cover of Joplin's and Hayden's "Something Doing" had stepped down from the observers' stand and were cakewalking across their parquet floors themselves. William K. Vanderbilt had hired a cakewalk teacher and Theodore Roosevelt had led a cakewalk through the East Room of the White House.[33] If white America knew the mocking origins of this dance they didn't let on, but participated as gleefully as their housemaids in the fun. But first they had to learn to dance, and it was African America who taught them.

The African American cakewalkers might have fallen into the sterility of their social superiors with their parodic display of costumed elegance, might have been as socially useless, as steeped in invidious competition as the participants in the parade of carriages and walking sticks up Fifth Avenue, but for one thing: their dance had entered the vestibule of art.

Thus the canes and the top hats, the watch chains and fans of the cakewalk, were played out on a symbolic register that was anything but meaningless. And no one, not George Washington Cable nor Mark Twain, understood this more than the African Americans who marched to the syncopated steps of Scott Joplin's and Arthur Marshall's "Swipesy." For after all, who knew better than the valets who shaved them and the coachmen who curried their horses and the maids who pulled the laces of their wives' corsets how empty was the distinction claimed by their masters? Who knew better than their servants the nuances of their masters' and mistresses' style, and the most elegant way to turn that style inside out? Or how to reconcile in a syncopated parade for a cake the instincts of envy and satire? The cakewalkers of the 1890s—absent the usual contingent of pimps—were anything but a leisure class; they were the working men and women of a new emancipation. Their finery, like that of the Astors and the Vanderbilts and the Whitneys, was weighed on the scales of social pride, but in its self-conscious exaggerations the cakewalk was played out not only parallel to that of the leisured white world, but also *against* it; it was both emulation and caricature at once, and behind the smiling leader of the cakewalk with his uplifted cane and beaming smile there was surely the mighty figure of the trickster god and interpreter Esu. It was a dance of assertion, of pride, surely. Yet for African Americans of the Gilded Age the dance could only go so far. You might be able to cakewalk athwart history, but you couldn't cakewalk out of it.

TWO PHOTOGRAPHS

It is not easy to look at this photograph [fig. 8]. A poster stuck to a brick wall. The paper has been partially torn away, so that it clings in shreds to the brick. It is as if a bomb has gone off inside it. The torn rags of paper carry exploded pieces of flesh and clothing flying from the center. A pickanninny leaps over a fence with a watermelon, a bulldog's teeth in his rump. Another sails into the air, clutching his rear from the kick of a mule. A pair of disembodied hands reach from an exposed section of brick to clutch at a chicken; truncated legs dive from the scene. In the top window of a broken house a razor-wielding ape rolls his eyes, menaces a banjo-playing darky in top hat and tails who is serenading a woman inside. A fat-lipped mammy in a bandana hurls a pail of slop from the porch.

The creatures in it are not human, not even the monsters of fantasy, but animals. They have the teeth and snouts and white, terrified eyes of animals, of apes, hyenas, baboons. Bodies are torn, beaten, kicked. The policeman's truncheon is a wrenched-off cock, and he will bludgeon the fleeing to death with it. The rumps of children are brutalized by the teeth of dogs, by the hooves of mules, by buckshot. Water sloshes everywhere in incontinent fantasies. The gelder's blade flashes from a window.

Other pictures surround the photograph of the minstrel show poster in Walker Evans's books. Pictures of the dead and dying towns of rural counties in the Depression-era South. Mules stand slack-necked in front of the courthouse; a heavy touring car simmers in the noon heat. The stores are blank and gaping, covered with peeling advertisements for chewing tobacco and liniment. Their emptiness is not a significance, a fictive or a sentimental value: we look at the minstrel show poster in the perspective of these empty streets. Such vacancy is the place where cruelty and sentimentality meet. It is a mirror which reflects our own pale dreams of grace, our bloody visions of violence and despair. There is another playbill caught by Walker Evans's camera [fig. 9]. Blacks promenade in impossible elegance at a ball. They swirl in crinolines, in swallowtail coats. Their hair is brilliantined, their skins polished like rare wood. Their faces are the smooth, dreamless faces of manikins in the windows of a store.

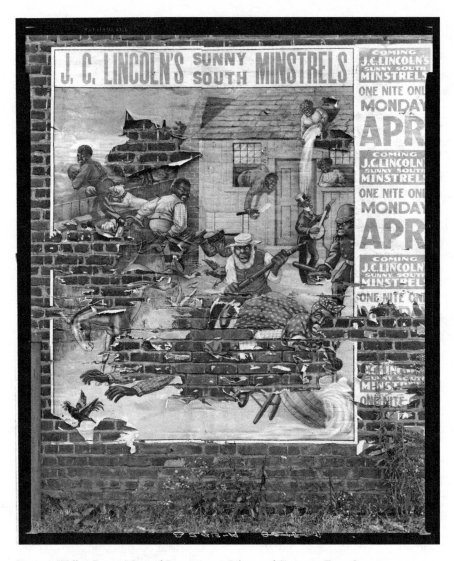

Figure 8. Walker Evans, Minstrel Poster, 1936. Library of Congress, Farm Security
Administration / Office of War Administration, Black and White Photograph Collection.
LC-USF342-008243-A-B [P&P]

Figure 9. Walker Evans, Minstrel Poster, detail, 1936. Library of Congress, Farm Security Administration / Office of War Administration, Black and White Photograph Collection. LC-USF342-001136-A [P&P]

Minstrels

Who are these gibbering, hyperkinetic idiots? Faces blackened with burnt cork, mouths smeared with white until their grins and grimaces take on a life of their own, they prance and parade, fidget and fight—or just prepare to fight with elaborate boasts—exchange repartee with the elegant gent in the middle of the row of chairs (those chairs they can't manage to sit on for more than a second at a time) rattle their tambourines, plink their banjos, clack the bones, and tell sappy jokes that only a yokel could love. They are Bones and Tambo, named for the primitive instruments they slap and click. Not men, not Negroes even, but somebody's nightmare, and withal as gentle as idiots.

Who knows where they came from? There were blackface performers in England, but Constance Rourke in her still excellent *American Humor* sees the American minstrels as Irish roustabouts (what's a minstrel dancing a jig, after all, but a corked-up Irishman?). Yet here in Jacksonian America there was being created on the stage a new language and a continuation of its war against black humanity under another name.

The Irish connection that Constance Rourke suggested is more than interesting: one proscribed and caricatured race puts on the mask of another and creates a kind of immunity and freedom. Scholars dig through the by now ancient minstrel show scripts to find social satire in a space where class and race slip in and out of the exchanges of meaning, and evoke the old tradition of the immunity of the fool. There might be traces too of magic in all this, the magic of kings and hunchbacks, the erotic and chthonic power of the exotic that once lured a king of France to dance as a Moor to the strains of Lully in a hall of mirrors.[34]

Yet beyond the class satire masked as race, or any ancient magic, there was the overwhelming attraction of the songs, the dances, the slapping banjos, the bad jokes. For the Minstrel Show—and it is difficult if not impossible now to understand how this was so—was beloved.

There was in Beauty, Edmund Burke thought, something that approached more nearly to contempt than was most generally thought. This might be true of love as well.

For if love in its far reaches might be a form of self-despising, another reach might be the sense of power that shows itself in condescension. The two sides might even be held in one consciousness. The minstrel show would develop from two end men and an interlocutor to more and more elaboration. Along the way there would rise strange hybrid forms, nostalgia for a South that never was, tearjerkers about slave girls sold away, black minstrels blacking up, black musicians and performers appropriating the Coon Song, all meeting in the tragic figure of the best beloved figure of the twentieth-century American stage, a thoughtful and elegant black man coming out from behind the curtain in ostentatious rags and blackened face.

Nobody

This must be a dream. But whose? The white-gloved hand groping from out of the curtain, tentative, wiggling, trying to find a way to pull the cloth aside.

> Hesitantly the hand followed the fingers, then an arm, a shoulder, and finally, with awkward reluctance, a tall man in a shabby dress suit pushed through the curtains and walked slowly to the front of the stage. The applause started before he reached the footlights, but the face behind the mask of blackface remained downcast. As if resigned to some inevitable and unending stroke of bad fortune, he shrugged his shoulders. With exaggerated care he searched his ragged coat pocket, pulled out a small leather notebook, and slowly turned the pages of the book until he found what he was looking for. Audiences settled into their seats expectantly when nodding in satisfaction, he began to half-sing, half-recite:
>
> > When life seems full of clouds and rain,
> > And I am full of nothin' but pain,
> > Who soothes my thumpin', bumpin' brain?
>
> He paused and shrugged with a sigh,
>
> > Nobody[35]

He was the most successful vaudevillian of his age, the highest paid, the best known. Among the Micks and the Sheenies and Dutchmen and Highland Flingers and Wops and Greeks and Swiss Yodelers of the vaudeville stage, he was the most admired. But finally, as he well knew, nobody.

He hadn't started out to be a travesty. He was born Egbert Austin Williams in Antigua, the West Indies, in 1874, though like many show people his biography is conjectural. His grandfather was the Danish consul in Antigua and he had white ancestry on his grandmother's and mother's side as well. He was handsome, over six feet tall, light-skinned, with a talent for mimicry. He said his grandfather lost most of his money, and when he was ten or eleven years old, his family emigrated to the United States and finally settled in Riverside, Southern California. He set off for Stanford. Whether he spent a couple of terms there, as his biographer Ann Chartres says, or simply never made it in the first place, 1890 found him traveling up and down the coast in shabby touring companies playing farm towns and lumber camps and hanging around the seedy bars of San Francisco singing, or trying to sing, for his supper.

In 1893 he met George Walker, an African American from Kansas who was a year older and who had been banging a tambourine in medicine shows. They came to call themselves "The Two Real Coons." They wanted to distinguish themselves from the blacked-up white men on the vaudeville circuit, and they caught the eye of promoters.

Bert Williams had to learn to be a coon. The language of the "stage Negro," he said, was "just as much a foreign dialect as that of the Italian." Williams and Walker worked on their act, settling into their roles of the Dandy, who was Walker, and the shiftless down-and-outer, Williams. One day in Detroit, at a theater called Moore's Wonderland, Bert Williams blacked up. It was the first time he had, and the results, he said, were electric. *Then I began to find myself. It was not until I was able to see myself as another person that my sense of humor developed.*[36] But the other person wasn't another person at all. He was a fabrication of the white imagination. Behind the terrible projection of this mask Bert Williams worked at perfecting his art. It was an art of conscious study—conscious, he says, "as soon as I began to get next to myself." But getting next to himself meant, as he put it, seeing himself as someone else, as if that volatile blend of whoever and whatever Bert Williams needed to be was poured into some imaginary bottle and decanted into laughter. He said what he was after was naturalness.

> I try to portray the shiftless darky to the fullest extent; his fun, his philosophy. There is nothing about this fellow I don't know. I must study his movements. I have to. He is not in me. The way he walks; the way he crosses his legs; the way he leans up against a wall, one foot forward.

He said he found much of his material by knocking around in out-of-the-way places and just listening. Eavesdropping on human nature was one of the most important parts of a comedian's work.[37]

Behind this mask he perfected an art of great subtlety. His voice, whether he sang or spoke, was soft, the dialect a suggestion. The humor was in his consummate timing, the rises and falls of inflection, the way he would freeze a facial expression and break it at exactly the right moment, the sweetness of the characterization. Singing, he moved from the most delicate of syncopations to a kind of spoken prose. Somehow, through that genius that the greatest actors have, he got to you.

Williams and Walker made a name for themselves as comedians and cakewalkers (it is their crudely drawn figures, copied from a lithograph, who cakewalk across the cover of Scott Joplin's "Maple Leaf Rag"). After the dance had become a fad with New York high society they challenged William K. Vanderbilt to a cakewalking match for the title of champion cakewalker of the world. Louis Chude-Sokei counts the erasure of Bert Williams from the history of the Harlem Renaissance as the embarrassment of a later age. In his thoughtful and wide-ranging book *The Last "Darky"*[38] he sees Bert Williams as playing a complex game of appropriating the white man's caricature of the black man and turning it inside out. But it is a particularly subtle reading and if it was all some colossal in-joke Williams himself never laid claim to it.

The black opera Joplin dreamed of was dead. The white audience that it needed to attract was not interested in fables of African American striving, but in seeing its own racial expectations singing and dancing on the stage. (One of Williams and Walker's songs was titled "The Coon's Trade-Mark: A Watermelon, Razor, Chicken and a Coon.") If black talent and wit were to be seen at all, they were to be seen in the musical revues, such as *Clorindy: The Origin of the Cakewalk* or *A Trip to Coon Town*, travesties of black life put on by blacks themselves that centered on the artifact called the Coon Song. "We wear the mask," Paul Laurence Dunbar said, "that grins and lies." But are you the mask, or is the mask a way of saying this is not me? For a black singer or songwriter or comedian, in some complex psychological tangle, it might be the latter; for a white audience at a vaudeville review it was a distinction without a difference.

That white audience was the crucial difference for the big shows, with their dancers and comedians, choruses and orchestras. For it was the Coon Shows that permitted black performers and composers an entrée to the legitimate theater in productions that only a ticket-buying white audience could support. The cost was great for Ernest Hogan, who wrote the hit song

"All Coons Look Alike to Me," and for educated men like Paul Laurence Dunbar and the classically trained musician Will Marion Cook.

In Dahomey of 1903, a collaboration by Cook, Dunbar, and Jesse Shipp, was the first full-length black musical to be performed in a major Broadway theater. Scholars, among them Marva Griffin Carter and David Krasner, have looked closely at shows such as *In Dahomey* and see more complexity than simple acquiescence to the minstrel show travesties that would satisfy the white audience's expectations. The same joke or story might be read differently by an African American than by the white sitting in the same theater. A song might carry a coded message for a black audience, or it might push a line that a white audience might miss.

> Come along Mandy,
> Come along Sue,
> White fo'ks a-watchin'
> An' seein' what you do,
> White fo'ks jealous when you'se walkin' two by two
> So swing along chillun
> Swing along.

It is a lovely invitation. But the Africa of *In Dahomey*, this place "where a coon is no longer a coon" and every darky is a king, is a swindle, a satire on white colonization schemes to solve the "Negro Problem" that went back as far as Thomas Jefferson, as unreal in its promise to African America as that of the still racially restrictive America. The theme of Emancipation Day that concludes the show is a secular resurrection, a judgment posited in another world outside the frame of the story and outside of time.

> On Emancipation day,
> All you white folks clear de way . . .
> When dey hear dem ragtime tunes
> White fo'ks try to pas fo'coons
> On Emancipation day.[39]

For Bert Williams and George Walker, two black men who made their fortune passing for coons, Emancipation Day had yet to come.

In Dahomey was Williams and Walker's greatest hit, touring England for a year, presented as a command performance in the garden of Buckingham Palace and making Bert Williams and George Walker social lions for a season. They must have known how tenuous their triumph was.

George Walker had few years left to sip the wine of his success. By 1909 syphilitic paresis had impaired his speech so much that he was unable to continue in Williams and Walker's *Bandana Land*. Two years later he was dead.

Without Walker, Bert Williams worked for a time as a single act in vaudeville, then mounted a new show, *Mr. Lode of Koal*. In 1910 he signed on to appear in the new edition of Florenz Ziegfeld's *Follies*. At the time he was seen as a race traitor. Yet he had integrated Ziegfeld's cast and opened the door for other African American performers in formerly all-white companies.

He was a trailblazer, the first black man to appear—and beyond that to star—in Ziegfeld's review, a man whose contract stipulated that the follies would not travel to the segregated South. But fame itself was dangerous to a black man. He surely remembered the forty-eight hours of racial mayhem in the theater district of New York in 1900. There would be no white chorus girls opposite him on Ziegfeld's stage if he could help it, and he spelled that out in writing in his agreements. He was left to play opposite a blacked-up Eddie Cantor, both of them singing Irving Berlin's "I'd Rather See a Minstrel Show."

Booker T. Washington said that Bert Williams had done more for the black man than he had. He had smiled his way into people's hearts while Washington said he had been obliged to fight his way.[40] Success, the great American solvent that could turn any Wall Street swindler with enough booty and perseverance into a social benefactor, was not enough in Bert Williams's case. He could wash the grease paint off his face after a performance, but he could not wash away the stain of race.

> I shuffle onto the stage, not as myself, but as a lazy, slow-going negro. . . . The real Bert Williams is crouched deep down inside the coon who sings and tells stories. . . . I'd like a piece that would give me the opportunity to express the whole of the negro's character. The laughter I have caused is only on the surface. Now I'd like to go much deeper and to show our depths that few understand yet. . . . [I]f I could interpret in the theatre [an] underlying tragedy of the race, I feel that we would be better known and better understood. Perhaps the time will come when that dream will come true.[41]

For all his success, he couldn't get a meal in a hotel or ride in the passenger elevator. "I am not complaining," he wrote,

> particularly since I know this to be an unbelievable custom. I am just wondering. I would like to know when (my prediction) the ultimate changes

come, if the new human beings will believe such persons as I am writing about actually lived?[42]

W. C. Fields, who counted Bert Williams as a friend, recalled Williams telling him of his experience on the first night of the Actors Equity strike of 1919. Williams emerged from his dressing room to find the theater dark. No one had bothered to tell him about the strike. He went back to his dressing room, washed the makeup off his face, and dressed. He found the theater manager up on the roof who asked him if he was with them or against them. Then he went home and closed the door to his library and asked himself if he had any views on Equity and found he had.

> Then I arranged some chairs in a semi-circle and held a meeting. I started the Bert Williams Equity. I was all the officers and all the members of both sides. I thrashed out the subject in true parliamentary order. First I was the president and opened the meeting, then I was each succeeding officer and I made speeches—anyway I had my own little equity and that is what I called it. I held briefs for both sides, because you see, I don't belong to either side. Nobody really wants me.[43]

David Belasco talked of other roles with Williams, but nothing came of it. Belasco thought Williams had been "overcome by diffidence and modesty."[44] "Bert Williams was the funniest man I ever saw," as W. C. Fields famously said, "and the saddest man I ever knew. I often wonder whether other people sensed what I did in him—that deep undercurrent of pathos."

Stunned and fluttering in a spotlight, Williams had become trapped in his audience's gaze. You can't finally sustain being two beings: the one who wears the mask and the one who sees the one wearing the mask. You can't be the picture and outside the picture at once.

> Before I got through with "Nobody" I could have wished that both the author of the words and the assembler of the tune had been strangled or drowned or talked to death. For seven whole years I had to sing it. Month after month I tried to drop it and sing something new, but I could get nothing to replace it and the audiences seemed to want nothing else.[45]

Now we know whose dream it is: it is Bert Williams's dream, one that he could not awaken from. If in putting on the burnt cork he learned to be funny, he had left the complex racial environment of the Caribbean and of his own aspirations and at the same time entered the simplifications of what Chude-

Sokei calls a bichromatic world, a world of black and white. For he himself had written the music to "Nobody," he knew it, and he knew you knew that. He was a king, but a king without the power to either abdicate or command. There were things America could let no black man or woman forget.

Nobody as Everybody: The Universal Coon

Yet caught in the grinning figure of the Coon, deeper perhaps than the racial travesty, is a desire, black or white, for our own emancipation. For the Coon is a fiction. A nobody. He is the other side of the Nigger. His liberty is absolute. You can't lynch a Coon. You can't destroy him.[46] His absurdity is beyond fear or rage. It was Bert Williams's genius to humanize this fiction: starting at that zero point, he moved beyond it; the stage sadness of Williams served as the medium in which we could meet, sympathize, and in some sense be the Coon: Williams had attempted to give the Coon an inner life. That inner life, too, is one shared by all of us, in our doubleness, in the face we hold out that the world, like we ourselves, may not quite believe in. Perhaps the pathos in Williams comedy does not come from his conventional pose of the Jonah Man, stepped on and ignored, but from the pathos we recognize in someone compelled to wear somebody else's face. William James claimed that we are all fabrications presented to the social world, held together by the glue of selective remembering and forgetting. If an Irishman or a Jew could enter American life by corking his face, why not a black man? The Coon is in this reading an imaginary location where white and black can meet. Yet we come to his image trailing our histories and the histories of our representations behind us. Clear as newsprint, they are read in our faces, they become us. "The declaration of an American identity," Ralph Ellison wrote, "meant the assumption of a mask, and it imposed not only the discipline of national self-consciousness, it gave Americans an ironic awareness of the joke that always lies between appearance and reality, between the discontinuity of social tradition and that sense of the past which clings to the mind . . . the "darky" act makes brothers of us all."[47]

Chapter 4
Monsters

The Sage of Milford

Around the town of Milford, Pennsylvania, in the triangle where New York and New Jersey meet Pennsylvania along the Delaware River, there was in the late nineteenth century a pleasant spot of farms and resorts, the estates of the rich a few hours by stage to the railroad terminal in Port Jervis, and from there to Manhattan in another few hours. It was to a farm near Milford that in 1887, burdened by his inability to earn a living by either his science or his philosophy, burdened by a sick wife, burdened by his tormented psyche, but above all burdened by his genius, C. S. Peirce retreated. The death of his mother and an aunt left Peirce enough money to begin the project of remodeling the farmhouse into a mansion fit for his grandiosity and a repository for his wife's taste. He called his house Arisbe, after that mainland colony of brilliant Greek Miletus. And in a way, the farmhouse itself was an intellectual outpost of Miletus, whose philosophers Peirce was studying keenly in a new start on what he would call an Architecture of Theories.

It was the mark of his overweening ambition, hubris even, to embark on the creation of a philosophical system as complete as Aristotle's, a structure comprising the entire work of human reason, from philosophy and psychology to mathematics, from physics to sociology, a plan so comprehensive that new discoveries, new sciences would be, as his biographer Joseph Brent has said, "a string of footnotes" to his plan.

Peirce began life with extraordinary promise. Tutored by his father, Benjamin Peirce, preeminent scientist and mathematician of his day, Charles Sanders grew up in a culture of relentless scientific discipline. His life itself was another thing. There was something cracked about him, something that would not take to any discipline but his own. He was erotically impetuous, grandiose in both his social pretensions and his intellectual ambitions, and as a scientist and logician he exhibited a strange blend of arrogance and an almost abject willingness to find himself corrected. He had trouble finishing his projects. His attempts to ingratiate himself with those who might employ him range from the insultingly arrogant to the sadly transparent. He did not know the world. Brent sees him as a Dandy in the mode of Baudelaire, someone who deliberately created a rigidly aestheticized persona in defiance of the society. There is a good deal of truth to that. Henry James, just beginning his career as a novelist, knew C. S. Peirce in Paris, and commented on Peirce's "beautiful clothes" as well as on his complaints of shabby treatment by the Parisian scientific community. A letter by William to Henry James at this time is worth quoting for its picture of Peirce.

> I am amused that you should have fallen into the arms of C. S. Peirce, whom I imagine you find a rather uncomfortable bedfellow, thorny & spinous, but the way to treat him is after the fabled "nettle" receipt: grasp firmly, contradict, push hard, make fun of him, and he is as pleasant as anyone. . . . I confess I like him very much in spite of all his peculiarities, for he is a man of genius and there's always something in that to compel anyone's sympathy.[1]

Early on, Peirce laid the foundations of what William James would come to call pragmatism, America's first homegrown philosophy, and had made impressive advances in formal logic and mathematics: he had moved beyond promise to mature achievement.

In 1867 Peirce would commence what he called his great *saltus*, the leap beyond the logical systems he had found wanting with his "New List of Categories." In that year, at the age of twenty-seven, after what he called three years of "almost insanely concentrated thought, hardly interrupted even by sleep,"[2] he presented a paper in which he laid out a tripartite categorization of the conditions of knowledge, a list in which with sublime self-confidence he challenged the basic categories of human understanding of both Aristotle and Kant. Peirce's categories were quality, relation, and representation, later to be labeled Firstness, Secondness, and Thirdness (Peirce chose willfully flat or awkward names for the components of his discoveries). Firstness was the immediate brute feeling of some external thing; Secondness was reaction to that stimulus; and Thirdness was mediation between the first two categories. Thus Thirdness is how we might understand and convey to ourselves or others the experience of the world. It was Thirdness that was the lynchpin of his logic. Soon after Peirce's New List of Categories came three articles in which he laid down the foundations for a necessary extension of that list, a science virtually invented by him and which he called the study of *semeiosis*, the study of signs. "For Peirce," Joseph Brent writes, "the fact of representation is the link—the sign—embedded in the otherness of the finite thing and is the bond between the inescapable duality of our inner world and the world without."[3] As the Yoruban devotees of Esu knew, it was the act of interpretation that gave meaning to the world.

A year after his New List of Categories Peirce published a series of three articles further extending his thought. The child, he said in a remarkable feat of counterintuition, learns it is a private self through ignorance and error. It is the learned distinction between desire and failure that separates his body from the bodies of those around him. There was, then, no inborn intuition for Peirce. If Descartes had said I think therefore I am, Peirce cut deeper still and asked what was thought itself, and what he found was that it, like the self, was a construction of the constant layering of representation on representation. For the sign always addressed somebody. It was not part of a sterile algebraic equivalence for Peirce, but created in the mind of its observer another sign, a sign that could be even richer, more developed.[4] The world was thus a construction of signs, one sign representing the next, as room led to room in the chambers of Peirce's mind. Just as one said a body is in motion, not that motion is in a body, so we ought to say that we are in thought, not that thought is in us. Man had no knowledge of the world outside of the signs he created to know or imagine it; man was a sign himself. Perhaps it was like the labyrinth that Peirce once sketched, where one came eventually to the Monster of Crete. The universe was a sign, and man was a sign, and to know meant to study these signs and to understand their manifold workings.

Beware the Syllogism

Civil wars, Ralph Ellison has said, have a way of continuing long after wars between nations are resolved

> because, with the combatants being the same people, civil wars are never really won; and because their most devastating engagements are fought within the individual human heart.[5]

Heir to an older tradition of the academy as a refuge for gentlemen scholars, and the government work that patronized them, Peirce would find himself at odds with a system of federal and university employment that in an increasingly utilitarian culture demanded results. For a man who began with such promise it would take only a few years for this culture to take its toll on his career, but it would take a lifetime to recognize the devastation a kind of civil war within himself had wrought. With the end of the four brutal years of hostilities between the North and the South, Peirce was at the height of his confidence and had already begun dismantling the logical systems of his predecessors. Writing in 1866, the year before his great leap, he illustrated his attack on the facile reasoning of the syllogism with an illustration.

> All men are equal in their political rights
> Negroes are men
> ∴ Negroes are equal in political rights to whites.

"Far be it from me," Peirce continues, "to say anything which could hinder justice from being done to that people whose guardianship the people of the North have assumed. . . .

> The Declaration of Independence declares that it is "self-evident that all men are created equal." Now men are created babies and therefore . . . nothing can follow from the argument relatively to the rights of Negroes which does not apply to babies as well. The argument, therefore, can amount to very little.[6]

What is self-evident for Peirce is that the newly freed slaves of the South and the freemen of the North are not equal in their political rights to white men. The Negro had been sucked into the funnel of his imperious logic. Yet was not this new creation, the Free Negro, not merely a step in a syllogism, but a man, and as a man part of a community of men?

In this world of obdurate opinions, of adamantine languages of exclusion, how does one live? Veiled from the world and from oneself, how does one contrive a set of signs by which one can be known and recognized, and neither be crushed by the dominant culture with its nomenclatures and prejudices and iron logics, nor submit to a secondary role, the nonbeing of imitation? For those spiritual isolates in this country, the thinkers like Peirce, the eccentrics and artists, it could be a matter of carving out a private space in the larger culture; for the African American in a white world, it could be a matter of life and death.

Thirty-one years after his attack on the logic of the syllogism, Peirce, the Dandy of 1866, found himself starving in an unheated, unfinished house in Milford, Pennsylvania. The death of his influential and brilliant father in 1880 left him reeling. It had deprived him not only of a powerful protector but also of a kind of touchstone and center, for he saw himself in many ways as carrying on his father's work. Because of his irascibility, because of the tardiness and incompleteness of his researches, in themselves meticulous, he had been fired from the Coast Geodetic Survey, the chief source of his financial security. The scandal of a marriage with a woman he had openly traveled with before his divorce from his first wife had made him in the American university of that day unemployable.

Slowly starving to death in Milford, Peirce could not know that in England Stephen Crane was writing *The Monster*, a novel set in Port Jervis, New York, a few miles away. Like Crane's black hero, Peirce had become a kind of monster, a pariah in the realm of American science, virtually erased from the contemporary world of philosophy and philosophers. The logic of his theory of knowledge led him to see that what we called reality was a social product, the project of generations of thinkers and scientists; that society itself was rooted in symbolic representation.[7] Peirce's tragedy was that as far as America went, he didn't understand or wouldn't live by the social code. With his wife and with only one true friend and protector, William James, he was virtually alone, as Henry Johnson, the black protagonist of Crane's story was alone with only a small-town doctor as a protector and his mutilated face and the ruins of his dandyhood.

Whilomville

Whilomville is a comfortable town. There are band concerts in the summer, and new, fancier neighborhoods going up; there are social worlds within social worlds, each with its own rituals and its social codes. The world of children, the world of the young men idling at the edge of the bandstand, not wanting to appear too close to it, for it is gospel in their group that the band is awful, nor too far away, for the young girls are listening to the music; the world of those girls, of younger girls too, and birthday parties

and volunteer fire departments, the poker game in the back of Whiteley's
cigar store, the kitchen where a cranky old maid holds forth, and the bar-
bershop through whose windows the men waiting for a shave observe their
fellow Whilomvillites floating by as if through the glass of an aquarium. It is
a town in which everyone knows his place.

Relations are easy between the whites of Whilomville and their black
neighbors. Each group circles to the steps of its own social dance, and their
rituals of courtship and polite behavior parallel each other. The worlds of
white and black intersect in work and in mutual observation. But it is an
observation that at first goes only one way.

> When Johnson appeared amid the throng a member of one of the pro-
> fane groups at a corner instantly telegraphed news of this extraordinary ar-
> rival to his companions. They hailed him. "Hello, Henry! Going to walk for
> a cake to-night?"
> "Ain't he smooth?"
> "Why, you've got that cake right in your pocket, Henry!"
> "Throw out your chest a little more."
> . . . .
>
> Young Griscom, the lawyer, was just emerging from Reifsnyder's barber
> shop, rubbing his chin contentedly. On the steps he dropped his hand and
> looked with wide eyes into the crowd. Suddenly he bolted back into the
> shop. "Wow!" he cried to the parliament; "you ought to see the coon that's
> coming!"[8]

"It was not altogether a matter of the lavender trousers, nor yet the straw
hat with its bright silk band," the author of this tale has said earlier. "The
change was somewhere far in the interior of Henry. But there was no cakewalk hyperbole in it. He was simply a quiet, well-bred gentleman of position, wealth, and other necessary achievements out for an evening stroll, and
he had never washed a wagon in his life."[9] Henry Johnson, like the distin-
guished logician and scientist living a few miles away, was a Dandy.

Under the jibes of the white loafers Henry Johnson passed on his way
there was a menace, a menace that the story would only partially uncover. In
1892 a black man named Robert Lewis, falsely accused of rape, was pulled
from a wagon taking him to jail and lynched from a maple in front of the
Port Jervis Reformed Church. Crane's brother, Judge William Crane, whose
house was directly opposite, vainly tried to save the man from the mob of
about two thousand who gathered. The lynching roils under the story, never

breaking through. It gives, in retrospect, a terrible resonance to the jibing loafers as Crane's hero walks by them.

Like the citizens of Whilomville, Crane too knows his place, and he dances through the tropes which at one time white America amused itself with at the expense of black America. He follows Henry Johnson across town to "a row of tumble-down houses leaning together like paralytics" that is Watermelon Alley and reports on his courtship of Miss Bella Farragut, as supervised by Bella's mother, with its "tremendous civilities." "They bowed and smiled and ignored and imitated until a late hour, and if they had been the occupants of the most gorgeous salon in the world they could not have been more like three monkeys." It is an ugly little passage, but the story will soon take a more profound and disturbing turn, with the burning of the house of Henry Johnson's employer.

Fire is like a mob. It starts as a whisper, and gathers, and becomes a roar. It is doubtful that anyone has ever written of a fire moving secretly through a sleeping house with the power of Stephen Crane.

> A wisp of smoke came from one of the windows at the end of the house and drifted quietly into the branches of a cherry-tree. Its companions followed it in slowly increasing numbers, and finally there was a current controlled by invisible banks which poured into the fruit-laden boughs of the cherry-tree.
> . . .
> After a moment the window brightened as if the four panes of it had been stained with blood, and a quick ear might have been led to imagine the fire-imps calling and calling, clan joining clan, gathering to the colors.[10]

After the fire, Stephen Crane does not so much know his place in the story. For that resplendent Henry Johnson, coachman of Dr. Trescott, rushes into the burning house to rescue Trescott's young son, and in doing so is horribly disfigured. Lingering near death, Henry Johnson is the nexus of a fictional town, a town that loves its heroes and its stories and likes to think well of itself because of them. Bella announces that she and Henry had been engaged, and even the little boys of the town who had been wont to follow Henry Johnson in his resplendent march buried that fact in the bottom of their hearts, as they buried the odious couplet they had chanted.

> Nigger, nigger, never die.
> Black face and shiny eye.

For in the terms of the story, Henry, who emerges from his ordeal without a face, can never die. He is brought back from the edge of death by the ministrations of Trescott, though perhaps it would have been better, says old Judge Hagenthorpe, to have let him die.

A monster is a prodigy. It is a portent, a warning. A monster might be shown, displayed. But in Crane's story Henry Johnson is something to be hidden. He is a curious being: a spectacle that men do not wish to see.

Trescott sends Henry Johnson to the ramshackle farm of a black ne'er-do-well, but even among his own people he becomes a terror, a devil, and he is kept locked in a side room. Then he gets out. In his monstrous parade through town Johnson terrifies a girl at a birthday party who sees him looking through the window; he pays court to Miss Farragut and the family breaks apart in horror and fear; when he appears on Main Street an Irish girl is thrown into a fit and a mob chases him, throwing stones. The sheriff advises the doctor to come for Johnson late at night at the jail where he is being kept, for there is likely to be a crowd around the door. And, the sheriff is embarrassed to add, to bring a mask, or some kind of veil. Dr. Trescott takes Johnson into his rebuilt house, but even as someone unseen the monster roils the social worlds of the town. He is an emptiness, a vortex into which the social worlds fear to be sucked.

Veiled, hidden, we cannot see—if we ever could—Henry Johnson. He has been effaced. We see only an absence and imagine it filled with pain and longing. Even the doctor's son, who loved Henry in the days of his splendor as his father's coachman, sees him only as a monster, not a man, the object of a challenge by a gang of little boys who dare him to touch Johnson as he sits warming himself on a box in the yard, a heavy crepe veil shrouding his face.

As a penalty for harboring Johnson, Dr. Trescott is shunned as if he were another version of this monster. He turns his back on the embarrassed delegation of town fathers who want him to send Henry away, to a "no good farm" up beyond Clarence Mountain or to a public institution. His patients abandon Trescott, as the town has abandoned him and as the world of women abandons his wife. Like the algebraic equal sign, the faceless man is a bridge that allows us to cross to another side, where everything that was a positive becomes a negative, where everything that was a negative becomes a positive, and makes visible what has always been there. The social forms of white Whilomville that were *aped* by Johnson and his girl's family—recall that Crane imagines their bowings and scrapings as like that of so many monkeys—are themselves horrible and as empty as the unused teacups that signal Mrs. Trescott's social despair.

"The individual man," Peirce wrote in 1868,

> since his separate existence is manifested only by ignorance and error, so far as he is anything apart from his fellows, and from what he and they are to be, is only a negation.[11]

Then he went on to quote Shakespeare's *Measure for Measure*:

> . . . proud man, . . .
> Most ignorant of what he's most assured,
> His glassy essence . . .[12]

Glassy because it was brittle, glassy because it was vain, a thing of mirrors. Glassy because, finally, it was for Peirce no essence at all, but a reflection of a reflection of a reflection ad infinitum, a self we only knew as we knew the world, through the reflection of sign on sign on sign . . .

Charles Sanders Peirce had seen truth as something fated to happen to an opinion, a kind of social convergence in the work and minds of investigators. For Stephen Crane, too, the world was a changing specter of signs, signs that reduplicated each other, reflected each other, canceled each other. But for Crane a lie might be the same sort of collaboration that made Peirce's truth, and in the conflict between the individual and the society he found himself in, truths themselves might be contingent, and for the moment multiple. Such a world would be a world of bluff, irony, and creative improvisation, a cakewalk of a world. One met it on its own terms, with courage and panache, dancing, as Nietzsche would say, on the feet of chance. Crane came to this position not through philosophy, but through some inner urgency of experience and the necessities of his art. He found, in an incident of race hatred played out a few miles from the proscribed philosopher, and in the horrifying image of a faceless black coachman, a sign that would draw to itself and reflect in the unblinking eye of his protagonist the glassy essence of a whole society. By the time Crane wrote his great story, Peirce too had become an unseen spectacle. Like Crane's Henry Johnson, the breath of madness had passed over him: he had become, in America's social syllogism, a man without a vote.

The Color of the Sky

> Conceive yourself, if possible, suddenly stripped of all the emotion
> with which your world now inspires you, and try to imagine it *as it
> exists*, purely by itself, without your favorable or unfavorable, hopeful
> or apprehensive comment. It will be almost impossible for you to
> realize such a condition of negativity and deadness. No one portion
> of the universe would then have importance beyond another; and
> the whole collection of its things and series of its events would be
> without significance, character, expression, or perspective. Whatever
> of value, interest, or meaning our respective worlds may appear
> endued with are thus pure gifts of the spectator's mind.
>   —William James, *The Varieties of Religious Experience*

There were four of them. Lost in a slate-gray sea whose white-topped waves
they rode and dipped below in the lifeboat, in a world without horizons.

At first none of them had a name. They were labels: oiler, captain, mate,
correspondent. They had no personal histories. They did not know exactly
where they were—off the Mosquito Inlet? off New Smyrna? St. Augustine?
Daytona Beach? The waves rose up and came crashing down and the boat
was always on the point of being swamped or overturned. None of them, the
tale begins, knew the color of the sky.

In the middle of the night of the second of January 1897, the steam tug
Commodore, carrying a band of *filibusteros* bound for Cuba and a cargo of
contraband weapons foundered and sank off the Florida coast. Among the
passengers was the writer Stephen Crane, headed for the Cuban insur-
rection as a reporter for the *New York Press*. When dawn came he found
himself on the open sea in the ship's dinghy with the oiler Billy Higgins,
Captain Edward Murphy, Montgomery the steward, and Gaines the mate.
The newspaper reports Crane would file after the incident are replete with
the facts of the case, the revolution in Cuba, the American naval blockade,
then the leak the pumps could not keep up with, the call to abandon the
tug. Crane reported the horrible moment when an overloaded raft was cut
loose from the dinghy, and the look of the men who had for some reason
gone back to the tug and waited on its deck to drown. He reported the thirty
hours tossed in the dinghy and the decision to abandon it and risk the waves
pounding against the shore, the swim to safety, the death of Billy Higgins in
the surf. But when Crane came to write his great story "The Open Boat" a

month later, he stripped the fiction of everything but the boat itself and the great fact of the sea. Except for a brief head note telling us that this is a tale inspired by the sinking of the *Commodore* there is no other explanation. But even this is forgotten when we enter the story. Of what has come before we get only a shard of the Captain's memory of seven upturned faces in the gray dawn—the men left on the sinking tug, a stump of a topmast that went low, and lower, and down. There is no history and no reason. The story is peeled away from the chain of cause and effect. There are only four men in an open boat. Looking at the sea, the correspondent, who might be Crane himself, knew everything except why he was there.

The men in the open boat see the shore and put out again because of the danger of the surf and spend another night at sea. They only know the coming of the dawn by the change in the color of the waves. There is, says Crane in his story, a "subtle brotherhood of men that was here established on the seas."

> There was this comradeship that the correspondent, for instance, who had been taught to be cynical of men, knew even at the time was the best experience of his life. But no one said that it was so. No one mentioned it.[13]

They were, in that dinghy, four friends.

Crane

Two years before the sinking of the *Commodore*, at the age of twenty-three, Crane had achieved an auspicious success with a Civil War novel in which he reconstructed battles that had happened before he was born. But his interest hadn't been in the battles, precisely, or the history. He might have written from the point of view of a general or an officer, or with the retrospective and omniscient view of a participant in the great battles like John De Forest. Instead he constricted the scope of his narrative to the point of view of one man, Private Henry Fleming. Further, one could say that his interest wasn't in Fleming as a piece of the great puzzle; his interest was in Fleming's psychology, and in a point of view deliberately limited to the chaos of battle, and the emotional chaos within. Of the memoirs he read he said, "I wonder that *some* of these fellows don't tell how they *felt* in those scraps!"[14] He called his book a "psychological portrayal of fear."

For Crane experience *was* psychological. He dropped—or it may be plummeted—out of college and into New York City, living with painters and illustrators in a series of cheap apartments, writing for whatever newspaper or magazine would buy his sketches. A first novel, *Maggie: A Girl of the Streets*, was based on his imagining the New York City slums before he even got there, and had been privately published out of a small inheritance. Then came *The Red Badge of Courage*, written, he said, when the only thing he knew about battles was what he had learned on the football field. It hardly mattered, for his interest was in the aesthetic and the psychological possibilities of his subject.

Crane has often been called an impressionist for the quick dashes of observation, of color and image that make up his works, but the comparison is misleading, for the Impressionist painters of Paris were interested in the changing play of light on the surface of the world; Stephen Crane was interested in the play of experience on the mind. Far from portraying the surface of the world, his imagery overwhelms it; color, metaphor—color especially—jump off the page as if they have a life of their own, as if the whole order of things were reversed, and the world existed only as a reflection of his ferocious imagery.[15] It is a world not merely real but intensified, as if seen through the medium of mescaline or the opium Crane experimented with among the bohemian artists of New York. Frank Bergon, whose 1975 study *Stephen Crane's Artistry* skillfully examines this imagery, says of the opening chapter of the early novel *Maggie*—but he might have been speaking of almost any of Crane's fictions—that it "draws us into a realm of experience where normal frames of reference are immediately shaken. . . . Not only are we in a strange world, but in that world we become strangers to ourselves."[16]

He seemed, Crane did, to live athwart the universe. In a battle or a barroom, he was always somehow both in and apart from himself. It was a kind of courage, perhaps. But it was more an observation post from which he watched himself and the world. He could be romantic and gallant about women and a bit foolish as young men tend to be, but about life itself he was a realist, and his intimate relations—the ones not thwarted—became relations with prostitutes and women otherwise proscribed. He took up, finally, a liaison with a divorcée and something of an adventuress named Cora Taylor who ran a swank nightclub and house of assignation in Jacksonville called the Hotel de Dreme.

Crane spoke very slowly, deliberately, and he could be both amusing and blunt. People liked him. But there was something else in him that people caught a glimpse of occasionally. "Stevie is not quite at home here—he'll not remain so very long," one woman said of him. To an early and unrequited love he wrote, "The lives of some people are one long apology. Mine was once, but not now. I go through life unexplained." He said he couldn't help vanishing and disappearing and dissolving. He said it was his foremost trait.[17] A young Willa Cather interviewed him in Lincoln, Nebraska. Very thin, seedy, coughing, he was on his way to Texas and Mexico. He wanted to see the West.

The West provided him with the material for some of his finest stories. He found in playing off the West of Pullmans and streetcars and towns that were beginning to support front lawns and Pollywog Clubs against the romantic expectations drawn from dime novels and the paintings of Frederic Remington the sort of ironic possibilities that gave his work its energy. But in all these scenes he found danger, expected and unexpected, and the overwhelming presence of nature in the form of blizzards, immense deserts, and great, empty skies.

A man plays poker for any of a number of reasons. He plays to pass time or kill time. He plays for money. Or for companionship. Or as a sublimated form of war. Or he plays for the moment when everything balances on a hair, the moment just before the card is turned that shows whether he has won or lost. Baching it among the bohemian artists of New York, waiting for a boat to carry him through the American blockade to Cuba, killing time, Stephen Crane played endless hands of cards. In the imagination of Crane the poker player, the moment when the last card was turned was a moment of extraordinary psychological and existential richness. It was the moment in which a man might know himself in the universe.

In the Labyrinth of Signs

When we think, then, we ourselves, as we are at that moment, appear as a sign.

—Charles Sanders Peirce

For that difficult genius Peirce, as for Crane pondering whether to fold or draw, we know the world by guessing. Early on in his investigation of logic Peirce discovered that the familiar processes we imagine we understand by induction and deduction are in fact sterile. They cannot proceed in any new direction. On their own they can really only discover themselves. If we think we are reaching a new place by inductive reasoning, by the patient gathering of facts that will lead to some inescapable conclusion, we have obscured the real process. Something is missing, the essential thing that causes us to jump the familiar tracks. If we think we are recreating a process by deduction from its conclusion, we have forgotten something else. What we have forgotten is the process of guessing. Strictly pursued, both induction and deduction are mechanical processes whose outcomes are already implicit in their operations. Causality itself, the links in the chain that leads to our conclusions, that gives such symmetry to the natural processes of the world, is itself a kind of illusion, the illusion of a world that has lost its originality—the creative originality of chance—and has settled into the ruts of habit. Peirce created the term *abduction* to describe this necessary piece of his logic, this informed and sometime unconscious process of guessing.

As a careful research scientist, measuring with delicate pendulums the earth's gravity from various locations for the Coast Geodesic Survey, Peirce knew that even the most meticulous observation did not yield uniform results. How would one know the truth of an observation if subsequent observers and subsequent moments provided different data? How would one guess at the answer to the riddle of the universe if all life and the cosmos itself seemed the product of the free play of chance in a world Lyell and Darwin had shown to be a mindless geologic process, an endless brute struggle for existence? But chance itself might be fertile, and just as one could cluster the errors of observation around an unseen center, tightening the probability of truth, so one might see chance in cosmological terms, a universe congealing its random variation around habit, so that the laws of the universe themselves—it was a startling idea that anticipated the most radical speculations of contemporary cosmologists—might be the products of an evolution of more and more habitual recurrence. Like players in a cosmic poker game we cannot know the world with perfect accuracy, so we guess; but our guesses are informed by the knowledge we have of the world, by the facts we can observe, by our experience, by the unconscious processes of our psychology, and our ability to read its language. For the world, for nature itself, speak to us in signs.

The signs create a language, but language is a social phenomenon; it is a transaction between us and another, between us and future generations, and finally it is a transaction between us and the cosmos, nature, the past. Thus signs for Peirce, as they were for the Medieval Realists, were not figments of some ghostly mechanism behind the screen of the world, but the world itself. For signs, like ideas, were real, as if the world were turned inside out and its many descriptions, its way of naming itself, were the ultimate reality, and the gross material facts were simply places to start from.

Up on a ridge in Cuba, indifferent to the bullets of the Spanish Mausers crackling all about him, a man stands waving a checkered piece of cloth to a ship far below. The positions of the cloth in the man's hands correspond to a letter in the alphabet, and out of these letters are made words. But the words themselves correspond to a code shared by the man with the flag and the navy officer watching through his field glasses, a code that will tell him where to direct the guns of the warship.[18]

Such moments, for Stephen Crane, are at the center of his stories. The signals must be noted, but perhaps they can never be finally interpreted in a world that wig-wags its flags back at us with sublime indifference. For Crane never constructed the signs of his world into a system as Peirce aspired to do. Crane's world is contingent, fleeting; chance—and danger—illuminate a moment in a man's psychology. Those brilliant, hallucinatory, odd, sometimes deflationary images of his prose create only the spark of illumination of a world that is indifferent. There was a fellowship on a battlefield and in an open boat, but it was fragile and temporary, perhaps an illusion itself. Hope, Crane once wrote, was the most vacuous emotion of mankind.[19] At the poker table or in a showdown on a Mexican street you had only your own guesses. One was essentially alone.

So there is something proud and brave and even a little stupid about the wig-wag. Its register of signals and meanings, so absolutely definite, so clearly seen, become questions in the midst of the sizzle of gunfire and the conflicting signs and signals of a world that is not so clearly read, a world whose message may finally be untranslatable or absurd. The positions of the wig-wag are signs and the words put together from the alphabet of the code are signs and the brown hills and sparkling sea are signs, and the war itself is a sign, and the man with the flag, who stands there with his back to the bullets of the guerrilla Mausers is a sign. A tiny speck of human consciousness in the midst of a universe of chance. If we approach the meaning of the Riddle, Peirce says, we do so by the convergent guesses of our peers, scientists if we are scientists, mathematicians if we are mathematicians, but by shaking the dice out of the cup if we are Stephen Crane, or watching the fall of the cards if we are in a Blue Hotel waiting out a Nebraska blizzard, or by trying to understand what is happening on the shore if we are four men bobbing on the sea in an open boat.

Landfall

A man said to the universe:
"Sir, I exist!"
"However," replied the universe,
"The fact has not created in me
"A sense of obligation."

—Stephen Crane, *War Is Kind*

Slowly the land arose from the sea. From a black line it became a line of black and a line of white—trees and sand. The men in the dinghy saw what they thought was a lighthouse on the shore. They thought that soon the keeper would make them out, drifting on the sea, and send the life-saving crew in their boat after them so they would not have to risk running the dangerous surf.

"Funny they haven't seen us."
"Maybe they think we're out here for sport! Maybe they think we're fishin'. Maybe they think we're damned fools."

Little dots appeared on the shore that seemed to indicate a city. They speculated on what it might be. They talked of rowing, exchanging places so the rowers could rest.
Then:

"Look! There's a man on the shore!"
"Where?"
"There! See 'im? See 'im?"
"Yes, sure! He's walking along."
"Now he's stopped. Look! He's facing us!"
"He's waving at us!"
"So he is! By thunder!"
"Ah, now we're all right! Now we're all right! There'll be a boat out here for us in half-an-hour."

The men in the boat picked up a bath towel that was by some weird chance there and tied it to a stick they had found floating in the sea and signaled to the shore. The man at the oars could not turn his head. He could only ask questions.

"What's he doing now?"

"He's standing still again. He's looking, I think. . . There he goes again. Toward the house. . . Now he's stopped again."

"Is he waving at us?"

"No, not now! He was, though."

"Look! There comes another man!"

"He's running."

"Look at him go, would you."

"Why, he's on a bicycle. Now he's met the other man. They're both waving at us. Look!"

"There comes something up the beach."

"What the devil is that thing?"

"Why, it looks like a boat."

"Why, certainly it's a boat."

. . . .

"No, by——. It's—it's an omnibus."

"I tell you it's a life-boat."

"It is not! It's an omnibus. I can see it plain. See? One of those big hotel omnibuses."

There is a temporary brotherhood of the men found by chance in an open boat tossed on an indifferent ocean, and there is a brotherhood of the shore, with its hotels and teas and social conventions, but the worlds might never merge. What the shore sees of the boat might seem a game, and what desperate and exhausted men see of the shore might be a wish, a hallucination, or a terrible joke. Abandoning the open boat and risking themselves in the surf, three of the men survive, the fourth does not. The world chance presents is, ultimately, unknowable.

A Tale of Two Houses

What if a man should build a house out of paper? A question Charles Sanders Peirce proposed in his paper on the architecture of theories. Peirce imagined this man, thinking that paper was a good material, building his entire house out of it, doorknobs and floors, oiled paper for windows, papier-mâché for walls and roofs. Stephen Crane had built such a paper house, not ordered but ramshackle and sporadic with brilliant flashes of symbol and image that came together on the page. There was no grand theory, no planning such as Peirce insisted upon. Both of them found in chance the creative spark of their universe, but Peirce had tamed chance: his theory gradually congealed around it.

By 1892, while the young Stephen Crane was just beginning his career as a writer, studying the life of the slums for newspaper articles and what would become his first novel, Charles Sanders Peirce was in severe economic distress. His life was falling apart. It had a plan, a wonderful plan, but there was no mortar in the joints, there were no beams and joists to hold it together.

Peirce had once been diagnosed as being on the verge of madness, and he felt himself always on that edge. Financial worry, coupled with the intense mental labor of his philosophical speculations, which he never abandoned, and the illness of his wife, unmoored him. He went for weeks without sleep, sustained by drugs, living he knew not how, writing reviews for *The Nation*, living on advances. Or not living. By 1894, broke and unable to find either a university appointment or a job in science, Charles Sanders Peirce, this eminent scientist and logician, this friend who gave William James the seed James developed into the philosophy of pragmatism, overwhelmed by debts and disappointment, was virtually homeless.

He prowled the Century Club, cadging cheese and crackers from the buffet, almost his only form of nourishment for months, conspiring with his chums on schemes he thought would make his fortune overnight, patents and inventions, power stations and acetylene lights. More than once he wrote of suicide. He must, in those days, have bumped into another Centurian, a raconteur like him, who was also in desperate financial straits, the eminent geologist, writer, and mountain climber turned mining promoter Clarence King. King and Peirce might have recognized each other, as they passed through the reading room or the buffet, as fellow bearers of a psyche that had cracks no philosophy could manage to glue together. Peirce knew King's revised view of natural selection, a modified catastrophism that was a parallel to what Peirce was working toward, a pacifying of chance at what for King was the service of an ultimately divine architecture.[20] But unlike Peirce, King kept his scandalous marriage secret, and while holding himself out to be the most charming of confirmed bachelors, growing bald and portly in his celibacy, he hid a beloved biracial family in Brooklyn.[21]

Stephen Crane had no such home as Arisbe, nor did he seem to care for one. Not yet thirty, exhausted, like Peirce burdened by debt, and wracked with tuberculosis, he was living in 1899 in England in an almost uninhabitable relic of the Elizabethan age, a manor house called Brede Place, equipped with almost nothing but a ghost. He had been housed anywhere he dropped: the bohemian tenements of New York, the Jersey shore, the Hotel de Dreme in Jacksonville, Havana, a bivouac in northern Greece—now Brede Place. His home, it seemed, was an open boat.

In the last days of the old century he and Cora gave a Christmas party at Brede Place. One of the guests, A.E.W. Mason, remembered Henry James greeting him from behind his garden gate at Rye and being warned that he might find an actress or two at the party, and that he should be careful not to get caught. James himself, a neighbor and admirer of Crane's, stayed home; it was very much not his sort of party.

There was a tremendous fall of snow. H. G. Wells and his wife invented a game of racing on broomsticks over the polished floor. There was a musical play put on—a farrago of lines by the guests, nonsense verses set to Gilbert and Sullivan tunes. There were "bevies of beautiful American girls" and fires and almost no indoor plumbing. Another of the guests, C. Lewis Hind, remembered Stephen Crane sitting in a corner of the great fireplace in the hall, among the clamor and festivities, "not unamused, but very silent. He seemed rather bewildered by what had happened to him." It was during that three-day party that Crane suffered his first hemorrhage of the lungs. He died in June of the new century, in a sanatorium in the Black Forest.

Freighted with mortgages, unpaid debts, lawsuits, Arisbe hung over Peirce like a self-imposed penance. Finally, it became a prison. He had been at one time exiled from it, a fugitive from justice, and now he could neither sell it nor leave it. One by one, he sold off the paintings, the fine furniture, his books. Arisbe fell into disrepair.

Peirce could not afford to heat Arisbe and in the winter he and his wife froze and starved and lived off the occasional charity of wealthy neighbors. Finally, it was William James, most steadfast of his friends, who arranged a subscription for Peirce and his wife's maintenance. Arisbe, the house Peirce imagined as a mansion of elegance and learning, even in its decay, with room added to room, addition on addition, could stand for Peirce's genius itself, his tendency to brilliant starts and unconcluded finishes, of powerful new insights—like the plans for Arisbe itself often mere scraps of paper—unpublished and unedited, eighty thousand pages of manuscript, thousands on thousands of words, unsorted, incomplete. He was content to imagine that he had laid the foundations strong and deep. "Systematic completeness," he wrote, ". . . is about the idlest decoration that can be attached to philosophy."[22]

His building at Arisbe stopped. The house remained a kind of American folly, a constructed ruin. But side by side with that house that had become his prison rose another house. In 1900 he began his intense work on phenomenology and the study of signs.

His house of logic, founded on a new science, which he called the semeiotic, was one of great beauty, a palace of the mind, where chamber opened onto chamber, sign led to sign, as in a sort of penetrable glass, Firsts, Seconds, Thirds, so beautiful, so lucid, a glassy palace where the soul could live, that "glassy essence" of man now not fragile and full of deceptive reflections of the self, but lovely in its symmetries. Peirce had rejected his early atheism, and in a Manhattan church had had a mystical experience. God was at the final portal, though we would never get there. With persistence we might catch a fragment of the thought of the Living Mind by guessing at its answers.

For Peirce had gone far out on a limb. The development of his later ideas might be seen as an attempt to work his way back to his New England beginnings, without abandoning the discoveries he had made. Plato, who in his youth had bored him, now proposed a model of a universe pervaded by, if not exclusively composed of, signs. All ideas, Peirce came to see, spread out from themselves, affecting other ideas, losing their intensity in the process, but gaining in generality in a world that moved more and more toward a final reasonableness, impelled not by Darwin's cruel and mindless struggle for existence but by the binding power of love. Toward the end of his life he was rereading the *Timaeus*.

Peirce stayed on at Arisbe, its furniture and paintings and fine artifacts sold, and was content in his empty and unfinished house to look back on his life and puzzle out his failure. Impoverished, he worked on, suffering two nervous collapses, finally dying of cancer in 1914. Once Peirce compared his perseverance to that of a wasp beating against the sides of a bottle. Peirce had stopped buzzing angrily against the glass. His was a universe that had, finally, signaled its meaning.

But the universe had signaled nothing. This is what, finally, Stephen Crane knew. Inexorable, poker-faced, the universe would finally call Peirce's bluff, as it would, Crane knew, his own. So Peirce might have spotted the coastline of the new century, but it was Crane who washed ashore on it.

Chapter 5
The Soul Shepherd

Fathers

"Where do we find ourselves? In a series of which we do not know the extremes, and believe that it has none. We wake and find ourselves on a stair; there are stairs below us, which we seem to have ascended; there are stairs above us, many a one, which go upward and out of sight. . . ." "Ghostlike we glide through nature, and should not know our place again." Emerson continues.[1]

On January 11, 1842, William James, the first child of Henry James and Mary Walsh James, found himself being born in the Astor House in New York City. Two months later, now in the Jameses' own house at 5 Washington Place, according to a family tradition, Emerson himself went up to see the infant and gave him his blessing.

Such blessings are like wishes in fairy tales, unforeseen in their consequences. Perhaps Emerson had whispered in the sleeping child's ear what was his most startling discovery: that consciousness is what we called the Fall of Man.

Experience, for Emerson, was a kind of intellectual inconvenience, something to be overcome with salutary doses of transcendental optimism. For William James experience was the foundation of his work and thought both as a psychologist and as a philosopher. Unlike Emerson, he did not grieve that he could not feel—nervous, tightly strung, volatile, self-lacerating, William James felt, perhaps, too much. Like Sigmund Freud, whom he would meet in the penultimate year of his life, he was soul-doctor to his age, but a troubled and sometimes reluctant one who both fought and helped to change a world which tugged at him with fierce resistance.

If Emerson was an intellectual godfather to William James, as he was to all New England, there was James's actual father. Henry James Senior lurched through life on one good leg. The horrors of a childhood amputation were deep in him, deep as his sense of sin. His excellent biographer Alfred Habbeger calls him a "blocked and monomaniacal hierophant."[2] His "paradoxes, ambiguities, and contradictions," says Habbeger, "were so deep-seated and intricate his children could not really grasp them. . . . [His] ideas were a kind of therapy, serving to neutralize his early religious training or quiet his torments. . . . The children couldn't catch on, couldn't see how their parent's domestic fatherliness was a performative version of himself—a statement, a demonstration, an expression not of a natural self but of a self-created self."[3] Erik H. Erikson describes him as making his family life "a tyranny of liberalism and a school in utopianism in which every choice was made from the freest and most universal point of view and, above all, was to be discussed with Father."[4]

It was a family of tingling wit and vehement argument and a kind of self-secreted glue that might have been love, and in the midst of it was Henry James Sr., at once paterfamilias and most privileged child, spoiled and indulged, his whims and his extravagances and his own vehemence unchecked. Whatever rage there was in him expressed itself on the occasions when he dipped his pen into his interior poisons, and in that stutter that he passed on to his second son and namesake. He jolted through Europe and the American Northeast with his family in tow under the rubric of giving his children an education, but his constant decampments from country to country made it impossible for them to really get one, except as they caught it on the fly (Henry Junior, who William would once in a fit of sibling pique call his "younger and shallower and vainer brother," thought it was the absolutely best education for a novelist; William thought it was no education at all.) The deepest education they received was not from the series of schools they passed through, but from the mysteries of their father's character. It showed young Henry James that beneath the social surface of life were whole worlds of complexity and conflict revolving around money, power, and erotic passion; but the future novelist chose or was chosen by his devotion to his art and by his celibacy to stand apart from those worlds. What this maimed and mercurial father gave to the elder son was the life-long struggle to undo the religious and psychological knots he first tied for himself and in which, like some latter-day Laocoön, he had implicated his children. If Henry James Senior left for his two oldest children a patrimony of complex and imaginative thought, as well as his interior shifts and contortions, for the remaining three children, the two youngest sons and the one poor daughter, there was only misery and failure.

Like all his tribe, including his daughter and sad younger sons, he could write with grace and fluency and wonderful wit and inventiveness—until he sat down to write of religion (having read his *The Secret of Swedenborg* William Dean Howells quipped that Swedenborg's secret was one James kept, though interestingly, Charles Sanders Peirce had admired one of James's early Swedenborgian texts). He was a hard father to bear, and his eldest son, for whom he had the highest hopes, did much of the bearing. Constantly the father, who had no occupation and who had been as he put it "leisured for life" by his successful challenge to his own father's punitive will, while pressuring William to embark on a career, at the same time undercut that pressure by warning him not to settle too early on any one path. Henry Senior had in mind a scientific education for his eldest son, for science would prove the invisible world that floated above his head. But what science might that be? Zigging and zagging from country to country and school to school, William, as was predictable, zigged and zagged through possible careers, thought he might paint, thought not, visited Brazil with Louis Agassiz, and settled finally, almost by default, for a medical degree.

William called Henry Senior after his death his "sacred old father" but it was Alice—poor, miserable Alice—who may have seen him most clearly when, watching his back bent over his endless writing, she had the sudden impulse to knock his block off. When he died it was William who took upon him the thankless task of poring through those numberless pages that few had read or wanted to, to make a memorial volume of extracts, and thus he entered his father's world more fully than he had before.

These fathers, Emerson and Henry James Senior, gave William James a world. He would have to cast this world away from him, but like the colonial, he never fully lost its manner. He never picked up from Emerson the habit of stringing together a series of apothegms as an essay, but like him he could on occasion talk like a Rotarian or a football coach and like him he had a gift for astonishing sayings. If he was wracked like his father, he picked up neither his nor Emerson's fatal smugness. Rather he used his inner world, tormented as it often was, as a mine for his own study. If he tried to pull himself up by his bootstraps into action and moral force, he never had the trick of forgetting where, psychologically speaking, he came from. High-strung, intense, a man whose nerves were always twanging, seeking repose, not finding it, he was an impossible husband, a kind friend, sometimes spontaneous as a child—who could imagine Emerson running around his yard naked in the middle of the night, as James had once done, while another eminent philosopher (it happened to be his friend and sometime philosophical opponent Josiah Royce) played a garden hose on him?

If for Emerson consciousness was the Fall, for William James it was a lifelong study. His project was to work his way back to innocence *through* consciousness itself, through the rigorous scientific discipline of his study of how the mind really worked. Yet his scientific materialism hid a wish, a desire for reconciliation with the world of his father and of Emerson. He was fully a man of his age, a scientist, a positivist, a believer in action and the will, yet he was a divided man. Somewhere in the mechanism of consciousness there might be a chink, an unexplored trapdoor that would lead to the Eternal.

The Other Side

He was never what one could call well. Headaches, neurasthenic doubts, bouts of near suicidal despair, lifelong insomnia. He suffered all his life from indecision, from lethargy. Later on would come angina pectoris. He found some solace in mountain hikes—he was indefatigable. But there was less help in the European spas he collapsed in. Then there were the Mind Cure practitioners, one of whom resembled the "Venus of Medicine," Mrs. Lydia E. Pinkham, whose bespectacled Puritan visage graced the bottles of the patent medicine of choice. None was ever able to cure him, for what he was suffering from was life itself.

On April 30, 1870, he wrote a passage in his diary.

> I think that yesterday was a crisis in my life. I finished the first part of Renouvier's 2nd Essay and saw no reason why his definition of free will—the sustaining of a thought because I choose to when I might have other thoughts—need be the definition of an illusion. . . . My first act of free will shall be to believe in free will. . . . My belief, to be sure, can't be optimistic but I will posit it, life (the real, the good) in the self-governing resistance of the ego to the world. Life shall be built [on] doing and creating and suffering.[5]

William James was twenty-eight.

In spite of Renouvier, James could not will himself into health, as his father, who saw ego as the great sin, would have told him. Two years later he had the experience that uncannily reproduced one his father had experienced in Windsor Forest, a terrifying vision that had led the elder man to Swedenborg. In *Varieties of Religious Experience* William James ascribed this vision to an unnamed French correspondent, but the image of the idiot boy hunched on a ledge in a sanatorium, which I described in the first chapter of this book, was undoubtedly his own. With that horrible image, something solid within his breast, James wrote, gave way entirely. He became a mass of quivering fear. The universe was changed for him altogether, and if he had not repeated like an incantation a handful of scriptural texts, he said he might have grown really insane. The vision gradually faded, but for months he was unable to go into the dark alone.[6]

It was as if the son was condemned to reenact his father's despair in order to find his own way out into the light. He remained in some fundamental way unhealed for most of his life, but he turned his longing into an investigation of the meaning of the world, an investigation, that like his own healing remained unresolved.

What James longed for was a final vision, the obverse of the despair that dogged him through his life, one like those experienced by the saints and the religious prophets. That vision, which he once called "a season ticket over the Stygian ferry" and the daily enjoyment it conferred of "correspondence with the 'summer-land'" was never permitted him; he was never to taste the ecstasy of the mystic, that inarguable experience that put God back into the world. He kept looking for it. Those dreary séances, whose trivialities, while they might seem amazing feats of mental telepathy or even the possibility of survival beyond the grave, ended up wearying him to death. ("I confess that the human being in me was so much stronger than the man of science that I was too disgusted with Phinuit's tiresome twaddle even to note it down." "Did you see me in your dream with my trousers rolled up at the bottom?" asked another voice from the spirit world. "Do you remember anything about celery root?") He wondered what good would come of holding the feet of a libidinous, illiterate Italian peasant under a table to be sure she didn't move it with her knees—she would cheat when she could get away with it. He gave fakes and eccentrics and Mind Cure practitioners their due, and more than their due—there might be something to learn from them, and after all, his father was one of their tribe.

The most remarkable of these outsiders was a man named Benjamin Paul Blood. Blood might have been just another village crank, expounding his ideas largely in local newspapers, except that he happened to be an original thinker and master of a powerful prose. James came across Blood sometime after 1874, when his privately printed pamphlet *Anaesthetic Revelation* fell somehow into his hands. "It begins," as James describes it,

> with dialectic reasoning of an extremely Fichtean and Hegelian type, but it ends in a trumpet-blast of oracular mysticism, straight from the insight wrought by anaesthetics—of all things in the world [Blood had described the experience of coming out of drug-induced sleep]—and unlike anything one ever heard before.[7]

It was the trumpet-blast, not the dialectic that fascinated James, so weirdly, as he put it, that it became one of the stepping-stones of his thinking ever after. For somehow and someway (James himself could not understand this fully) Blood's transcendental idealism, his monism, became mystical and pluralistic. Blood wrote to James a succinct description of this turn. "I am more and more impressed that Heraclitus insists on the equation of reason and unreason, or chance, as well as of being and not-being, etc. This throws the secret beyond logic, and makes mysticism outclass philosophy. The insight that mystery—the MYSTERY—as such is final, is the hymnic word."[8]

Ether, the chloral hydrate he dosed himself with to treat his habitual insomnia, amyl nitrate, the mescaline Weir Mitchell supplied him with, and which left him with nothing but a crashing hangover, alcohol, tobacco even—these had done nothing to ward off the lurking horror of that vision James had had long ago and that seemed to stand behind the fringe of consciousness. Nor could they take him to what he called *nirwana*. The exception might have been nitrous oxide, the very substance Paul Blood had found as an entry to another vision of the world. James kept track of his experience as he fell under the influence of the drug:

> What's mistake but a kind of take?
> What's nausea but a kind of -ausea?
> Sober, drunk, *-unk*, astonishment.

It sounds like the kind of thing his student Gertrude Stein might have written, or perhaps something from the experiments at the psychological laboratory he set up at Harvard.

Everything can become the subject of criticism—how criticize without something *to* criticize?

Or perhaps the kind of note a philosopher, dozing off, might scribble down in his bedside notebook for further elaboration.

Agreement—disagreement!!
Emotion—motion!!!

Or perhaps it is part of some Futurist Manifesto. Or might it be the production of some contemporary language poet scissoring through a philosopher's wastebasket?

Die away from, *from*, die away (without the *from*).

But under the initial elation of this dance of opposites, there was a note of something slipping away, not quite graspable. What James saw finally was that the identification of contradictories was not the self-developing process that Hegel supposed, but really a self-consuming process, "passing from the less to the more abstract, and terminating either in a laugh at the ultimate nothingness, or in a mood of vertiginous amazement at a meaningless infinity." A "pessimistic fatalism, depth within depth of impotence and indifference, reason and silliness united, not in a higher synthesis" but in the fact that whichever you chose it was all one.

Reconciliation of opposites; sober, drunk, all the same!
Good and evil reconciled in a laugh!
It escapes, it escapes!
But——
What escapes, WHAT escapes?
. . . .
And it fades! And it's infinite! AND it's infinite!
. . . .
It fades forever and forever as we move.
There *is* a reconciliation!
Reconciliation—*e*conciliation!
By God, how that hurts! By God, how it *doesn't* hurt! Reconciliation of two extremes.
By George, nothing but *othing*!

The oppositions force themselves up into the consciousness, obtrude themselves in the voice, while another voice, perhaps a deeper one? yearns for their cessation, for reconciliation, for stasis, for peace, for an end to language.

> That sounds like nonsense, but it is pure *onsense*!
> Thought deeper than speech——!
> Medical school; divinity school, *school!* SCHOOL! Oh my God, oh God, oh God![9]

The rapture of beholding a process that was infinite changed into the sense of a dreadful and ineluctable fate, with whose magnitude every finite effort is incommensurable and in the light of which whatever happens is indifferent. The instantaneous revulsion of mood from rapture to horror was, he said, perhaps the strongest emotion he ever experienced.

The Living Stream

In the beginning, there was a primordial chaos of sensations, "a black and jointless continuity of space and moving clouds of swarming atoms," which science called the only real world, given out indifferently to all men and all creatures, to the ant or the cuttlefish or the crab.

It was a frightening world, this world as defined by science, for there was no single intelligence, no meaning illuminating it; the process of creating human consciousness was the step-by-step building of a ladder into the light out of this chaos of pure sensation itself, and at any given moment, for any individual, the ladder might give way, plunging one into some other space, some other consciousness, like the idiot boy William James had the vision of, or those other poor souls he had seen in those "castles of despair," the asylums, strutting or swaggering, grinning with self-satisfaction, or locked in a rictus of self-abasement. Yet slowly, by cumulative strokes of choice, human beings had extricated themselves from the primordial chaos like sculptors paring away, bit by bit, portions of the given stuff, agreeing on what they shall notice and name, and out of that agreement selecting what of the remainder should be accentuated or preferred, what subordinated or disliked.[10]

By 1875 James, teaching at Harvard, was immersed in the new field of psychology. Always, as his biographer Robert Richardson has insisted, James began with experience. His own experience, of course, but the sheer physical experience of others, of the subjects of his experiments, of what the experiments and case studies he read about reported. To study consciousness then was to start at the beginning, with the anatomy of the brain, with what could be learned of the seats of sensation. The metaphor James discovered for these physiological processes, so hard in themselves to witness or note or describe, was a stream; the stream of thought, a Heraclitean river into which we never descended twice, but which was in some sense always the same: the same because consciousness was not a collection of distinct perceptions; it was a process.

> The traditional psychology talks like one who should say a river consists of nothing but pailsful, spoonsful, quartpotsful, barrelsful, and other moulded forms of water. Even were the pails and the pots all actually standing in the stream, still between them the free water would continue to flow. It is just this free water of consciousness that psychologists resolutely overlook. . . . The significance, the value, of the image is all in this halo or penumbra that surrounds and escorts it—or rather that is fused into one with it and has become bone of its bone and flesh of its flesh; leaving it, it is true, an image of the same *thing* it was before, but making it an image of that thing newly taken and freshly understood.[11]

Thus James built his account of consciousness from the ground up. He rigorously excluded, and had no need for, any concept of something outside the material world—no appeals to the soul or to a world-soul or to a creator. It was the world of Darwin, not of Plato or Aristotle or Kant.

But if human beings on the whole were in agreement on the selected and rejected portions of the original world-stuff, of what they should notice and name and what not, there was one entirely extraordinary case in which no two human beings ever were known to choose alike. That was the division of the universe into the two halves that James called the *me* and the *not me*. What was significant was that everyone drew the line between them in a different place.[12]

Like his approach to consciousness itself, James built this consciousness of the me and the not me step-by-step from observation. There was no mystical self, no self serving as a conduit for some over-soul; there was only the accretion of experience: but the line between what a man calls *me*, James wrote, and what he simply calls *mine*, was difficult to draw. In this fluctuating relationship between the me and the mine, the line sometimes disappeared, sometimes was clear, at other times had no relevance to a mind that had ceased to have any relation to it at all. Ultimately a man disappeared into his possessions. Not only into his body and his psychic powers, but his clothes and his house, his wife, his children, his ancestors, and his bank account.[13]

It is to James's great credit that this view of the self as an accretion never slipped into a sterile determinism; the world that he saw and knew and studied was far too complex, paradoxical, and interesting for that. Yet this sense of an incremental making of the self is a startling one: he was stepping to the very brink of modern thought.

James ends his very long chapter on the self in his monumental *Principles of Psychology* at a disturbing juncture. Why was it that the successive passing thoughts should be able to pass on their feelings, intuitions, discoveries to other thoughts, and those thoughts accept, modify, add to them in the constantly moving stream that, in James's reasoning, was the very nature of the self? The answer to that question, if answer there be, he said, must be "where all real reasons lie, in the total sense or meaning of the world." It followed that the thought itself was the thinker, and psychology, as a science, need not look beyond. The only other possibility would be to deny that we could in fact have any direct knowledge of the passing thought. But if so, there must be a knower correlative to all this known. The problem then became a metaphysical one: who was that knower? With the question once stated in these terms, "the spiritualist and transcendentalist solutions must be considered as *prima facie* on a par with our own psychological one, and discussed impartially." But that, James wrote, "carried us beyond the psychological or naturalistic point of view."[14]

G. Stanley Hall, psychologist, philosopher, and rival to William James, read *Principles of Psychology* and detected, no doubt in passages such as this, a strain at odds with the methods of experimental science, a yearning for, as James's biographer Richardson translates Hall, "the old-fashioned idea of soul."[15]

James left his further speculations on the ineffable concealed in a footnote in his *Principles of Psychology*, as if he did not want to trouble the text of a work of science with something so personal. But the speculation refused to be so easily put away. What James characterized as "the fullness of the world" would lead in the final stages of his philosophical thought to what he would call "radical empiricism."

James never worked out these ideas in an orderly exposition in one book, and indeed he saw radical empiricism as more of a philosophical attitude than a doctrine. The method was empirical because, as in that of science, it regarded the most assured matters of fact as hypotheses, which themselves might change or be modified in future experience. The method was radical in that it treated the doctrine of monism, the idea that there was some over-arching cosmic law or idea—call it God if you like—as a hypothesis itself, "and, unlike so much of the halfway empiricism that is current under the name of positivism or agnosticism or scientific naturalism, it does not dog-matically affirm monism as something with which all experience has got to square."[16] There was no essential difference between mind and matter, be-tween the knower and the known. They were all part of the same continuum, a section taken from different perspectives of the process, part of the flux of the ultimate stuff of the world, which was neither mind nor matter, but what James called "pure experience."

James published the first of his essays on radical empiricism, "Does Con-sciousness Exist?" in 1904. Einstein proposed his theory of special relativity in 1905. Ten years later would come his theory of general relativity.

In reaching this stage James had taken himself well into the scientific thought of the twentieth century, a realm where the circle might never be squared, where light could be treated as a wave or as a particle but in which some ultimate reconciliation might never be found. It was the universe of Einstein and Heisenberg. A universe without a numinous envelope and William James was willing to embrace it.

Still, there was the problem of how a man so tormented, so pulled on one side and the other by his spiritual strivings and his materialist skepti-cism might live. James had given psychology a description of consciousness as something that could not be caught and measured by the pailsful or the bucketsful, but as a living stream, as true in its transitions and flow as in the pailsful we took of it. Perhaps you could extend that description to the moral world as well. Perhaps you could see that moral world as something living and evolving and ever-flowing.

In hindsight it would seem inevitable that James would take up the split be-tween the naturalistic and the numinous points of view, a split that existed not only in the culture of the late nineteenth century, but in himself. The solution to finding a purchase, however provisional, in these worlds in flux was in a philosophy outlined by a friend of James's youth, a method of thinking, really, that proposed a way of knowing that accepted the fragmented and unfinished state of the world and of the mind and of above all of raw experience. What was true was what worked.

> Thought in movement has for its only conceivable motive the attainment of belief, or thought at rest. Only when our thought about a subject has found its rest in belief can our action on the subject firmly and safely begin. . . . To attain perfect clearness in our thoughts of an object, we need then only consider what sensations, immediate or remote, we are conceivably to expect from it, and what conduct we must prepare in case the object should be true. . . .
>
> This is the principle of Peirce, the principle of pragmatism.[17]

Louis Menand in *The Metaphysical Club* has skillfully traced how this philosophy, beginning with the meetings of a group of young men in Cambridge, Massachusetts, in the early 1870s, among them William James, Peirce, and Oliver Wendell Holmes Jr., would have a profound effect on the intellectual life of post–Civil War America and through such reformers as John Dewey and Holmes and James himself on its practical life as well.[18]

For Peirce, pragmatism was not a philosophy, but a method of thinking. Truth was something that happened to an idea, happened in the course of experiment and careful measurement and trial. It was developed through a Darwinian struggle for existence in the realm of science and philosophy, and therefore, like Darwin's natural world, had no overarching finality. James's preoccupations led him to apply the pragmatic principle to moral, and finally to spiritual life.[19] It was this moral application especially that struck the minds of James's countrymen.

Pragmatism was a wonderfully apt philosophy for the post–Civil War United States driven by tremendous industrial expansion and the pursuit of personal fortune, and James had, significantly for the grandson of one of the wealthiest men of his day, the unfortunate habit of talking about the "dollar value" of an idea. But the pragmatic principle might be turned around to challenge the materialism of the age as well, a kind of biting of the hand that fed it. It was clear to James that the United States of the turn of the century was skating on very thin ice. Poised against the lure of what he called famously in a letter to H. G. Wells "the bitch Goddess success," might there not be another sort of success? Against the bombast of Theodore Roosevelt's call to the strenuous life—a life of military conquest, it should be said—might not a period of social service in iron mines or in the fishing fleet or washing dishes be an answer to the blood-tax of battle? For pragmatism was *the* philosophy of action. It was the special horror of the vision James had had of the epileptic patient that the patient was immobile, unable to act. His belief in the duty of the thinker to act took him beyond the quiet precincts of the laboratory and the classroom and into the public realm of a turbulent era, with his denunciations of war and imperialism and the epidemic of lynchings of African Americans, condemnations which for their passion and trenchancy still ring with authority. But there were other acts as well with which the pragmatic principle might deal, acts performed daily throughout the world, and that had moved men since almost the beginning of human life, acts of prayer and of belief.

The Soul Shepherd

At the borders between one precinct and the next, in the lands of the Greeks, there stood rock monuments called Hermes. Like the Yoruban Esu, Hermes was a god of the crossroads, and the monuments called by his name stood at such places and, outside of private houses, delineated the line between the public and the private. Sometimes they were just a crude boulder; at other times they were elegantly carved with the head of the god surmounting a square shaft, which exhibited on its front an erect phallus.

Hermes was not notably a god of eros, but like Esu, Hermes was the god of luck, and in that sense a god of the fertility of one's projects. He was also the god of highwaymen and swindlers and cattle thieves. But most notably, Hermes was the god who could transcend the borders of this world and the next. It was Hermes who, as a divine herald, brought messages and protection from the upper world of the gods, and Hermes who led one to the shadowy world below. The Greeks called him *psychopompos*, the shepherd of souls. Around his winged herald's staff twined a pair of snakes, those wise and undying reptiles who knew the secrets of what lay beneath the ground.

In an age of growing materialism and disbelief, William James attempted to leave the door open a crack for believers in another world, in God, in the soul. Bertrand Russell, who had great admiration for James's radical empiricism, which he said had made a fundamental change in his own philosophy, saw the pragmatic principle, which was the philosophic tool James used to accomplish this, as "an attempt to build a superstructure of belief upon a foundation of scepticism." Like all such attempts, it was dependent on fallacies, a form of the subjectivistic madness, Russell said, which was characteristic of most modern philosophy.[20]

Fallacious it might have been, but as he stood in the doorway of modernity, hesitating, a shepherd of souls who could not himself step over the sill, the attempt to find a way out of doubt and disbelief led, for William James, to a broad perspective; and if he conducted no souls to the underworld or brought them back, or ushered them into the realms of the undying gods, still he took them to the edge of lands full of richness and variety and insight. James had a tin ear and writhed under the conventions of Boston concerts, but if there was an unheard music beneath his philosophy it would not be the eternal concept—music circling eternally around itself, or the thin, noontide hum of the transcendentalist summer. It would have to be a music of earth, not of heaven, elegant or brazen and improvised, or both, but always playing doubt and belief against each other, always distinctly American.

The Varieties of Religious Experience

He couldn't pray. He wrote that it made him feel foolish and artificial. He believed in God, but not from any argument. He had never experienced God's presence. But believed, he said, because he needed belief, so that it "must"—and he put that word in quotation marks—be true. He never believed strongly in personal immortality, yet his belief became stronger as he grew older, because, as he put it in 1904, he was just getting fit to live.[21] In 1898, William James received the signal honor of being appointed the Gifford Lecturer at the University of Edinburgh for 1898–1899 and 1899–1900. A letter he wrote to Frances Morse as he planned his talks gives a succinct statement of what he was after.

> The problem I have set myself is a hard one; *first*, to defend (against all the prejudices of my "class") "experience" against "philosophy" as being the real backbone of the world's religious life—I mean prayer, guidance, and all that sort of thing immediately and privately felt, as against high and noble

general views of our destiny and the world's meaning; and *second*, to make the hearer or reader believe, what I myself invincibly do believe, that, although all the special manifestations of religion may have been absurd (I mean its creeds and theories), yet the life of it as a whole is mankind's most important function.

It was a task well-nigh impossible, James wrote to Morse, a task at which he would fail. But to attempt it was *his* religious act.[22]

Standing at the lectern, he set off boldly to talk about religion, not as refined in arguments of theologians and philosophers, or in the doctrines and conflicts of organized sects, but as the experience of men and women that was at its heart emotional. Emotional in its deepest sense for the lecturer himself; for the book that came out of these lectures might be read as containing in its pages a kind of spiritual autobiography. An autobiography finding itself more in baffled search and failure than in triumph.

> Unsuspectedly from the bottom of every fountain of pleasure, as the old poet said, something bitter rises up: a touch of nausea, a falling dead of the delight, a whiff of melancholy, things that sound a knell, for fugitive as they may be, they bring a feeling of coming from a deeper region and often have an appalling convincingness. The buzz of life ceases at their touch as a piano-string stops sounding when the damper falls upon it.[23]

This might well be William James at sixty—cursed with that profound vulnerability to deepest depression that afflicted his family—describing his own experiences. What he called "the religion of healthy mindedness" had the wistful appeal for him that the display behind the window of a butcher shop might have for a starving dog; what remained was doubt, yearning, skepticism, desire.

If the many eloquent passages describing the ennui and despair in the chapter titled "The Sick Soul" were called up by James's own experience, then we must see the central chapter of *Varieties of Religious Experience* as the one immediately following it, which he called "Conversion."

The cases James cites in the chapter he called "The Sick Soul" in *Varieties*, his father's own "vastation," the experiences of recovered alcoholics and addicts, the mystical "death" of a poor Nevada Indian that occurred in the year before James published his monumental *Principles of Psychology*—those stark visions of terror and emptiness—present a kind of bottom that must be hit, an emptying out of the pretensions of the ego, preparing the way for some vision of help that is at hand, of spiritual reintegration. That James himself had such a reintegration is witnessed by his long and impressive career as a scientist and philosopher and public man. But deliverance from such horrible despair as his vision describes, he thought, must come in "as strong a form as the complaint."[24] For James, this was never to be. There were for him no miracles, no supernatural operations. He declared himself, in one of the personal asides in his lectures, to be singularly resistant to mystical ecstasies. He had, it is true, one magnificent Walpurgis Night in the Adirondacks, brought on by his chronic insomnia, the beauty of moonlight, perhaps by the closeness of a vivid young woman, a night such as Thoreau might have enjoyed, and perhaps another in the Alps, but they were nothing compared to the transports of the saints. Still he kept trying. Always ill, neurasthenic, insomniac, he visited mind-cure practitioners of all stripes, injected himself with concoctions of bull semen and lymph, and surrendered himself to European spas. He always had a great tolerance for quacks, for anyone outside the ordinary realm of thought and "correct" society; the "lame ducks and neglected possibilities," as his colleague Santayana put it, the Gertrude Steins and W.E.B. Du Boises; and his cultivation of the "underdog and his insistence on keeping the door open for every species of human experiment" as another colleague put it, "sometimes brought James into alliance with causes his social set looked on with disfavor."[25] To the end of his days he busied himself with research into realms few reputable scientists dared to consider. For beyond the edge of consciousness there might be another world, peopled with the voices of other times, voices of the dead, a myriad of voices, if one could only hear them.

Somewhere, in all these searchings, in all these yearnings, in all these ecstasies of illiterate nuns and drunks and saints and philosophers, whether crude and even ludicrous or spun out by the finest sensibilities, there must be some common ground. That common ground was found in belief's *results*.

But if pragmatism might offer a way of dealing with belief through its consequences, there was still the question of the origin of these religious experiences themselves, a question of paramount importance for a man who was torn between the rigors of research, its demands for a theory of cause as well as effects, and the evidence of those experiences themselves.

Baffled in a search for some objective proof of the religious motive, he turned back to the mind itself. But now it was not the stream of thought with which he was concerned, but something deeper, something below the visible currents of the mind at work. You could call it what you would, the subconscious, the B region, but lying under consciousness it was for James obviously the larger part of each woman and man,

> for it is the abode of everything that is latent and the reservoir of every-
> thing that passes unrecorded or unobserved. It contains, for example,
> such things as all our momentarily inactive memories, and it harbors the
> springs of all our obscurely motived passions, impulses, likes, dislikes, and
> prejudices. . . . It is the source of our dreams, and apparently they may
> return to it.

In persons deep in the religious life, James concluded, the door into this region seemed unusually wide open.[26] He himself stood outside the door of the unconscious, listening.

Just as, in *Varieties*, the world of the spirit might make itself known in the guise of the shabbiest and poorest and most ignorant of saints and repro-bates as much as in the fine-grained spirit of an Emerson, so no one could know who might have the gift of being able to translate the voices from the other world. If they were dull and ordinary and their "controls"—the spirits who spoke through them—were clearly fictions, it could be that these fictions were the residue of some soul stuff seeking out weak spots in an individual human consciousness, finally leaking into the world and dragging scraps of truth with them but knowing little how to weave these into any important or significant story. But always James was disappointed. Always he wasn't able to tally up the evidence the scientist demanded with the need to hear some voice from the beyond. It was as if Hermes stood with his foot balanced unsteadily above the line that marked the other world with no ability to let that foot fall.

Dreams

Half past twelve a.m. In Palo Alto, William James awakened from his first sleep in the middle of a dream that had somehow become confused with two other dreams that shuffled themselves abruptly between the parts of the first dream. The content of the three dreams had no connection; the places, the emotional atmosphere of each was entirely different. He began to feel curiously confused and scared. Soon cold shivers of dread ran over him. Was he getting into other people's dreams? He wondered if this was a telepathic experience, or the invasion of a double or even treble personality. Or a thrombus in a cortical artery. Who knew how far this confusion and disorientation would go? All the while the vivid memory of the three dreams kept coming over him. Whose? *Whose?* WHOSE? He had had a paler dream experience the night before, but then it was simply curious, had only gone the first step. This was the second step. The thought of where he might be after a third step made his teeth chatter.

He was losing hold of himself.[27]

This experience of fear and confusion of mind was not in any way like the sense of wholeness and peace of mystical illumination, but the sense, for James, that reality was being uncovered was mystical in the highest sense. At the age of sixty-four, he had never had an experience anything like it. In his notes he speculated that the threshold between the rational and the morbid state had been temporarily lowered in him; but in point of fact he didn't know "who" had had those three dreams or which one "he" had first woken up from. He wondered if by waking up at certain hours we might tap distinct strata of ancient dream-memory. It seemed the curtain had been lifted on something in life, a realm of consciousness broadened. Yet it was terrifying to him.

James was in the last year of his life when he traveled to Worcester, Massachusetts, to hear Sigmund Freud. He had written perhaps the first notice in America of the work of Freud, his and Breuer's account of Anna O. and the "talking cure." But he wanted to hear Freud himself. In Worcester, amid the luminaries G. Stanley Hall invited to celebrate the twentieth anniversary of the founding of Clark University (the roster included two Nobel laureates), Freud gave five lectures, in the course of which he touched on nearly all of the main principles of his theory, and introduced to an American audience the notions of repression and sublimation, of libido and of the unconscious, of the role of infant sexuality, of the transference and the Oedipus complex.

It was the fourth[28] of these lectures which James attended. In it, Freud, speaking extemporaneously in German, dealt with slips of the tongue and other events that he labeled parapraxes, but spoke mostly of his theory of dreams. "The interpretation of dreams is, in fact, the *via regia* to the knowledge of the unconscious—the most secure foundation of psychoanalysis and the field in which every worker must acquire his convictions and gain his education," Freud said.

> If I am asked how one can become a psychoanalyst, I therefore answer: through a study of one's own dreams.[29]

At the home of his friend and rival G. Stanley Hall, where Jung and Freud were staying, James had several talks with Jung. Already the relationship between Freud and his Swiss disciple was unraveling, and Jung was exhibiting tendencies of what Freud would tell him was "the black tide of mud of occultism."[30] Perhaps James would have been attracted to Jung's later theories that linked religious life to the unconscious, as he himself had speculated, and in fact he hit it off with Jung. Yet it is clear that his distrust of all-encompassing systems would have also put him off Jung's theories as it had Sigmund Freud's—if he thought Freud's use of symbolism to explain dreams was a shaky foundation for science, what would he have thought of Jung's mandalas? James hoped that the exploration of the unconscious might be the route to the discovery of a spiritual world. But James himself could make nothing in his own case of Freud's ideas, though he hoped Freud and his disciples would push their dream theory to its limits. He thought Freud himself "a man obsessed by fixed ideas," or even more strongly, "a regular *halluciné*." To follow Freud into the world of dreams founded, as Freud at least explained them, in the repressed memories of infant sexuality and familial conflict would have required James to turn from the quest for a broadened and finally numinous mother sea of consciousness to the darkness underneath: for the journey began not in the light of effort and renunciation that Dante called Purgatory and Freud the sublimated Ego, but in the lurid light of the underworld itself. And here James, who had all his life struggled with the pull of the underworld's despair and horror, would not go.

James had one opportunity for a private talk with Freud, when Freud walked with him the mile and a half to the railroad station. What they talked of no one knows. It may have been Freud's criticism of the Emmanuel Movement of lay psychologists, which James, the pragmatist, upheld and Freud, the specialist, had publicly deplored in an interview on coming to this country. It may have been dreams. It may have been railway schedules. On the way James paused and asked Freud to carry his grip ahead. James was suffering an attack of the angina pectoris that would kill him one year hence.

James, the failed mystic, straining upward, had looked for the secret of life, yet the secret was not in a heaven of expanded consciousness but in the underworld of the mind, in dreams, in forbidden wishes, in a twilight realm driven by sexual conflict, forbidden aggressions, violent desires: it was not up there, it was in here. The horror of the epileptic patient James had seen in his youthful vision, the frightening view of the possibility of his multiple selves in his dreams in California, could never be examined by William James, because an inner world that led to the unresolved pain and fear of childhood, the complexities of sex and desire, was beyond the realm of the pragmatic principle that resisted the tragic, that resisted any world but God's beyond the will.

James never systemized his philosophy. It remains for this reason penetrable, experiential, and quite alive, almost a personality with its cranks and incommensurables, much like William James himself. Like the African Americans moving from slavery to an uncertain status as free men and women in a world of color lines that were blurring and sometimes disappearing, like the immigrants crowding the cities of America, William James was pushing into a new world. A world whose mental counterpart for him was philosophical pluralism, a world that stubbornly refused to revolve around a single center, a world of incessant change, ever flowing, and into a life that was lived as much in the transitions as in the things it connected, not static but heterogeneous, not ordered by ancient hierarchies but often chaotic and full of the unknown. A life of indeterminacy, of social engagement, not philosophic quietism. Of effort. Of will. Tough-minded and tender-minded at once. Suspended between disbelief and belief, it was neither the land of death nor of heaven above that William James was ultimately most equipped to traverse, but the very richness and variety and pain and occasional ecstasy of life itself. For, James wrote, "The only real truth about the world, apart from particular purposes, is the *total* truth."[31] Writing of Paul Blood in 1910, the last year of his—James's—life, he quotes a remarkable passage from Blood's own pen.

> Not unfortunately the universe is wild—game flavored as a hawk's wing. Nature is miracle all. She knows no laws; the same returns not, save to bring the different. The slow round of the engraver's lathe gains but the breadth of a hair, but the difference is distributed back over the whole curve, never an instant true—ever not quite.[32]

James ends his essay with a quotation from Blood that he adopts as *his* last word.

> There is no conclusion. What has concluded, that we might conclude in regard to it? There are no fortunes to be told, and there is no advice to be given.—Farewell![33]

William James died on August 26, 1910. He had promised his wife he would try to communicate from the Other Side if he could. His wife and his brother Henry sat in dismal séances, waiting for a message.

Chapter 6
The Return of the Novelist

The Restless Analyst

Everywhere he was confronted by ghosts. The last of the major novels, *The Golden Bowl*, had been written. The great themes of money and society and, above all, of the American in Europe, had been worked and reworked in all their subtleties and variations and surprises. And now at sixty-one, rotund, indefatigable walker, and note-taker and writer and talker and recorder of talk, the novelist had come home. The project he was to pursue, the American scene, was a travel book, such as he had written before. And as before, he proposed himself as the viewer of the scene, a sensitive surface upon which might be registered the slightest vibrations of the play of beauty and history and pleasure. A surface that might catch the most delicate impressions, the finest discriminations, the subtlest of paradoxes. But in fact, he himself was the subject of his book. The surface itself, the agitations and tremors of the impressions as they pressed upon it, was the theme.

A ghost is a kind of vacancy, a sense of the air all at once being sucked out of a room, and something that had once been, life, blood, desire, returned but as a vacuum to trouble the present. He felt that vacancy often enough as he visited places he had known and in which he had lived. Indeed, all of them had changed. His family home in Manhattan had been pulled down, and with it the more or less hallowed university buildings (with that tinge of irony with which he often touched his past, "hallowed" was in quotes), and a huge, impersonal square structure had been put in their place. The effect for him was of having been amputated of half his history.

For history was always personal in Henry James; it was lived in him and through him in his memories, impressions, ceaseless observations. And history was being erased in America, as he nervously wandered, noted, observed. Erased by the huge skyscrapers with their banks of windows that seemed to deny any privacies, their elevators that one was hustled into and squashed. What wasn't being torn down to be replaced by these monsters of greed was diminished by their shadow, threatened by their ominous tread. Few were the pleasure-giving accidents that provided a respite from the usual destruction, in our "vast crude democracy of trade" that held out to view only "the new, the simple, the cheap, the common, the commercial, the immediate," and, as James ruefully noted, "all too often the ugly." The human products too were most often explained by, involved in, these elements: they too were turned out to pattern.[1]

But even in the quieter places, the places, as he put it, that didn't bristle, there was the question of the past. *His* Cambridge, his "poor little personal" Cambridge of the "far-off unspeakable past years" hung there always behind the town to which he returned, "like a pale pathetic ghost" fixing him "with tender, pleading eyes, eyes of such exquisite pathetic appeal and holding up the silver mirror, just faintly dim, that is like a sphere peopled with the old ghosts."[2]

He found the graves of his family, "that unspeakable group of graves." "I walked," he wrote in *The American Scene*, "at the best, but on the break-water"—the breakwater of the critical responsibility against the "assault of matters demanding *literal* notation"—"looking down, if one would, over the flood of the real, but much more occupied with the sight of the old Cambridge ghosts, who seemed to advance one by one, even at that precarious eminence, to meet me."[3]

It was late, in November; the trees all bare, the dusk to fall early, the air all still (at Cambridge, in general, *so* still), with the western sky more and more turning to that terrible, deadly, pure polar pink that shows behind American winter woods. But I can't go over this—I can only, oh, so gently, so tenderly, brush it and breathe upon it—breathe upon it and brush it. It was the moment; it was the hour, it was the blessed flood of emotion that broke out at the touch of one's sudden *vision* and carried me away. I seemed then to know why I had done this; I seemed then to know why I had *come*—and to feel how not to have come would have been miserably, horribly to miss it. It made everything right—it made everything priceless. The moon was there, early, white and young. . . . Everything was there, everything *came*; the recognition, stillness, the strangeness, the pity and the sanctity and the terror, the breath-catching passion and the divine relief of tears.[4]

He stood in front of the little Florentine urn that held his poor, stunted sister Alice's ashes, and read the lines that his brother William had chosen out of Dante's *Paradiso*, his brother's gift to the family and to Alice herself:

ed essa da martiro
e da essilio venne a questa pace[5]

The quotation took him "so at the throat by its penetrating *rightness*," that it was as if he sank down on his knees in "a kind of anguish of gratitude" before something for which he had waited with "with a long, deep *ache*."

> But why do I write of the all unutterable and the all abysmal? Why does my pen not drop from my hand on approaching the infinite pity and tragedy of all the past? It does, poor helpless pen, with what it meets of the ineffable, what it meets of the cold Medusa-face of life, of all the life *lived*, on every side. *Basta, Basta!*[6]

But what the ghosts said to him, and he to them, remains unsaid in the notebooks and unmentioned on the page of his book. He refused "going to smash on the rock of autobiography." His eminence must be maintained at all costs, that distanced, elaborated eminence which was for James the written page. He would give, for his beguiled hours, only "the general happier drift."

In fact, everywhere in this book, where memories cluster, he was nervous about his living weight, and he himself pulled away from his text, through modesty or privacy or something else, some emotional strategy of living, really living, only on the page. For he knew that the artist was present "in every page of every book from which he sought so assiduously to eliminate himself."[7] He had become a ghost of himself.

But ghosts too must occupy themselves. If the living blood is denied them, there, in their Tartarus, they must nevertheless engage in ceaseless activity. That activity, for the returned novelist, was the constant agitation of finer discriminations of feeling and critical distinction on the surface of his sensibility. He was, therefore, the restless analyst, sometimes the brooding analyst. Once, the lone visionary. At other times, the pious pilgrim, and then he was the palpitating pilgrim and then again the musing moralist. Always, on the page, he was alone. Yet in truth, no one was more sociable or more eager for society. He was motored about western Massachusetts by Edith Wharton in the latest of her expensive autos; in Washington was the guest of Henry Adams, living out what Adams called his "posthumous existence" in his gloomy fortress of a house nineteen years after the suicide of his wife; the guest too of George Vanderbilt at his impossible château in North Carolina. The president, who found James's work effete and had said so in print (but then James himself had mocked Theodore Roosevelt's crude chauvinism in a published review) even invited him to dine. Everywhere the novelist went arrangements were made. Strings were pulled. Testamentary banquets proposed and declined. In every city women's clubs were speechified on Balzac and the young scholars of Bryn Mawr lectured on diction. And there were, of course, brother William and his family—but the story of that relationship is a long and complicated one that will exist for the most part off the margins of these pages. But even when accompanied, by the Yiddish playwright Jacob Gordin into the depths of the Lower East Side or by Owen Wister into the wan charms of Charleston, he was alone. The most vivid image of him is often that of the hapless analyst, as I may call him, standing in some friendless, shabby midnight railroad station, his traveling case in his hand—where, he moaned, is anyone less served than in America?—waiting for his connection.

The solitude of the restless analyst was a prerequisite. He was the unquiet shade, moving over the surface of the world, searching for something left behind, or something left undone. The trick was to stay on the outskirts of things, to be an observer. To be not a presence in the world, or even on the page, but to be the page itself. To be thus perpetually between things, between Europe and America, between Society and the bitterest critique of its emptiness and rapacity, for the restlessness of observation substituted for the life of action.

Coming into his own as an artist of twenty-four, and seeing his future project, he counted himself as an Emersonian young American. "We young Americans," he wrote Thomas Sergeant Perry, "are (without cant) men of the future. I feel that my only chance for success as a critic is to let all the breezes of the west blow through me at their will." Yet unlike Emerson or Walt Whitman, he did not see himself as creating some distinctly American voice. Rather, his ambition was to stand between two cultures, to serve as a kind of arbiter of taste and quality.

> To have no national stamp has hitherto been a regret and a drawback, but I think it not unlikely that American writers may yet indicate that a vast intellectual fusion and synthesis of the various National tendencies of the world is the condition of more important achievements than any we have seen.[8]

It is a critical and aesthetic position, to be sure. But as much as that, it is a decision about how he would produce the narrative of his life itself.

This position of being suspended between continents, and arbiter of both, came not without pain. Returning after a year in Europe and his first taste of Italy, he felt he had been wounded by the Continent, and that in the United States his experiences were closing over the bullet as a scar over a wound. But the missile was still there, if he probed for it. He had been fed, he said, too prompt a mouthful of the fruit of the Tree of Knowledge. And the taste of it, as a child and young man traveling with his parents, was queer. But the taste of the new America he found was queerer still.

The prolonged adolescence that Erik Erikson saw William James suffering was not to be for his brother Henry, the "angel," as William sarcastically called him. Henry early on knew his vocation and his social way and admitted to accepting a hundred and seven invitations during one London season. But in fact he was at home nowhere but in the midst of his family and in his own mind. He was the eternal observer, for whom life and its mysteries were seen through plate glass, as Leon Edel has remarked.[9] It was the curse—or was it a blessing?—of one condemned to be always looking from outside.

The Inconceivable Alien

After twenty years abroad Henry James was home, or as close to home as he could ever be. But whatever his questions about the sufficiency of that home itself and its ability to nourish him, he found that it was not finally his at all. He was displaced, displaced ironically by Europe as it was represented by the hordes of immigrants beating at the doors.

One's supreme relation, he always imagined, was to one's country. But one's country was finally one's countrymen and women. At Ellis Island—the terrible little Ellis Island—he was escorted about by the commissioner. There he saw the door of America open to the knock of the immigrants, but open only with "a hundred forms and ceremonies, grindings and grumblings of the key." The immigrants stood, "appealing and waiting, marshalled, herded, divided, subdivided, sorted, sifted, searched, fumigated for longer or shorter periods." An "intendedly 'scientific' feeding of the mill." It was a drama, James said, that went on without a pause, a "visible act of ingurgitation on the part of our body politic and social." Any sensitive citizen who may have happened to look in came back from his visit "not at all the same person that he went."

> He had thought he knew before, thought he had the sense of the degree in which it is his American fate to share the sanctity of his American consciousness, the intimacy of his American patriotism, with the inconceivable alien; but the truth had never come home to him with any such force. In the lurid light projected upon it by those courts of dismay it shakes him—or I like at least to imagine it shakes him—to the depths of his being; I like to think of him, I positively *have* to think of him, as going about ever afterwards with a new look, for those who can see it, in his face, the outward sign of the new chill in his heart. So is stamped, for detection, the questionably privileged person who has had an apparition, seen a ghost in his supposedly safe old house.[10]

It is easy to miss the note of comic hyperbole here in his summoning up of "the sanctity of his American consciousness" which the citizen of 1905 was called upon to share with the "inconceivable alien." James was such a horrified American, it is true; but he was also an intelligent one, intelligent enough to mock the very notion of "Americanism" as sported by the president, who proposed, wrote James in reviewing a book by Theodore Rex, "to tighten the screws of national consciousness as they have never been tightened before." But Henry James, who was just that sort of "undersized man of letters" Roosevelt condemned, "who flees his country because he, with his delicate, effeminate sensitiveness, finds the conditions of life on this side of the water crude and raw,"[11] knew very well that consciousness, even national consciousness, was a process of accretion; it was not a piece of Chicago or Manhattan real estate that had its boundaries recorded in a book. "Mr. Roosevelt makes very free with the 'American' name," he wrote in his review in 1898,

> But it is after all not a symbol revealed once for all in some book of Mormon dug up under a tree. Just as it is not criticism that makes critics, but critics who make criticism, so the national type is the result, not of what we take from it, but of what we give to it, not of our impoverishment, but of our enrichment of it. We are all making it, in truth, as hard as we can, and few of us will subscribe to any invitation to forgo the privilege—in the exercise of which stupidity is really the great danger to avoid.[12]

Still, here they were, the immigrants. And in James's view, much as in his story of the expatriate Spencer Brydon, who returns to confront in a safe old Manhattan house the ghost of himself as he might have been had he remained on this side of the water, it was the immigrants who were, in this new country, everywhere at home, and it was he, the restless analyst, squashed by them in the streetcars, confronted by their silence when he greeted them as they dug a ditch in a New Jersey estate, hearing the jabber of their children as they tortured the living idiom of our language into strange and terrible sounds among the tenements and skyscrapers springing hostile as erectile hairs from the landscape and in lovely Central Park (weren't the native sounds strange and terrible enough, he would warn the young women of Bryn Mawr)[13]—he, with his American pedigree and his sanctified American consciousness, who was the unhoused and dispossessed.

Nowhere was the immigrant more to be confronted than in New York's Lower East Side. James's reaction was squeamish in the extreme, a visceral fear of propinquity. He confessed the fear of being asked, figuratively, to eat from the same greasy ladle of the immigrants, but now it was a fear, finally, of being consumed—ingurgitated, he might have said—by the horde of immigrant Jews in the Hebrew conquest of New York. He thought of the long, warm June twilight, in which he first entered the ghetto.

> It was the sense, after all, of a great swarming, a swarming that had begun to thicken, infinitely, as soon as we had crossed to the East side and long before we had got to Rutgers Street. There is no swarming like that of Israel when once Israel has got a start, and the scene here bristled, at every step, with the signs and sounds, immitigable, unmistakable, of a Jewry that had burst all bounds.[14]

Everywhere we see him, his good, bourgeois anti-Semitism assaulted by the swarm of Jews, this soul who lamented the absence of penetralia, private nooks in the vast hotels and clubs, now forced into the crowd. But his artist's eye found in all of the scene a kind of incredible beauty, the beauty of history that he found denied and plowed over in the restless expansion of his country, but which expressed itself in the individual countenances of the dwellers of the Lower East side, in the "intensity of the Jewish aspect."

> There are small strange animals, known to natural history, snakes or worms, I believe, who, when cut into pieces, wriggle away contentedly and live in the snippet as completely as in the whole. So the denizens of the New York Ghetto, heaped as thick as the splinters on the table of a glass-blower, had

each, like the fine glass particle, his or her individual share of the whole hard glitter of Israel.[15]

Worms and snakes, it may be, beak-nosed fish bumping at the bottom of some sallow aquarium in another of his images, or like the caged simians in the zoo, gazing through the bars of the fire escapes, yet to his discriminating eye, glowing golden with a kind of Renaissance movement and beauty, a ghetto beauty he could not find in the solitary, empty mansions of the rich farther up the East Side, or in the factitious splendor of the hotels, whose inhabitants trailed their wealth from one of them to the next, houseless and bespeaking, finally, of an intense loneliness.

Through the Glass

His journey was one of railroad trains shuttling back and forth across the continent, south to Florida, then across the "illimitable Texas" he called so "stopless and so appalling."[16] Now he was literally seeing his native land through plate glass, the glass of the ersatz luxury of Pullman cars that were like rushing hotels, just as the hotels that James imagined were the supreme social expression of this country and carried almost all the facts of American life were like stationary Pullmans.[17]

As James traveled south, he saw through the windows of the car a land no one cared for, a land, moreover, that seemed to deny its blood-soaked past: Richmond, the capital of the Confederacy, looked to him simply blank and void, but James would see that it was precisely from this blank that the great emotion was to come.[18] And it did come, with intensity, when he saw that what he was feeling was the "far consequences of things made absolutely majestic by their weight and duration."

> I was tasting, mystically, of the very essence of the old Southern idea—the hugest fallacy, as it hovered there to one's backward, one's ranging vision, for which hundreds of thousands of men had ever laid down their lives. I was tasting of the very bitterness of the immense, grotesque, defeated project—the project extravagant, fantastic, and today pathetic in its folly, of a vast Slave State (as the old term ran) artfully, savingly isolated in the world that was to contain it and trade with it. This was what everything round me meant—that that absurdity had once flourished there.[19]

But always on the lookout for some aesthetic payoff, it was in this sense of failure, of "weakness" as he called it, that James found what would be "the prime source of beauty."[20]

James walked among the shabby displays of the Confederate Museum in Richmond, daubs of portraiture, scrawls of memoranda, old vulgar newspapers, old rude uniforms and unutterable mid-Victorian odds and ends of furniture. America, for Henry James in 1904 and 1905, was a land without history. Because for James history was not a process, a violent or steady collision and conflation of economic interests, desires, religions, peoples; it was a settled aesthetic accretion, like the sedimentation of a geologic section, a patina of past cultural glories and fadings and failings that deepened the surface of the present. Thus it was the poverty of glorious monuments of the past, the destruction of even the humbler monuments of other times that made America seem empty and heartless to him. His Americans, indeed, the nouveaux riches in their faux châteaux and the tinny splendor of their hotels and Pullmans, the immigrants swarming in the streets of New York, the black laborers and porters he observed through the windows of his car, were for him historyless; they lived in a kind of eternal present which was the surface of his consciousness.[21] Even here, in the Confederate Museum, confronted by the terrible remnants of the recent past, of his own youth, in fact, and of the wounds and traumas of his own younger brothers, there was no sense of powerful engines of historical impulsion; there was only a poverty of *la gloire* of the sort that he found in the memoirs of Napoleon's marshals, of which he was an inveterate reader, and of the aesthetic artifacts that could have drawn him into the past. There was none of this. There was only blankness. Illiteracy "seemed to hover like a queer smell"; the war, the subsequent social revolution, had "begotten neither song nor story—only, for literature, two or three biographies of soldiers, written in other countries, and only, for music, the weird chants of the emancipated blacks." The only "Southern" book of any distinction that had been published for many a year, James said, was a book by a Negro, one of his brother's students at Harvard, and its name was *The Souls of Black Folk*.

Always James was aware of the presence of the Negro. The whites of the South, he saw, were no less "imprisoned in it and overdarkened by it" than they were in the time of their "fallacious presumption." In Washington James had encountered an "African type or two" and had been attended by the black servants in what he called the niggery wilderness of George

Vanderbilt's North Carolina estate. But here, waiting for his luggage in a cab outside of the Richmond railroad station, he saw, in a group of "tatter-demalion darkies" who "lounged and sunned themselves" in front of him, a warning and a threat.

> To take in with any attention two or three of these figures had surely been to feel one's self introduced at a bound to the formidable question, which rose suddenly like some beast that had sprung from the jungle. These were its far outposts; they represented the Southern black as we knew him not, and had not within the memory of man known him, at the North; and to see him there, ragged and rudimentary, yet all portentous and "in possession of his rights as a man," was to be not a little discomposed, was to be in fact very much admonished.[22]

So Henry James moved through his southern journey, staring through the glass at the denizens of an impoverished land, a land that was living off the dregs of a lie.

> It was a monstrous thing, doubtless, to sit there in a cushioned and kitch-ened Pullman and deny to so many groups of one's fellow–creatures any claim to a "personality"; but this was in truth what one was perpetually doing. The negroes, though superficially and doubtless not at all intend-ingly sinister, were the lustier race; but how could they care (to insist on my point) for such equivocal embodiments of the right complexion? Yet these were, practically, within the picture the only affirmations of life except themselves; and they obviously, they notoriously, didn't care for themselves. The moral of all of which was that really, through the more and more southward hours, the wondering stops and the blank renewals, it was only the restless analyst himself who cared—and enough, after all, he finally felt, to make up for other deficiencies.[23]

He cared enough, even, when he was roused in the middle of the night for an unpremeditated transfer to a dark and friendless void—some forlorn and nameless country station—where he waited with what grace he could for the February dawn and another train. He cared because in a strange way the world he saw through the glass mirrored his own inner world.

One sees, in the window of a train at night, or in the reflected light of day, the landscape one rushes through, the people along the way; but one sees them through a reflection of oneself. Europe, the Europe he had fled to as a young man "seeking impressions more numerous and various and of a higher intensity than those he might gather on the native scene," that Europe which he embraced in order to become the novelist Henry James, had lost "its primal note of mystery," had little by little ceased to be "strange, impressive and august."

> The European complexity, working clearer to one's vision, had grown usual and calculable—presenting itself, to the discouragement of wasteful emotion and of "intensity" in general, as the very stuff, the common texture, of the real world.[24]

It was, then, to his native land he perforce turned for that thrill of romance and mystery. Wracked with homesickness for his house in Rye, his study, his mulberry tree, his garden, he was seeking the intensity that he had once experienced in Europe here in America, and especially in the South. The calculation, for the expatriated observer, was simple: "Europe had been romantic years before, because she was different from America; wherefore America would now be romantic because she was different from Europe."

But it was not so, it was not so especially in the South, whose romance, like its absurd dream, was a fallacy. Here was no place for an artist to drink in romance; the artist must make romance out of its very absence. So, may we not read in this shabby South in which the restless observer found himself, though James himself did not make the connection, a figure for that glittering European society James knew best, living out the impoverished and facile glamour of a social lie?

The Double Self

A few years before James made his tour of old Confederate states, another disaffected American, a young Harvard Ph.D. from Barrington, Massachusetts, had also traveled south by railroad coach. Like Henry James he had studied in Germany and had had his stay in Paris, though it was only a month. Like James he was a man of wide culture, a scholar who had studied philosophy not only with James's brother but with George Santayana and the eminent idealist Josiah Royce, and had worked under Max Weber in Germany. But W.E.B. Du Bois was traveling in the Jim Crow car. His alienation was as deep as James's, deeper still, for if James came back to his native land a stranger to its ways and economic power and social pretensions, W.E.B. Du Bois was born a stranger.

"After the Egyptian and Indian, the Greek and Roman, the Teuton and Mongolian," Du Bois wrote in a celebrated passage,

> the Negro is a sort of seventh son, born with a veil, and gifted with second-sight in this American world,—a world which yields him no true self-consciousness, but only lets him see himself through the revelation of the other world.

"It is a peculiar sensation, this double-consciousness," Du Bois continues, in a passage that has reverberated through the study of race in America, "this sense of always looking at one's self through the eyes of others, of measuring one's soul by the tape of a world that looks on in amused contempt and pity."[25] The germ of this passage might have come from Hegel's master-slave dialectic, but the words struck a note of special poignancy for black men and women who still lived under the shadow of racial opprobrium and for whom slavery was not the theoretical speculation of a German philosopher but a living memory.

One cannot imagine that observing the black porters, the laborers lounging in the shade of the country stations, the ragged people in the stubble fields, Henry James sensed any kinship. Yet for the expatriated artist, Du Bois's passage, if he had looked deeply enough, might well have touched a note of personal recognition. For like Du Bois's Negro, if James was burdened by the double vision of the expatriate critic, he too was a sort of seventh son, with the gift of second sight, that uncanny ability to illuminate the shifting needs and hungers beneath the social world; he too was a sort of visible ghost in a society that paid homage to his name but that, in 1905, had ceased to read him. An American in Europe, a European in an America that assaulted him with its venality and vulgarity and its incessant destruction of its own history, he was homesick for a country that he scarcely recognized. Spectator to the social dance, this hedonist child of the Puritans, this celibate voluptuary, whose own deepest erotic nature was hidden from the world and, it could be, from himself, lived out the kind of doubleness that Du Bois found in his veiled and second-sighted African Americans, and shared with them the struggle to attain self-conscious manhood. That struggle, which black men and women were compelled to fight often publicly and violently in a brutal and racist land, James carried out immured in his art. It was here that he worked out the "complex fate" of being an American, pitting the Old World denizen against the New in the social and psychological textures of his novels, and in that mediated life on the page found a place both to show himself and to hide himself. Reading James's newly published *The Golden Bowl*, his brother William asked, "Why don't you, just to please Brother, sit down and write a new book, with no twilight or mustiness in the plot, with great vigour and decisiveness in the action, no fencing in the dialogue, or psychological commentaries, and absolute straightness of style."[26] William James had tried to cure his neurotic hesitations and his despair by thrusting himself into science and into the world. He had become a public man. His younger brother could not and would not do this. He could not trade in his painter's brush for the slate pencil, could not write such a book on the "two and two makes four system" (though, tongue in cheek, he promised William he would). He looked about him and saw nowhere done or dreamed the things that alone for him constituted the interest of the novel, the very things William would have him sacrifice. He preferred to remain the "curiosity of literature" that his brother accused him of becoming on reading the published *The American Scene*.

James once wrote a story about a literary master whose secret was embedded in his work as the figure was embedded in the carpet. But James's secret was his art itself. The figure is not in the carpet, it *is* the carpet. And like Poe's purloined letter, it is there before us, in plain sight, all the time, in its lights and shades and lovely colors, in its darkness and its brightness, in its long looping arabesques of language and its intricacies and its subtleties—it is there because it is all figure. Nothing is hidden, after all. Nothing is left unsaid. The Pullman carried the novelist Henry James across a vast landscape, and like the way he chose to live his life, he didn't impel its motion; he was a passenger, a witness to the scene outside its window, a scene that he deciphered through its hints and what its surface presented.

In Saint Louis, he wrote his brother William, "This vast grey, smoky, extraordinary *bourgeois* place" that seemed to offer "in a ceaseless mild soft rain, no interest and no feature whatever," his sensitive ear could not catch, beyond the breastworks of his social pretensions, the syncopated sounds rising up from the pianos of the bordellos and social clubs on the dark side of town. The cakewalk itself had almost died out as a social diversion in black America, just as Henry James's elaborate and half-veiled novels, with their subtleties and reservations, were beginning to lose their appeal. But had he ventured to Chestnut Valley with some intelligent guide, as he had ventured into London's Soho with Clarence King and into New York's Lower East Side with Jacob Gordin, he might have found a black pianist named Scott Joplin elevating ragtime syncopation into the realm of art. One could imagine their meeting—and their mutual incomprehension.

He was, after seventeen days in the great Middle West, spent and weary,

> weary of motion and chatter, and oh, of such an unimagined dreariness of *ugliness* (on many, on *most* sides!) and of the perpetual effort of trying to "do justice" to what one doesn't like. If one could only damn it and have done with it! So much of it is rank with good intentions. And then the "kindness"—the princely (as it were) hospitality of these clubs; besides the sense of *power*, huge and augmenting, power, power (vast mechanical, industrial, social, financial) everywhere![27]

Chicago. Huge, infinite, "black, smoky, *old*-looking, very like some preternaturally *boomed* Manchester or Glasgow, lying beside a colossal lake (Michigan) of hard pale green jade, and putting forth railway antennae of maddening complexity and gigantic length." He began to loathe his talk on the Lesson of Balzac. In California, in the brief respite of San Diego, the days of heavenly beauty, and the flowers that fairly *raged* with radiance, were worthy "of some purer planet than this." He lived on oranges and olives fresh from the tree, and lay awake at night to listen to the languid lisp of the Pacific. There he tried to catch up with his impressions of the early winter, but it all got beyond him, beyond the process of what he called his precious, his "sacred little record and register." But the history was written "in my troubled and anxious, my always so strangely more or less aching, doubting, yearning, yet also more or less triumphant, or at least uplifted heart."[28]

But then it was north to Portland and back to New York across Canada on the Canadian Pacific. Then, in July of 1905, he was home—home to England and the house in Rye. He finished what he was able to finish of his scheme of an American journey. He planned to write a second volume, to speak of the universities, of California. His book ended with him on the train going across the vast reaches of America. "Is the germ of anything finely human, of anything agreeably or successfully social, supposably planted in conditions of such endless stretching and such boundless spreading as shall appear finally to minister but to the triumph of the superficial and the apotheosis of the raw?" he asked. "Oh for a split or a chasm, one groans beside your plate-glass, oh for an unbridgeable abyss or an insuperable mountain!" But this same "criminal continuity" scorned its grandest chance to break down, it made "but a mouthful of the mighty Mississippi." And that, he wrote, was to be his very next big impression. But he never brought us to the Mississippi. The line that was to lead to the next volume led only to its absence. He had said enough.

The Sacred Fount

For a long time, since he was stricken with severe writer's cramp during the composition of *What Maisie Knew* he had in his practice become his story. The hand that held the pen, the hand that wrote and thereby apprehended the world, had failed. He had been compelled to hire a stenographer. Now he paced about his work room at Rye declaiming his work, a kind of latter-day Homeric bard, his stammer transformed into a rhythmic cadence, with the click of the Remington like the strokes of a lyre, the necessary punctuation to his thought and the "strong, slow stream of his deliberate speech"[29] that played over his imaginative life.

For all his denunciations of his brother's novelistic subtleties, we are in Henry James's late novels often in the realm of William James's psychology of consciousness. The metaphor William James discovered for these physiological processes, so hard in themselves to witness or note or describe, the stream of thought, was like Henry James's novels not a collection of distinct perceptions, of scenes and chapters, but a process.

Dictating to his amanuensis, over the clatter of the Remington (only a Remington would do), talking to himself about his characters, pacing rhythmically up and down, sounding out his periods in "tones of resonant assurance" and oblivious to the wailings of the cats outside his windows and the hoots of automobile horns bringing visitors, he composed, stopping only to rest his elbows on a bookcase or mantelpiece, head in hands, audibly pursuing a word that eluded him, his very stutters and pauses becoming part of that living stream. Every image, every scene, was as William wrote of consciousness itself, "steeped and dyed in the free water that flows around it." and contained the "dying echo of whence it came to us, the dawning sense of whither it is to lead." [30] This was the world of *The Golden Bowl*, of *The Ambassadors* and *The Wings of the Dove*, the world of dawning realization that the reader and often Henry James's characters are plunged into.

A Final Return

The death of his brother William in 1910 brought Henry James once more to the United States. But on his re-establishing himself in England, he began a final return to America, this time in his memory, a return to the America of his boyhood. *A Small Boy and Others* is a family story, to be sure, but it is also the story of his aesthetic education and the first stirrings of his vocation.

He remembered the August day on which he went with his father to Mathew Brady's daguerreotype studio on Broadway to have their portraits taken. The daguerreotype was meant for one of the surprises that his father could never quite keep. It documented, did that portrait, his father's cultivation of the small boy's company, and the "romantic tradition" of the value of being taken up from wherever the Jameses were then spending their summer to the "queer empty dusty smelly New York of midsummer." He remembered the boat, the rank and rubbishy waterside quarters, the big loose cobbles wrenched from their sockets of pungent black mud, the green grocers on what seemed every corner, the carts and barrows, boxes and baskets elbowing the bumping hack they rode in, the fruitage of that more bucolic age, as he had it, of America ("Where is that fruitage now, where in particular are the peaches *d'antan*?"). He remembered feeling somehow that the adventure of the daguerreotype was improvised, for he might have worn something other than that little sheathlike jacket with the single row of brass buttons. Thackeray, on a lecture visit to the United States, had a short time before seen the small boy lurking about the father's library and called to him: "Come here, little boy, and show me your extraordinary jacket!" The novelist informed the boy that in England, were he to go there with that jacket, he would be addressed as "Buttons." "It had been revealed to me thus in a flash," James wrote, half a century later, "that we were somehow *queer*." He was never, he said, exactly crushed by it, but he remembered that he felt so, standing there, with his head in Brady's vice, during the interminably long exposure of the beautiful, lost art of the daguerreotype.[31] Yet he knew he must preserve the boy he had been, the boy we see in that old daguerreotype, standing with his pensive yet eager look, his gray eyes faded into nothing but two sharp, bright pupils, examining with deep interest what was going on in the mechanism before him, his hand resting a bit uncomfortably on the shoulder of the seated man beside him, so sure and comfortable and perhaps a bit loony, who was his father. The boy looking out of the old picture must have been very precious to Henry James. He kept that little boy's jacket for over sixty years.[32]

Was it that day, too, he wondered, that after the lunch at Union Square, and more ice-cream and more peaches after that, that he went with his father to Mrs. Cannon's shop just off Fourth Street? To look back at all, to stop however idly at a moment such as this, was for Henry James to meet the apparitional and "to find in its ghostly face the silent stare of an appeal." When he fixed it, this hovering shade of a person or place, it fixed him back and seemed the less lost, not to his consciousness, for that was nothing, but to its own.[33]

Mrs. Cannon's was at once a parlor and "a shop in particular for the relief of gentlemen in want of pocket-handkerchiefs, neckties, collars, umbrellas and straw-covered bottles of the essence known in old New York as 'Cullone'—with a very long and big O." It was also a sort of discreet hotel, with an array of furnished apartments for gentlemen—the same gentlemen for whom she imported the Eau de Cologne and neckties, among them the small boy's remarkable uncles, desiring more intimacy of comfort than the New York Hotel provided. So Mrs. Cannon sat in that parlor, in her rocking chair, sedately hemming handkerchiefs, while Miss Maggie and Miss Susie sat with their own needles in their own rocking chairs, discussing the comings and goings of these uncles, and how they last appeared and that their consumption of neckties and Eau de Cologne was somehow inordinate. Over all the sedate atmosphere there hovered secrets unknown to the boy, only hinted at in the memoir, about these profligate uncles, immersed in lives of gambling, debt, alcoholism, adultery, and at last, to go even beyond the reach of life, suicide.

> If I didn't understand, however, the beauty was that Mrs. Cannon understood (that was what she did most of all, even more than hem pocket-handkerchiefs and collars) and my father understood, and each understood that the other did. Miss Maggie and Miss Susie being no whit behind. It was only I who didn't understand—save in so far as I understood *that*, which was a kind of pale joy.[34]

We are never far from the fairy tale in Henry James. His novels are full, after all, of princesses and near-princesses,[35] and he was prone to make of the center of his life, insofar as he wrote of it, a kind of fairy tale too—the fairy tale of the boy who would not grow up. Because fairy tales are full of sights that must not be seen and words that must not be spoken and doors that must not be opened. The penalty for this knowledge is to be thrust into the realm of time and time's decay. Sigmund Freud thought that the voyeur's wish to see the hidden was in fact a wish to be seen. The wish in James was the reverse, a wish *not* to see, a wish *not* to be seen.

Yet there is a counter fairy tale, a fairy tale about a boy entering the tale itself. In his late and very poignant book *The Ambassadors*, a man in many ways like Henry James, who had deferred much, imagines entering a painting of a foreign land. That was the pull always for James, to enter his fiction, to become it. Yet what if one could not return? He explored such a nightmare in his late book *The Sacred Fount*. The narrator, who has no name and therefore is both the center and the circumference of the book, explores such a fairy tale, a story of social and sexual vampirism about couples who feed off each other, waxing and waning according to whether they are the feeder or the fed. The narrator wants to *know*, yet not to *see*; to prove his theory without being the vulgar detective at the keyhole, just as doomed Milly Theale tried to read the signs of London society from its surface. James's narrator is trapped in a "crystal cage" in this tale, the cage of his social world, but also the cage of his own obsession. It is a wonderful interior joke, that phrase, for we remember James's story of the poor London girl stuck in the cage of a telegraph office, similarly living a life by proxy, who must decipher the mysteries of the aristocrats of a glittering world who stop in to drop cryptic messages containing the secrets of their love affairs and betrayals. Henry James was both of them, knowing and articulate actor in the glittering world, and impoverished girl. The issue became what was most crucial to him, for beyond his friends, his society, beyond everything, was his work. He lived in his work. His inspiration—what he called amusingly his *bonne*—had never failed him. It was his own Sacred Fount.

So Henry James the novelist mused over those early days in New York, days in which he groped for his earliest aesthetic stirrings. It was all there, really, everything that was to come. There was Barnum's Museum, "ignoble and awful," as it must have been, and of "the last meanness."

> Its blatant face or frame stuck about with innumerable flags that waved, poor vulgar-sized ensigns, over spurious relics and catchpenny monsters in effigy, to say nothing of the promise within of the still more monstrous and abnormal living.[36]

Yet he would resist, with the effect of a "passionate adverse loyalty," the impulse to translate into harsh terms any "old sorditities and poverties," since it was there, in the museum and in the city itself, that he "plucked somehow the flower of the ideal." He recalled sitting inside the lecture hall with William and perhaps a friend and the "weary waiting, in the dusty halls of humbug, amid bottled mermaids, 'bearded ladies' and chill dioramas," for "the true centre of the seat of joy" to open. For it was the theater, with those florid and inept performances in Old New York, that gave him his earliest sense of the power of art, and it was comparing performances of *Uncle Tom's Cabin* and recognizing the gap between the absurdity and crudity of the performance and the pleasure it gave that awakened in the boy his earliest sense of a critical faculty.

Others might wish to thrust themselves into life as had William, who seemed to him as a boy so full of efficacy and knowledge and who once explained to him why he couldn't accompany him on some adventure by saying with all the superiority of an older brother, "*I* play with boys who curse and swear." But Henry James stood still, and he didn't seem to mind.

We see him, then, as the boy he was in New York, in his bright-buttoned coat, taken by the hand of his father; and we understand his literary project, the project of a small boy, an observer whose powers were sharpened by the very poverty of his own experience, as they say a blind man or a deaf man might compensate for the loss of one sense by the special acuteness of another. A small boy peering between the iron rails at the browsing and pecking and parading fowl on the lawn of a New York house or looking at the freaks and tawdry wonders behind the glass of Barnum's Museum. A boy the aging artist always imagined as alone, wondering and dawdling and gaping.[37] It was his innocence that made his art possible, the art indeed of a world seen through a window or the bars of a cage; but the window had become that special aperture in his own room in the house of fiction, his unique view of the world beyond the glass. There, he said, "there . . . was the delicacy, there the mystery, there the wonder, in especial, of the unquenchable intensity of the impressions received in childhood. They are made then once for all, be their intrinsic beauty, interest, importance, small or great; the stamp is indelible and never wholly fades. This in fact gives it an importance when a lifetime has intervened."[38] Underneath everything the man Henry James became was the overwhelming need to preserve at all costs that gaping boy, the boy in the buttoned coat; to preserve, through all its vicissitudes, through all weariness and disillusion and horror, the essential wonder of consciousness. Always the most powerful emotional connection he made in his work was to the world of children. Children abandoned, often dying in the care of negligent, exploitative adults, and always essentially alone. What is the doomed Milly Theale in *The Wings of the Dove*, that almost unreadably moving book, but a child at the edge of womanhood, and fated not to be able to cross its threshold? It is significant that only in that book is the sexual passion that James so scrupulously left between the lines of his page fully and emotionally believable: it was the world Milly Theale would never know.

Lying ill of typhus in Boulogne-sur-Mer, at about the age of thirteen, alone in a great old room behind green shutters, the small boy found himself already aware "that one way of taking life was to go in for everything and everyone, which kept you abundantly occupied, and the other way was to be as occupied, quite as occupied, just with the sense and the image of it all, and on only a fifth of the actual immersion." It was a circumstance, he thought, extremely strange—"Life was taken almost equally both ways"— that was the strangeness.[39] Walking in the old streets of the *haute ville* of the town, amid the ramparts and "scattered, battered benches of reverie," thinking of real history in the form of Catherine de' Medici, who had so dismally sojourned in the citadel, and the fictional history of Thackeray's Newcomes, and peering at the old, anciently odd houses, he wondered "what human life might be tucked away in such retreats," so absolutely appointed and obliged did he feel "to make out, so far as I could, what, in so significant a world, they on their part *represented*."

> I think the force mainly sustaining me at that rather dreary time—as I see it can only show for—was this lively felt need that everything should represent something more than what immediately and all too blankly met the eye. . . . What I wanted, in my presumption, was that the object, the place, the person, the unreduced impression, often doubtless so difficult or so impossible to reduce, should give out to me something of a situation.[40]

When he recovered from his illness he found that he was no longer the small boy. His way was not yet clear to him. It was not yet clear to him that in fact he had been all this time educating himself in the most rigorous way for his vocation, a vocation after all of gaping and dawdling and delineating on the page the most subtle and complex of representations. Near the conclusion of his book he recounts a remarkable dream or nightmare or both, much commented on, which he had many years after his illness, of triumphing over some ominous specter that had tried to come for him in his bed, of his trying to bar the door against it, but then turning the tables on it at last by thrusting the door open. For the specter was more afraid of him, he imagined in his dream, than he of it. Once opened, the door revealed the long Galerie d'Apollon in the Louvre, and the specter fled, retreating through the splendor and power of art. It was the specter of life. James had looked at its Medusa face and found neither the nightmare paralysis of fear nor that of defeat, for he had looked at it, in his dream, through the lens of art. He would continue his autobiography in *Notes of a Son and Brother* and the unfinished "The Middle Years." But the pattern of his vocation, of his whole approach to art, had already been set. William James had overcome the doubts and neuroses and false starts of his lengthy adolescence by pulling himself up by his moral bootstraps, by will and science and by thrusting himself into action, by a politics of pragmatic engagement. His younger brother engaged only with the challenge of his art. It was, for him, enough. "We work in the dark—" he wrote in the persona of his fictional writer Dencombe, "we do what we can—we give what we have. Our doubt is our passion and our passion is our task. The rest is the madness of art."[41] To the end of his days he insisted that he had been right, that art *made* life, made interest, made importance.[42] He was sure of it.

The Cakewalk of Mister Henry James

So private a man, so full of exquisite perceptions, so fastidious, so rich a consciousness—but a man who burned his letters, who hid himself by distributing his persona, his emotional life, in the thousands of pages of his work, sitting now on shelves, revered, largely unread. In a civilization that demanded of its artists the moral certitude of a ledger, James could not get his representations of the world to balance. "Ah, is not that the trick that life plays?" he asked. "Life itself leaves you with a question—it asks you questions."[43] For James, one of the greatest questions was that of his relation to his native land. But the complexity of that relation, the bareness of its soil for one so constituted, had left him alone. In 1915, during the Great War, he became a British subject. But in fact, he was at home only in his art. To write, to see, had been for him, and would remain, "an act of life," and he steadfastly lived on, "that queer monster, the artist, an obstinate finality, an inexhaustible sensibility,"[44] an isolate observer of the human dance. Yet once, at a festive gathering of the artists and writers of the near-bohemia of his literary circle in the Cotswolds in 1886, he had in fact joined the fun. His friend Edmund Gosse remembered it. "Benign, indulgent, but grave, and not often unbending beyond a genial chuckle," as Gosse remembers him, the only sedate one of the party, who once "nobly descending, took part one night in a cake-walk."[45]

How finally could James fully know himself without that most intimate relation with another being, what he called "the great relation," that between lovers? He once wrote a little story about an artist who so split his private life from his personal that he was at work on a novel while some simulacrum of himself played the social game. It was James's loneliness, finally, that was the essential thing. It was the port, he wrote, from which he set out and to which he finally was to return, "the deepest thing about one." Deeper in him than his talent, his discipline, his pride. "Deeper above all, than the deep countermining of art."[46] But lest he disappear entirely into it, that other self, that simulacrum, the affable, indulgent, benign novelist, Henry James, must join now and then the dance. A grave tournament of deportment, as Mark Twain had said, yes, was the cakewalk of Mr. Henry James, yet the prize was no mere confection, but life itself. Disguised among the masqueraders in this impromptu minstrel show—for who really knew this small boy playing the man?—he performed his dance. Many and many were the women in his life who might take his proffered arm, those matrons whom he found so comfortable and comforting and for whom he was a sympathetic ear; the young men, too, those beautiful young men, the artists and writers whom he loved and to whom he wrote—he might only imagine them in the dance—but they too would take the proffered arm. But finally, in his integrity, we must imagine him treading his cakewalk alone, nodding gravely from side to side, doffing his silk hat in time to a cadence only he could hear, gesturing with one of the walking sticks that were so much a part of him, a bit ludicrous in the bright vests and tight pants he favored, a bit vaudevillian even while playing that complex game he had perfected to an audience that only imagined they saw what they saw, and finally, dancing to the pulse between insufficiencies—Europe and America, the public and the private, the rich and the not rich, the innocent and the serpent wise—in that space between what he gave of himself and what he withheld, the art of misunderstanding.

Chapter 7
An Innocent at Cedro

The Spring of 1909

America in the spring of 1909 was, as usual, going to hell in a handbasket, and as usual, it was the professors who were swinging the basket by its strap. The titles of the first two articles a journalist named Harold Bolce wrote for *The Cosmopolitan Magazine* on American institutions of higher learning pretty much give the gist of it: "Blasting at the Rock of Ages" in May, then, in June, "Polyglots in Temples of Babel." The final piece in the series, "Avatars of the Almighty," came in July. The whole thing was really quite terrifying, according to the *Cosmopolitan* lead. In hundreds of classrooms it was being taught daily that the Decalogue was no more sacred than a syllabus; that the home as an institution was doomed; that there were no absolute evils; that immorality was simply an act in contravention of society's accepted standards; that democracy was a failure and the Declaration of Independence only spectacular rhetoric; that the change from one religion to another was like getting a new hat. The list continued. Moral precepts were passing shibboleths; children were an encumbrance to the climb from one class to the next; there could be holier alliances without the marriage bond than within it. . .

Bolce had spent two years sitting in classrooms and interviewing professors and college administrators. The serious, thoughtful men—and one or two women—he listened to were able to espouse the most radical doctrines from the sanctity of the lectern. If *Cosmopolitan* played up the shock value, Bolce himself, it seems, found it rather exciting. At Syracuse, a church school as it happened, Bolce directed a question to Professor Edwin Earp, a former clergyman, about whether or not he believed Moses got the Ten Commandments as Scripture told it. Earp smiled. "I do not," he said.

"It is unscientific and absurd to imagine that God ever turned stone-mason and chiseled commandments on a rock." At Yale William Graham Sumner was saying that those ethical notions were "mere figments of speculation" and "unrealities that ought to be discarded altogether." The academy was a slough of cultural relativity. There might be nakedness without indecency and adultery without lewdness. It all depended. Then at Harvard there was Professor William James. "The nihilists, anarchists, and free-lovers," Bolce quotes him as saying, "the socialists and single-tax men; the free-traders, the prohibitionists, the anti-vivisectionists, the radical Darwinians with their idea of suppressing the weak—these and all the conservative elements of society arrayed against them are simply deciding through actual experiment by what sort of conduct the maximum of good can be gained and kept in the world." Yet somehow Bolce missed one of the worst of the worst, at once one of the most famous yet most reclusive of American scholars, who had been since 1907 living among the pines and cedars a mile from the Stanford campus.

This was Professor Thorstein Veblen. But anonymity was exactly what this quiet professor wanted, for his life, his very style of writing at this time, was one long parade of artifice, irony, and circumlocution, an elaborate mystification of who he really was and what he really believed. Those cakewalking African American waiters and housemaids competing among themselves and against a hostile or indifferent white world, and striving to learn where real freedom lay as the twentieth century dawned, had, with their stylish satire, touched on the glittering surface of America's dream of success. But to fully understand the dream we must look beyond the superficial flounces and top hats and fans and go more deeply into *what* exactly the African Americans were mocking and envying at once, at its structure and its meaning. It would take someone like Thorstein Veblen to do this, a theorist of leisure and investigator of the origin of the aesthetic impulse, a mocker himself who still could probe beyond mockery, someone who quite likely had never seen a cakewalk.

In a beautiful essay written nineteen years after Veblen's death, Max Lerner tried to sum up this strange and difficult character:

> He was a lone figure, the man nobody knew—not even his family and friends, not even his warmest disciples. He was a man living in a shell formed by long years of alienation and hurt, and perhaps also by the

glimpses of terror he had when he probed into the nature of institutions and the course of history. As with all great satirists, there was passion underneath everything Veblen wrote. It was the passion of a man whose sense of reality was so shattering that he had to turn aside from it and fashion for himself a mask of mockery and indirection. That mask was Thorstein Veblen's style, as it was his life.[1]

Veblen was the most impossible of professors. A student watching him ambling across the quad at Stanford with a slouch hat pulled down over his brow, his coat and trousers hanging, hair and mustache untrimmed, could have taken him for a tramp. His collar was a couple of sizes too large and his stockings were held to his trousers with safety pins. In his classroom he would sit down ponderously at his desk and produce an enormous watch that was attached by a black ribbon to the front of his vest—which rarely matched his coat—with another safety pin. A useful gadget, the safety pin.

He lectured in a low, monotonous voice, without raising his eyes, which were frequently closed, stopping sometimes to ask a question. He might talk about southwestern Indian festivals, Viking pirates, or prehistoric European artifacts, all of this tumbling out in a disorganized jumble, which seemed far from the subject at hand. His students found him an enigma—the few who remained in his classes. In fact he usually seemed intent on having no students at all.

The rituals and requirements of academic life that bored or burdened him he did his best to shrug off, ignore, or subvert. He shuffled his roll cards, gave an entire class the same grade, and committed the heresy of imagining that students came to the university to learn, which of course made grades, examinations, roll books (not to mention football and clubs named by Greek letters) irrelevant. He confused the marks of the idlers with those of the industrious and showed no remorse. "My grades," he explained, "are like lightning. They are liable to strike anywhere."

What this odd and solitary man would have read into the cakewalk, if he had seen one, is debatable. Would he have seen only what Mark Twain had, a crude and childish imitation of the rich? Or would he have seen under an elaborate camouflage the very sort of subversive satire he himself practiced with such telling effect? Or would he have gone further still, and discovered in the cakewalk that creative energy he found at the heart of human behavior, that spirit of pure play that animated real, disinterested scientific investigation and that just might have animated, beyond the competition for a cake, those working-class African American men and women who were creating with their flounces and furbelows a poetics of gesture and emulation both beautiful and complex and very much like art? Both his life and his writings give room for speculation.

Eight years before he came to Stanford, this obscure professor had overnight become famous for a book, *The Theory of the Leisure Class*. His method was anthropological and the mode comic. Veblen had been a student of Peirce's during the latter's short career at Johns Hopkins, and his analysis may have owed a good deal to Peirce's thinking. The accoutrements of the conspicuously paraded leisure of the rich, as Veblen described them, had a meaning. They were signs. They were a language of difference and discrimination. Dogs and carriages, dresses and walking sticks—it was a grand American potlatch, a kind of plutocratic cakewalk of corsets and courtesies, of snubs and snobberies, of spaniels and jewels and privileges. It was a language that might have at first rankled Veblen, that practitioner of rural thrift *ad absurdum*, but ended up as the source of endless amusement. Through thirteen chapters of elaborate Victorian verbiage he mercilessly deconstructed the rituals and institutions of the ruling class, their carriages and colleges and churches and sports and clothing.

Alas for Veblen's style! For all his protestations of linguistic precision there is a circumlocutory, deliberate inflation of the language that seems to defy clarity. Mencken hated it and saw Veblen as something of a quack. "Futile, archaic and cumbrous," one early critic of *The Theory of the Leisure Class* called it, though Howells thought the style "graphic" and "easy" with a "delightful accuracy of characterization." At times it is hard work to immediately grasp the riot of scorn and rage that Veblen chose to camouflage under the polysyllabic verbiage of this elaborate cakewalk of self-mockery and verbal effusion which he chose to call a "morally colorless" language. But stay with him: it is a style that begins by leading you all around Robin Hood's barn and ends by kicking you in the pants. After a while you discover under the elephantine, Oliver Hardy sort of tread of Veblen's prose an epic hilarity, a satire more intense than anything Mencken or Twain ever dreamed of, for Veblen went beyond the warts and bumps on the surface of human behavior; he cut to the very bone. Lévi-Strauss says that the function of anthropological thinking is to make the exotic ordinary; Veblen inverts this and makes the everyday accoutrements of the world of the rich as exotic as the paraphernalia of a barbarian chief.

Consider the walking stick.

> Taken simply as a feature of modern life, the habit of carrying a walking-stick may seem at best a trivial detail; but the usage has a significance for the point in question. The classes among whom the habit most prevails—the classes with whom the walking-stick is associated in popular apprehension— are the men of the leisure class proper, sporting men, and the lower-class delinquents. . . . The walking-stick serves the purpose of an advertisement that the bearer's hands are employed otherwise than in useful effort, and it therefore has utility as an evidence of leisure. But it is also a weapon, and it meets a felt need of barbarian man on that ground. The handling of so tangible and primitive a means of offense is very comforting to any one who is gifted with even a moderate share of ferocity.[2]

It is a wonderful passage. The walking stick is both an emblem of perfect leisure and a reminder of perfect ferocity: its symbolism makes brothers of J. P. Morgan and the most unregenerate pimp in your town's Tenderloin.

So Veblen's book goes on, a deadpan send-up of what he called the predatory class, of its propensity for violence and plunder, which when not enacted in actual armed conflict express themselves in displays falling under the head of "sportsmanship," from which even children are not exempt, boys of the ruling class being enrolled in "pseudo-military organizations" under the tutelage of "clergymen and other pillars of society." The organizations justified themselves as developing the manly virtues, but what they really developed, it turned out, were "truculence and clannishness" on the playing field and the leisure-class huntsman (Theodore Roosevelt immediately comes to mind) who is really a superannuated boy, and who keeps all nature in "a state of chronic desolation." Women, too, as much trophies of this prowess as the stuffed buffalo and grizzlies adorning the sportsman's lodge, were paraded for their uselessness (another form of conspicuous consumption), and their costly, archaic, and uncomfortable dress attested to the fact that they would find it impossible to do any work should they be for some reason inclined to it. If Marx discovered the fetishism of the commodity, it was Veblen, as his scholar John P. Diggins points out, who understood why such magical power lay embedded in the necessary accoutrements of wealth.[3]

Like any good caricaturist Veblen's verbal hyperbole turns pimples into mountains and noses into fire hoses, and if this is exaggeration it is exaggeration at the service of making us see something that we haven't seen before. The hick-town banker and the hick-town merchant seen in Veblen's habitual language as reliable, conciliatory, conservative, secretive, patient, and "prehensile" (the "prehensile" is a masterstroke)—are only versions of the Captains of Industry and Finance who rule our world. Veblen's method is often stereoscopic. He discovers, for example, a certain moment in history where intense competition among companies was fast becoming intolerable, and describes how there arose a man to set things straight, "a man of far-seeing sagacity and settled principles, of executive ability and businesslike integrity, who saw the needs of the hour and the available remedy, and who saw at the same glance his own opportunity of gain."[4] Yet that man is not some nineteenth-century robber baron but a tenth-century Viking pirate: put Pálnatoki on one side of the card and John D. Rockefeller on the other; put the card in the stereopticon and adjust the focus: the pirate and plutocrat become moral equivalents of each other. Veblen was even quite prepared to extend his theory of the leisure class into the celestial realm itself, and described Heaven as a kind of sempiternal country club, with its hierarchies of angels and saints leisured beyond the touch of history and time.

Eighteen ninety-nine, the year that saw *The Theory of the Leisure Class* come into print, was, as it happened, the year a similarly corrosive book was published in Vienna by Sigmund Freud (Freud postdated his book to 1900, to have it ring with the authority of the new century). *The Interpretation of Dreams*, like Veblen's book, quite literally got under the skin of its society—we recall Freud's famous quip on seeing the Statue of Liberty from the ship that was bringing him on his first and only trip to America: "Don't they know we are bringing them the plague?" The comparison of Veblen to Freud is not too much of a leap even in its biographical and social implications. Like Freud and other secular Jews, Veblen, as a child of immigrants in largely Norwegian-speaking farming settlements in Wisconsin and Minnesota, was born at the margins of two cultures. In fact Veblen once wrote an article on the Jews that described the fate of the Jewish intellectual who has left the security of the traditions he has grown up in and yet is outside the conventions of the Gentile world into which he is thrown.

> He becomes a disturber of the intellectual peace, but only at the cost of becoming an intellectual wayfaring man, a wanderer in the intellectual No

Man's Land, seeking another place to rest, farther along the road, somewhere over the horizon. They are neither a complaisant nor a contented lot,
these aliens of the uneasy feet.[5]

This might have been, as a number of commentators have noted, Veblen's
description of himself. There was, however, a kind of intellectual culture in
his Minnesota settlement and a relation to the nonimmigrant world, and certainly there was a superior intellectual inheritance that showed itself in his
father's determination to procure for his sons an education that was broader
than that prescribed for the usual ministerial occupation—practically the
only respectable intellectual one in his Norse community. It was, in his family, an intellectual inheritance overlain by a profound silence. One day, the
story goes, Veblen was called from the fields, found his bags already in the
family wagon, and was driven to college by a hired man. Veblen did not find
it strange that his father said nothing to one of his sons he bumped into in
town one day, since, after all, he had nothing to say. The silence of that family became Veblen's own.

Thorstein Veblen was born in 1857. "I grew up in a laboratory," he
was fond of saying of the rural communities of his childhood and early
youth, and his view of that laboratory would only be magnified by the
larger laboratory outside. He witnessed the swindles and chicanery of the
small-town merchants and bankers and saw the frugal, hard-working farmers turning from producers to land speculators. It was all one big poker
game, as Veblen observed. In the United States the years of Veblen's youth
were years of smashups and head-on collisions of the runaway trains that
were propelling American industrial growth. Financial panics wiped out
fortunes large and small overnight. Strikes on the railroads and in mines
and steel mills rose at times to the level of local and even national in-
surrections as labor unions with ever-more-militant missions pushed back
against employers and were met with the guns of private police forces and
state militias. A radical populism raged through the prairie states, and the
unemployed gathered in militarized companies and commandeered railroad trains to take their case to Washington. Over all of this Veblen cast
the cool and distant and often ironic eye of the scientific observer. The
books he gave to a colleague when he finally left Stanford are significant:
the nineteen volumes of the United States Industrial Commission; a number of volumes of the ethnological reports of the Smithsonian Institution;

a set of Herbert Spencer. The ethnological reports must especially interest us, for Veblen had searched for the origins of economic man beyond the fringes of the rational calculations of self-interest and capital accumulation, where the classical economists and Marx himself had searched for them. If Freud went in, Veblen went back. Back to the primitive instincts of power, possession, and emulation.

Against the prevailing Social Darwinism preached in the best churches and the most elite American universities, Veblen reconstructed humanity's earliest societies as egalitarian and cooperative, rather than competitive. As a young man Veblen, with his first wife, Ellen Rolfe, read Edward Bellamy's utopian novel *Looking Backward*. It made, Ellen said, an epoch in their lives. The novel created a world without money and almost free of labor, where technology and systematized human goodness had triumphed over the grinding competition of capitalism. Veblen outgrew the bland rationality of Bellamy's insufferable Doctor Leete, but the book had given him that great gift of all literary utopias, a place outside history—if only imaginary—from which to evaluate society's accepted truths. Darwin might be understood by one sort of reader, say Herbert Spencer, to show that nature itself was a form of cutthroat competition, the "survival of the fittest" in Spencer's rephrasing of the process of natural selection, but Veblen did not think that was by any means the whole story, so he wound the skein back, looking for other evidence.

The most primitive instinct, beyond the sheer will to survive, was what he called the "Instinct of Workmanship," which expressed itself in this hypothetical primitive world in a spirit of emulation, a peaceful competition to be the best practitioner of what Veblen named the "Industrial Pursuits"— the best basket maker, say, or wood-carver. But with the advance of technology came the ability to hunt and make war, and the useful industrial pursuits, now largely the work of women, became humiliating, tabooed. The warrior became the leader of this divided society; his predations were sung and praised, the new objects of competition and emulation. Finally, the skulls and scalps he accumulated, the women he stole, became uniquely his, a sign of his prowess and the origin of private property. It was only a few short steps from actual war to pecuniary competition and the sterile, wasteful, and finally socially useless battles of the robber barons.

Yet for all his many publications, it was often difficult for people to know what, exactly, Thorstein Veblen *did* believe, and he took pains to keep it so.

The socialists liked to claim him, and indeed he once said he was surprised that they hadn't made more use of his work. But if the socialists claimed him, he didn't exactly claim them. He learned from Marx and held him up as one of the world's great minds, yet he saw him as in reality only continuing the thinking of such English economists as Ricardo and Adam Smith. For Veblen found in all of them a teleological bias smuggled into their science, a kind of subjective magic he called animism. Marx's view of history as class struggle was just another version of the Victorian myth of progress, his dialectic a leftover from the orgy of German Romanticism. Veblen's view of capitalism was unique, for unlike the classical economists and the Marxists, he did not hold it to be a necessary stage in historical development. He thought it might be a sort of moment and he did not respect it. He was nobody's man. He liked to have it so. He read William James's psychology with great care, but had no use for his pragmatism; he satirized the church and he quarreled with the academy. "The outcome of any serious research," he said, "can only be to make two questions grow where only one grew before." Other professors thought he wore a mask. He rarely spoke in public, rarely took the floor in a meeting. Perhaps it was the sin of intellectual pride.

The Innocents at Cedro

Sometime after Veblen's arrival at the Cedro Cottage at the edge of the vast Stanford campus, his household had resolved itself into himself, three college students, two Indian ponies, two cows, forty or so chickens, and numberless cats. The youngest of the students, Robert Duffus, has left the elegiac memoir from which this section takes its name. The students looked after the place, cooked, milked the cows, hitched up one of the ponies to the two-wheeled cart or saddled it as Veblen's pleasure might be, tended to the chickens and the cats—Veblen thought dogs unclean and worthless sycophants—and did the general chores around the place for their board and room, all without touching, as Veblen put it, "the cash nexus."

By summer the hills of the Santa Clara Valley had turned brown, and above the tops of the redwoods that marked the crest of the coast range sea fog lay like a blanket of fleece. The fog never came down in the valley, but dimmed and softened the outlines of the hills. Dust lay on the roads and there was the good smell of tarweed in the air. It was beautiful. At night the boys might hear the thin rattle of the wheels of the cart or the clop of the pony's hoofs, and might imagine Veblen going about among the small sounds of the night in this little utopia. Where William James, who was teaching at Stanford at the time, made a moral lesson of the 1906 earthquake that turned San Francisco and a good part of the Peninsula into rubble, Veblen "borrowed" the wreckage of the Stanford family's chicken coop and improvised a mountain cabin. It was a simple, sparse affair, with furniture of his own making. But it had a view of the valley from one side and of the ocean on the other, and of the fog sifting through the trees. Gossip circulated that Veblen would take his concubines there for a weekend, but there were always stories of that sort around him. It may be that he went up there to be alone.

At the dinner table Veblen might talk, or he might not. The worst way to get him to talk, the boys discovered, was to ask him a question, for his habitual answer was "I don't know." In the classroom, paying close attention to his uninflected monologue, you would become aware that he had interpolated some sly joke, or quoted a line from a popular song, or inserted a bit of contemporary slang. He might talk about Viking pirate trusts or Inuit economics, but always it turned out that he was making some point—illuminating, often startling—that led him back to the business of the modern world. If his agonizingly slow delivery and his monotone were part of a strategy, the strategy was to present his evidence in such a way that the contradictions, the absurdities even, of contemporary economic life and culture convicted themselves with very little help from this most erudite and for the most part imperturbable professor. At Cedro he was more straightforward than in the classroom and let go of the protections of his baroque terminology, but he continued to teach on his own terms. "He was a kind of god," Duffus says, "a minor god, possibly, but still a god—considering things mundane with humorous disapproval. He did not denounce institutions. He was not indignant at strutting figures of men. They just seemed ridiculous to him."[6] So, if it was one of his evenings to talk, he talked of ludicrous customs and social rituals, of nature and its economics, and quietly exploded all the accepted theories about how society, beneath its conventionally described skin, in fact worked. Then around the dining-room table it might happen that one of the boys who was taking an elementary economics class might ask why rent was not a component in the cost of production, and the author of *The Theory of Business Enterprise* and the most original economist of his generation would say he didn't know.

He told them once about the female ichneumon wasp (he thought it a fly, but no matter) which laid its eggs in the folds of an unsuspecting caterpillar, and how, when the eggs hatched, the grubs feasted on it without the caterpillar knowing it, until it was too late. He might have been such a wasp himself, laying his little eggs of irony and mirth in the body of capitalism. Veblen had made a simple but fundamental distinction between Industry and what he called, in his mock-heroic style, pecuniary gain. The two were usually coupled, as classical economists would have it, in the industrialist's quest for profits through greater efficiency and greater production. But to Veblen the industrialists, finally, were not concerned with efficiency and production. They were concerned with profit, profit, and only profit. Thus the hallowed connection between efficiency and production, which gave a moral and heroic tinge to the economics of the Gilded Age, was merely adventitious.

Veblen on one occasion told the boys a story about a farmer who had a mud hole in the road in front of his house.

> At first he used to get out his oxen and haul travelers out of the mud because he was sorry for them. So many got stuck that he felt justified in charging a little to cover expenses and overhead. After a while he gave up his farm work and specialized in hauling people out of the hole. When a dry season came his income fell off. He thought about this, and then took to bringing water from the creek after dark to keep the mud hole in revenue-producing condition.[7]

"Veblen," Duffus wrote, "believed that a great deal of modern business was maintaining mud holes for the purpose of charging people to be hauled out of them." If you added to that the growing role salesmanship played in modern business (you imagine signs urging travelers to visit the world-famous mud hole)—the baleful role of credit, which lay at the heart of business cycles—you might come close to an outline of his theory of business enterprise. Yet one evening he shocked Duffus by remarking that there was one thing to be said for capitalism: "It works."

In the years of Veblen's stay at Stanford the roads of California's valleys were full of men with bundles on their backs, itinerant fruit tramps and workers driven out of their jobs by the crash of 1907. A number of them

were members of the radical new union, the IWW—the Industrial Workers
of the World—the Wobblies. The oldest of the boys, the stoical, tubercular
Harry George, had a job as gatekeeper and would talk to them.

> He said these men weren't ignorant. Some of them had read a good deal
> and had ideas. These ideas weren't too far different from Harry's, or from
> Veblen's, either, though the language was different. A kind of ferment was
> stirring. A man who walked around with his blankets on his back, with no
> permanent home and no permanent woman, looked at institutions with as
> much aloofness and disrespect as any Norwegian agrarian.[8]

David Riesman said Veblen himself was something of a Wobbly,[9] and in his
own quiet way he was. The Wobblies had no hopes for political remedies,
and for most of his life Veblen was a silent pessimist on the front of political
action. But deeper still was his connection to Wobbly primitivism. What
this collection of tramps and social riffraff was after was more than the incremental gains—or "pork chops"—that a worker might bargain for or even
extort from the capitalists; they were after a fundamental transformation of
society and looked toward a world without bosses and owners, one great cooperative mechanism run by workers who used their hands and workers who
used their heads. In order to make that transformation, the Wobblies had
to transform the mind of the worker itself. Their method was in many ways
Veblen's method, cutting away at accepted truths with the tools of satire
and ridicule until the real truth emerged; and if Veblen exposed the absurdities of pecuniary culture to a middle-class audience that was largely that
culture's product, the Wobs filled their newspapers and the songbooks they
peddled on skid road with equally savage satires that sent up the whole capitalist establishment, from the street-corner preachers offering pie in the sky,
to the blockheaded workers buying the hogwash that emanated from the
front office, to the capitalist himself, always, in their cartoons, decked out
in cutaway and plug hat à la Scrooge McDuck. Like those Wobblies trudg-
ing down dusty roads and riding the side-door Pullmans through the West,
Veblen was an intellectual tramp, disdaining the pork chops of academe,
never acquiring rank and tenure, and being dumped at one university after
another; and if the Wobblies refused to disavow sabotage (their literature
and the little stickers they left stuck to water tanks and boxcars were replete
with wooden sabots, and black "sab cats"), Veblen too practiced a quiet sort
of sabotage on the time-honored practices of the university, boycotting cer-

emonies and committee meetings and mumbling through his lectures until
he had pared down his students to those few who could really *hear* him.
What was sabotage, after all? In his cool, detached way, Veblen failed to see
the difference between a radicalized worker throwing a handful of nails into
the gears of a threshing machine and an industrialist slowing down production for profit—what he called in a phrase he borrowed from the Wobblies,
which had the ring of his own kind of satire, the "conscientious withdrawal
of efficiency." Like those "masterless men" in the hobo jungles and on the
roads of the West, Veblen too had no place in the formal scheme of his
society. No place *in* it and therefore no respect *for* it.

The Bard of Idle Curiosity

At Cedro, The Professor, as the boys called him, was pursuing a curious
sort of hobby. He was learning to knap flints. Patiently flaking off an edge
(what was he making? an arrowhead? a tool to cut the pages of his Bureau of
Ethnology reports?), Veblen was going back in time to the origins of things
human.

Two hundred fifty miles or so due north, in the foothills below Mount
Lassen in the years that Veblen was at Stanford, there was living a Yahi
Indian who was possibly the last indigenous American to have never known
a white man. He made his fires with a wooden fire drill, lured deer close to
him with a deer head decoy, and shot them with a short-range bow and a
stone-tipped arrow. These arrowheads he chipped out of obsidian with
a metal point that, like the rough canvas of the shirt he wore, he had scavenged from some miner's cabin. Since childhood he and his small band had
been fleeing from the whites. He was the last of them. The world of his tribe
before the coming of the gold miners and Indian hunters, like the agrarian
world buried somewhere in the back of Veblen's consciousness, existed only
in his songs and stories. When, in 1911, he finally came into civilization,
he became a kind of museum exhibit for the anthropologists of the University of California, living in great dignity and great loneliness until his
death five years later. He taught the anthropologists the songs and stories
that but for their preservation on 148 wax-cylinder recordings would have
died with him, and he might, had Veblen been in California during this
Indian's brief stay in San Francisco, have taught Veblen many things, things

above all pertaining to the book Veblen was working on during his Stanford years. For this savage, who was called "Ishi"—the word for "man" in his language[10]—was a superb craftsman. The tools he made while under the protection of the anthropologists of the university, the arrowheads and fire drills and lengths of twine, have a simple usefulness that, in the case of the arrowheads, was astonishingly elegant.

Ishi called white men *saltu*, ghosts. They were simply another order of being. These ghosts knew how to make a number of things that were useful—matches, for one thing—and their indoor plumbing was good, too. But still, in their antics, in the things they seemed to care about, they were children, very clever children but children nevertheless. Veblen and this savage man might have agreed on a good many things. Like Veblen, Ishi was reticent about himself and his inner life. He, like Veblen, was from a tribe with only one member—himself.

Veblen might have recognized himself in Ishi's story of Lizard, who is patiently described in all the stages of his arrow-making. The arrow-making becomes a recurring chorus in the story, the scraping and straightening of shaft and fore shaft, their joining, the fletching of the arrow, its painting, and the chipping of the arrowhead. Necessary tasks to which Lizard patiently returns after each adventure. In one of these adventures, after a shaft breaks, Lizard gives over his arrow-making to join the night dance of a kind of "story-people," covering himself with their excrement as a hunter might rub himself in ashes to kill his human smell. At last Lizard has enough of this upside-down land, where one dances all night and sleeps all day; he cleans himself up and returns to his arrow-making.[11] Chipping away at his flints or at a chapter in his current book, Veblen may have felt, strange and solitary lizard that he was, that he had come back from one of his occasional forays into the social rituals of the academic *saltu* bathed in shit.

There was a good deal of the savage in Veblen himself, then, but it was a savagery that harked back not to the barbarian raiders carrying off women and booty but to the Stone Age toolmakers like Ishi and the southwestern Indian agriculturalists. The instinct of workmanship prized craft knowledge and grew out of a time when knowledge was held in the hands as much as in the mind, when craft knowledge was a value in itself, not something to be seized and exploited for the wasteful production of profit. The book Veblen was working on at Stanford was an elaboration of his 1898 essay on that all-important instinct of workmanship.

But there was a paradox: seized by the forces of capitalism, the instinct of workmanship might lead to the dead end of pragmatism, to processes that created a foregone material end, and thus to the instinct's own death. No matter how the moralists and the Social Darwinists might choose to read him, there was no foregone end in Darwin, only the blind forces of nature acting, reacting, leading on to an indeterminate future. And for Veblen there was something else. An instinct parallel to that of workmanship, and which Veblen called—and the name has a kind of savagery in it too—idle curiosity. For the worked piece of flint must not only be functional; it must be elegant. I do not know how beautiful Veblen's arrowheads were, but in that final stage he might have approached something he perhaps learned from Peirce, a kind of aesthetic, where both he and his teacher found the beginnings of ethics.[12] For real science to flourish, Veblen knew, it must be free of pragmatic ends; it must be motivated by the same primitive force that lay behind the beauty of an arrowhead or a woven basket or a Zuni pot, a free-flowing, improvisatory, impractical spirit of *play*. It was the same spirit animating the songs and tales of the creation of the world of men and animals that would be left by that Indian who lived in a museum.

Veblen was forced to leave Stanford finally in 1909, his peccadilloes and long-running battle with his first wife once more having gotten the better of him. It wasn't that his sexual behavior was particularly strange by the standards of current or possibly even Edwardian academia. It was just that he made no effort to hide it. For oddly enough, unkempt and wordless as he was, he was attractive to women. Perhaps it was his very silence, his hiding from, and need of, what Duffus calls the "emotional nexus," that inspired something maternal in the women who approached him. One story—and there were many about him in this connection—has Veblen called on the carpet by a university president, who told him he feared the baneful effect he was having on the morals of the faculty wives. Veblen reassured him a bit ruefully, the tale goes: "I've tried them all. They are no good." A woman, who didn't particularly like him, surmised that he had learned of his erotic power late and was making up for lost time. Women saw him as a project: he was the type of independent man who left room for a great deal of taking care of. More significant to his attitudes toward women than his sexual predilections might have been his research. For Veblen, women were the first private property. Trophies of war, they belonged not to the community, or to themselves, but to the successful warrior or chieftain as tokens of his prowess. Veblen may have needed women in some fundamental way, but he did not consider them trophies of war. They came and went through his life, and it seems clear that he was more often than not the pursued rather than the pursuer. At Stanford he continued to scandalize. When a female admirer followed him to Palo Alto, he asked a friend what you did if a woman moved in on you.[13] University president David Starr Jordan sent an emissary to deliver a message to Veblen: "The president is disappointed with the conduct of your domestic affairs." "So am I, sir. So am I," Veblen replied.[14] The long-suffering Jordan threw up his hands. "What can you do with such a man?" A nice question.

The Hunkey with the Shovel

> In the past the man has been first; in the future the system must
> be first.
>   —Frederick Winslow Taylor, *Principles of Scientific Management*

Out in the yard of the Bethlehem Steel Works are six hundred Hunkeys with six hundred shovels. Some of the Hunkeys are Irish Hunkeys and some of them are South Slav Hunkeys and some of them are Poles or Italians or Swedes. Say six hundred Hunkeys. The Hunkeys bring their own shovels to the yard. None of them knows how to shovel sand, or hard coal or soft coal or pea coal. None of them knows how to shovel at all. None of them knows how to work.

Cold in the yard this morning. A few grains of snow flutter down, fine as sand, landing on the sleeves of the Hunkeys' mackinaws, and down the necks of their shirts. Half of the Hunkeys rub their hands together and blow on them before picking up their shovels. Half of them stamp their feet in the thin snow. None of them knows what number Gandy shovel you need to handle the rice coal or Mesabi ore; none of them knows that to get the most out of a man in a day the right shovel load is twenty-one or twenty-one and a half pounds. Not twenty or twenty-two pounds, twenty-one or twenty-one and a half. None of them knows how you bend into a pile of sand from the bottom with your right hand against your side so you can put your back into it, or how to give the right little flip to the shovel to keep the load in. None of them knows that Frederick Winslow Taylor has put all of this into a code of laws and that if only they follow the code and the managers follow the code they will be the best friends in the world.

One morning the Hunkeys show up to work and find in their pockets a slip of paper. The slip sends them to the tool room the company has just built and tells them what number shovel to get and where to start in at the yard. (None of the Hunkeys can read, maybe someone reads it for them.) After a while they find another slip, that's either yellow or white. If it's the white slip, the Hunkey knows he has earned his sixty percent raise. If it's the yellow slip, he knows he hasn't. In the old days he'd look at the yellow slip and say, Oh hell, something is going to happen. In the old days the foreman would say, "Here, Pat (Pat is an Irish Hunkey), you have four or five yellow slips; you are no good; get out of here. You are not a high-priced man; get out of here." But now, under the new regime, someone teaches Pat how to shovel. It isn't the old fellow with glasses watching the shoveling in the yard, or some youngster with a college degree and a stopwatch, but someone like the Hunkey himself, a star performer with a shovel, a regular artist with a muck stick. To make the yard really work, you have to know every man. You have to know the men as well as you know shovels. You have to know the human instrument. Before long there are a hundred forty Hunkeys working in the Bethlehem Steel Works yard. That is what is called Scientific Management.[15]

It was an era when things were studied by taking them apart and breaking them into little pieces in order to understand them. Eadweard Muybridge had photographed the stages of a horse's gallop at Leland Stanford's farm in Palo Alto and biologists and physicists were cutting up the universe into ever smaller pieces in their labs and theoretical papers. In Paris Gertrude Stein was sorting out the tender buttons of language and recomposing them in her imagination and her teacher William James was studying passing time. Frederick Winslow Taylor knew how to cut up a Hunkey shoveling pea coal, but he didn't know how to put him back together again to make a whole man. Thorstein Veblen knew how to cut things up and how to reassemble them. He took apart clocks for fun and put them back together for more fun. Like Frederick Winslow Taylor he believed that the great issue in economics was efficient production. Unlike Taylor, he had a good deal of respect for the ability of the man behind the shovel.[16] And unlike Taylor he knew who would get the increased surplus and it wouldn't be the Hunkeys.

Veblen drifted for a time and ended up editor of *The Dial*. He was no revolutionary, in spite of his sympathy for the Wobblies and the Bolsheviks who had taken over Russia.[17] He was not even a reformer, and his stay at *The Dial* was a difficult one for him. Duffus, now a journalist, found him in New York looking quite miserable. Veblen had written some important books—*Imperial Germany and the Industrial Revolution*; *An Inquiry into the Nature of Peace and the Terms of Its Perpetuation*—and his *Dial* editorials and other pieces of journalism are still trenchant. "The Bread Line and the Movies," in which he compares the anodyne productions of Hollywood to imperial Rome's bread and circuses, is one example of a piece still worth reading; *Dementia Praecox*, on the post–First World War Red Scare is another. But his old satiric obfuscation was gone. Still his detachment remained in even his most provocative articles, and like his treatment of the women in his life, there was more than a touch of sadism in it. He started learning Russian and coolly envisioned the inevitable destruction by "selective starvation" of the whole bourgeois and "kept classes."[18] Still one wonders how much faith he had in the Russian Revolution, deep down. In 1919, during a period of intense industrial turmoil in the United States, *The Survey* asked him, along with other industrial experts, labor leaders, and employers, for his ideas on solving the economic clash. "To my great regret," he replied, "I have no answer. . . . In fact I find myself more interested in what is likely to happen than in what should be done about it."[19] Finally, this man whose stock-in-trade was puncturing myths, fell victim to one of his own: the myth of the Engineer. Unlike William James and John Dewey, as Murray G. Murphey explains in his introduction to *The Instinct of Workmanship*, Veblen believed it was not the individual but the group that carried social inheritance and hence was the only source of social change.[20] Thus Veblen thought that the discipline of the machine would develop in its workers and acolytes the sort of rationality that would overturn the long habits of mind that created superstition, obedience, economic hierarchy. In his pursuit of this discipline he elevated the engineer to a sort of god. It was the engineer, Veblen imagined, who would finally free us from the primitive animism that was found at the root of our economics and society, and he dreamed of a Soviet of Engineers, all laying down their slide rules and clipboards like shop-coat-wearing Wobblies in a General Strike that would reform our way of thinking and reform our world. But in spite of Veblen all that the discipline of the machine seemed finally to provide was the discipline of the machine, and we were soon to see that the most rational of minds could harbor side by side with advanced technological knowledge the most primitive genocidal aggressions. The very aesthetic that Veblen saw as a common fund of culture embedded in the instinct of workmanship was being crushed not only by bankers and capitalists, but by the very figure he saw as its salvation. In the factories and in war ministries as well, the barbarian chieftain with his plunder-lust was rapidly being replaced by technicians, and in Europe and Asia immense armies—those first machines Veblen's disciple Lewis Mumford would call them—would be marching once more.

In 1920 Veblen returned to California for a visit. He had had the mountain cabin he'd carted away when he left Stanford rebuilt and drove up to visit it with some friends. When he got there he found signs surrounding it, claiming it as part of someone else's property. It had been a mistake, but before anyone could explain what had happened, he seized a hatchet and was going around methodically breaking all the windows in a rage of destruction. When he was finished, everyone got back into the car, too stunned and embarrassed to explain. Finally, to break the heavy silence, someone asked Veblen what the title of his next book was to be. "Absentee Ownership," he said, and did not speak for the rest of the journey.

Two years before his death Veblen returned to Stanford once more, but not to teach. He built a shack across the road from Cedro, on Perry Lane, in a working-class neighborhood of Menlo Park, where forty years later a group of nonconformists fueled on hallucinogens and as dubious of American values as Veblen himself would find a home. What Veblen would have made of Ken Kesey and his entourage would be difficult to guess; he probably would have ignored them, or possibly have found them interesting specimens of a certain kind of savagery or maybe only of a faux primitivism. Walking up to the door of his Menlo Park shack he discovered that once again his property had been claimed, this time by a woman who simply refused either to pay rent or to leave. His first wife had also built a shack on the property, but this too was inhabited by a squatter, a cheerful old-timer who was similarly immovable. This time Veblen didn't go for his hatchet, but simply sat on the doorstep laughing silently, his shoulders shaking with the wonder of the whole thing.

Visitors remembered his house once he had finally gotten it back. It was bare, barnlike, dusty, surrounded by a jungle of weeds and overgrown shrubs, and "so devoid of ordinary comfort that one felt as if someone from a very alien culture were camping in it—someone to whom our chairs and beds and tables are but useless curiosities."[21] He had the mountain cabin repaired and spent days up there. Wood rats scampered through the place and got into the larder and once, as he sat perfectly motionless, a skunk came by and rubbed against him as if it were a tame cat.[22]

The country towns of the sort that Veblen had grown up in were effectively dead, nothing more than false-front charades built on paper and vacant as a drummer's smile; for behind their bankers and merchants with their smalltime extortions were bigger bankers and huge commission houses, and the real-estate schemes that propped up the whole aggregate were about to go bust. Yet if the small town was nothing but a walking corpse, Veblen knew that its soul would go marching on, because it had become what America conceived of as itself. The Stone Age Indian living in a museum in San Francisco, who measured white civilization with such imperturbable dignity, had died of tuberculosis in 1916 and his brain was swimming in a jar of preservative on a shelf in the Smithsonian. By now the cakewalk was a thing of the past, supplanted by other dances from the rich repertoire of African American life—Black Bottoms, shimmies, and Charlestons, loaded with fun and sex and improvisation. Whatever the promise of Bolshevism had been, it would become, under Stalin, a bloody reaction of purges, deportations, and liquidations, and among the first to go, of course, were the engineers. By now Veblen had turned to anthropological speculations on race and the translation of an Icelandic saga. He read Aldous Huxley, Norman Douglas, endless detective novels. Perhaps he found in Huxley the brave new world for which the machine and its discipline would prepare us. It may not have frightened him as much as it did its author.

Thorstein Veblen died in virtual obscurity in the first week of August 1929. He had looked on his own death with as much detachment as he had looked on nature and the world itself. He wished no memorial volume, no obituary or memorial tablet or slab, and asked that his ashes be scattered on the sea or in some stream emptying into it with no ritual or ceremony of any kind. He was an economic marvel, with an international reputation as a thinker and the greatest satirist of them all but now almost forgotten. There was in his character as well as in his thought an essential innocence, perhaps the innocence that resides at the heart of all great philosophers and artists, for they see the world afresh, and the hand-me-down assumptions and fenced-off intellectual real estate most of us meekly rent from the intellectual landlords of our age are not for them: they jump the fences and skylark in the pastures; they cakewalk through the halls of universities; and when they find the kind of cruelty and inequity we have become inured to, they fight back—with brains and sometimes muscles, surely, but also with sabotage and satire and subversive comedy. Three months after Thorstein Veblen's death the New York Stock Market crashed. He would not have been especially surprised.

Chapter 8
The Rise of Abraham Cahan

In the Tenement Museum

At 97 Orchard Street, on Manhattan's Lower East Side, is an old building, erected originally in the 1860s, that houses the Tenement Museum. You can visit the museum by appointment. You can speak with a docent dressed as fourteen-year-old Victoria Confino, from a family of Sephardic Jews who came from Greece in 1913, or choose to see the apartments of the Baldizzis from Sicily, the Irish Moores, the Levines or the Rogarshevskys or the Gumpertzes. You can visit the museum online as well, moving like a ghost through the invisible snow of cyberspace.

The artifacts that these people or others like them have left behind are monuments to the ordinariness of their lives; a hairbrush, a bottle of cologne, a much-used tea kettle. The touch of their lives still adheres to these things as perhaps to nothing else.

Where the denizens of 97 Orchard Street went can be documented in a few cases. Abraham Rogarshevsky, a presser in a garment shop, died of tuberculosis in this building at the age of forty-five. In a photograph in the catalogue of the museum the mirrors in the Rogarshevsky apartment are covered with cloths, the table laid with foods that replicate the circle of life and death—oranges, eggs, buns—that friends and neighbors have provided for guests who might come while the family sits Shiva. Others who lived here moved elsewhere in the city and outward and into the flood of American life. As much as Henry James, less articulately, more urgently, they were between two worlds. Outside the windows the streets teemed in their day with pushcarts and merchants crying their wares, with harried mothers, men and women bargaining, arguing, greeting each other, going to and from the *shuls* and their apartments and the sweatshops with bundles of clothing among a multitude of kids. The language was a mixture of Yiddish, American slang, Russian, Italian, German. They created their lives, as Emily Dickinson would have said, where the differences are. We look in the museum catalogue at the photographs taken by Arlene Alda—and they are beautiful—of the small rooms that held lives once so tumultuous, and we realize that the element proper to them is silence.

In one of the apartments of the Tenement Museum, placed near a window, is a sewing machine. If anyone were to make up a coat of arms for the Lower East Side it might be a shield halved by the blood red of socialism and the black of anarchism, or perhaps by the colors of any of the immigrants' native lands, or it might be cut in the shape of the Star of David, but no matter what its design, in the middle would be a sewing machine. Here is where one of the immigrants, Nathalie Gumpertz, a Prussian woman whose husband, like thousands in those hard days, had abandoned her, lived by her needle [fig. 10]. Thumping on the treadle of this machine, stitching fabric in front of that window, she raised her four children making clothing for the women of the neighborhood. Upstairs the Levine family kept a rudimentary sweatshop—baster, sewer, presser, finisher—completing the bundles of cut

Figure 10. Arlene Alda, "Nathalie Gumpertz's Room," in Linda Granfield and Arlene Alda, *97 Orchard Street, New York: Stories of Immigrant Life* (Toronto, Tundra Books; New York, Lower East Side Tenement Museum, 2001), p. 4. Reprinted with the permission of Arlene Alda.

clothing brought from outside, all of this in the midst of the cooking and washing and diapering of the Levine children.

For the dwellers of these tenements, the American frontier began at Cherry Street. It was a porous frontier—what we might prefer to call in today's reconsideration of the term a "zone of contact"—its indigenes the landlords and Irish cops, the WASP social workers and school principals, and the German Jews who initiated the new arrivals into their shops' dangerous mysteries. Pushing into America meant that history would no longer write itself in the common destiny of the *shtetl* or the Sicilian village but in the individual struggle with the demons of failure and of success.[1]

Henry James might see these streets as an aquarium of exotic-nosed fish or a biblical spectacle, but for James the world, it sometimes seemed, existed only as a surface to stimulate his imagination. Abraham Cahan knew the tenements from the inside. He had lived in them and written about them: their dark hallways, smelling of urine, cooking, mold; the noise of the neighbors carrying on their lives across the airshafts, their gossip and their arguments—fights about money, politics, the kids, sometimes love. They were more than subjects for his sketches and fictions. They were, like the newspaper he edited, repositories of the texture and animation of immigrant life itself.

The Rise of Abraham Cahan

In the second act of Jacob Gordin's 1892 Yiddish play *The Jewish King Lear*, we find Dovidl Moysheles's servant Trytle, who has accompanied his master and mistress on their unhappy journey to Palestine, putting his disappointment in what they found trenchantly:

> Ah, Land of Israel! Land of Israel! What a fine wedding feast you gave us! May I fall ill, if I ever say at the end of a Pesach Seder "Next year in Jerusalem!"[2]

How do you build a land out of an idea? Out of this place of longing and mourning, a place where a tragic past met a continually postponed and renewed "next year" at the Passover Seder, the Jews in exile had created a fertile absence, a homeland of the mind. Homeless, they carried their homelessness with them like the ark and at last it became a sort of home itself. But even the homeless must find a place, in their flight, to perch.

Abraham Cahan, as he tells us in his memoirs, surrounded by Jews flee-ing the pogroms of the 1880s and himself running from the czar's police, had been solicited to go to Eretz Israel, but instead decided to journey to another imaginary land and another promise: the socialist future. At first he had come to the United States with the idea of joining one of the Jewish communes then forming, and becoming a farmer-idealist. I do not know if Cahan ever read Crèvecœur, but in any case it took him only a few weeks in New York to disabuse himself of that dream. The freedom of America confused and liberated him at once. In the czar's Russia he had imagined no higher calling than distributing underground pamphlets in factories and on street corners, but in the United States one could buy the most radi-cal of newspapers for a penny at any newsstand. Cahan had been a Talmud student, then a teacher in Russia, and now he sat working in a cigar factory stripping tobacco leaves. Upstairs in the factory, though he didn't meet him, another immigrant and former Talmud student, Samuel Gompers, formerly of London, was rolling the cigars.

Looking back as a man of sixty-six, Cahan remembered with an aching presence his first years as an immigrant in New York. He remembered a city that had no subways, automobiles, phonographs, motion pictures. A city with few telephones and only one bridge—the Brooklyn Bridge—that was not yet open. The tallest building was eight stories high. Yet the streets were full of immense crowds, and in the Lower East Side there were thou-sands upon thousands of Jewish immigrants from Russia and Poland, from Germany and from German-speaking Posen. Hester and Orchard Streets swarmed with peddlers and their pushcarts and with the "customer ped-dlers" who sold to other Jews and to African Americans on the installment plan. Canal Street and East Broadway were filled with the shops that sold these men the clothes, the bolts of cloth, the cheap jewelry, and furniture they peddled. In the city there were thirty or forty thousand Jewish workers, many of them tailors from western Poland working for the German Jews manufacturing men's ready-made suits. The women's cloak business hardly existed: the women of America wore shawls.

Most poignantly, Cahan remembered the moments of agonized longing for his old home. His dreams were filled with images of Vilna, visions of his father and mother and his younger brother, his aunts and uncles, his comrades and acquaintances. Everything in America was strange to him. The more established workers lived like what would have been the well-to-do in Vilna. Yet did one really live better here than in Russia? It seemed to him that in America the furniture was not furniture; the carpet on his land-lady's floor was not carpet. An American apple was not an apple, cucumbers were not cucumbers. The songs he would hear from the girls visiting his landlady's daughter sickened him. They were not his father's songs, or the haunting Russian folksongs he had heard, or the chants of the synagogue. He noticed the way the Americans drank coffee, ate bread and butter. The language disgusted him. The Yiddish of the American-born children of the immigrants rasped in his ears, but that of their parents was just as bad: "er macht a leben," "er is vert tsehn toisend dolar"—he makes a living; he's worth ten thousand dollars. "vindes" were windows, "silings" were ceilings, "Pehtaytess" were potatoes. "Oil-rite" and "Never mine" and Hester Street sounding like Esther Street appalled him. The burning hot weather of July and August was unbearable compared to summer in Vilna. Quilts and mat-tresses hung from the fire escapes; garbage cans overflowed on the streets. Forty-odd years later, when the hot weather began in New York, he still re-membered those days, and the physical agony and the loneliness came back to him with an almost unbearable intensity.

Cahan set himself to learning English and soon moved beyond the Russian–English dictionary he had bought in Liverpool, beyond Appleton's *German–English Grammar*. He wanted correct pronunciation. He entered an American public school and was placed with the older children. Mr. Farrell, his teacher, reminded him of his *melamed* Elya Itche at the yeshiva. The English as spoken in America seemed even more unnatural than what he had heard in Liverpool. In McGuffey's *Fifth Reader* they read a poem about a bobolink. The children declaimed it as if they were reading a great poem.

Bob-o-link, bob-o-link
Spink, spank, spink!

The word "bob-o-link" was so odd, so strange, that he always remembered it. Years later, when Cahan became interested in American birds, he paid the greatest attention at first to the bobolink. "To this day," he wrote, "with the coming of spring, I listen for the clarinet-like sound of this American bird and if I do not hear it I miss it all year round."[3]

Cahan married early, and in one of the beautifully written moments of his autobiography he tells of the pleasures of the poor New Yorkers who, in the stifling heat of summer, could only afford to take the ferries endlessly back and forth, or ride the Grand Street boat to Williamsburg, then travel by horse car to Prospect Park to spend the day there with picnic lunches. The ride back produced in him a sad mood, like those which filled the Saturday dusk of the old-country synagogue before the candles were lit.

> The horse-drawn car picked up speed as it dashed through the vast darkness with its tightly packed human load. In the distance there were flickering spots of light which by their glitter made the darkness darker, the sadness heavier.
>
> Then, on to the ferryboat. The boats converse with whistles. Our boat shudders and starts and we hear the sound of the lapping waves. My wife and I take a position at the outside railing, where it is darker and lonelier. It seems that the ferry is being wafted across a dark abyss. The black water ripples with pale luminosity and makes a mysterious sound. In the distance—a thousand miles away, it seems—the countless city lights sparkle across the water.
>
> The native young people, the boys and girls, begin to sing, and their songs have a sorrowful sound, and my heart fills with a painful longing and with the memory of what has been lost.[4]
>
> Bob-o-link, bob-o-link
>
> Spink, spank, spink!

In 1898, Abraham Cahan, then thirty-eight, went to Madison Square Garden to watch a cakewalk competition. Cahan had helped found the Yiddish-language *Jewish Daily Forward* the year before, but now he was taking a breather from the infighting at the paper. He occupied himself working on his own fiction and reporting in English for Lincoln Steffens's *Commercial Advertiser*. As couple after couple emerged from behind the stage to a slow march, the vast space seemed all afloat with the music. "The walking," he wrote, "seemed to lend grace and spirit to the music, and the music seemed to heighten the charm of the walking."

The judge was a "sable-colored young negro" in a black fur cap who was bandaged up because of a toothache and who reminded a "Hebrew spectator," no doubt Cahan himself, of a Hasidic rabbi. On and on Cahan watched them walk: the powdered and painted young mulatto woman, "looking more like the patent medicine pictures of Emma Calvé than Emma Calvé herself," on the arm of a fellow who looked "like a parlor stove wreathed in smiles"; the young woman with "the color of a white girl and the features of a negress," performing a "grotesque" with her pitch-dark young partner; and the crowd favorite (alas to be denied the prize by the hometown judge), "A tall, lean young negro with dreamy eyes and with a coffee-colored companion, fleshy, genial and happy," going by in a "straight" walk. Cahan might not have known this, but a good many of the dancers may have been refugees like himself—migrants from a place as harshly punitive and dangerous to their race as Poland and the Ukraine were to the Jews. If they had arrived from the post–Civil War American South speaking the language of the new land, its freedoms and its more subtle forms of racism were as strange to them as to the immigrants stepping for the first time on American soil.

Like the African Americans in that contest, immigrants like Cahan were improvising on the theme of America. Against the familiar tempo of the old country, regular in its constrictions as the march time of the cakewalk, they played off what they would make of this new land, what syncopations they would contrive to the rattle of its subways and hum of its sweatshops and factories.

"Out!" the judge would say through his bandages to a couple whose steps were not up to the mark, and out they would slip—"shamefacedly, forlornly, but with perfect resignation to their fate."

> "Why did you reject that couple?" he was asked.
> "'Cause they didn't do it wid—what do you call it?—science—no, that ain't de word."
> "Skill?" his questioner suggested.
> "No, that ain't it neither," the rabbi answered, gruffly.
> "Grace?"
> "That's it. You've got to walk swell and nice, you know, jes' like a swell guy on de street. No foolin'."[5]

The phrase was both a judgment and a dream. One might perform this cakewalk Straight, Fancy, or Burlesque, as Cahan (or his editor) put it in the subheading to the piece and which might perhaps be convenient labels for our walk through life, but the performance was always judged, and the judgment could be cruel and final. Cahan too was judging and being judged in his description of the contest. In subscribing to the racial travesty expected of him, mild by the standards of his era—the image of the grinning parlor stove, the painted mulatto woman (and was that dreamy-eyed Negro *really* named Pickaninny?)—he was only following the path of entry into the larger American life worn smooth by so many others, including African Americans themselves. A generation later Jews like Asa Yoelson (Al Jolson) and Israel Iskowitz (Eddie Cantor) would go farther, putting on blackface themselves.[6] For the Jolsons and the Cantors it was a ticket to success in a larger America as it had been for the Irish blackface minstrels before them. The burnt cork and the white gloves were in a way the same sort of pass signs as the unsmiling smile that Cahan's hero David Levinsky would learn to use. But oh! To have the ease, the lack of remorse, the courage to walk swell and nice, you know, like a swell guy on the street.

Letters

Worthy Editor,
I am a workingman from Bialystok, and there I belonged to the Bund. But I had to leave Bialystok, and later came to Minsk where I worked and joined the Socialist-Revolutionaries. . . .

Worthy Editor,
I am a young woman, married eight years to a man who came from Russia, and we have four beautiful children. My husband's parents were killed in a pogrom and he alone barely escaped with his life. . . .

I, an old woman of seventy, write you this letter with my heart's blood, because I am distressed. . . .

We, the five brothers, always speak English to each other. Our parents know English too, but they speak only Yiddish, not just among themselves but to us too, and even to our American friends who come to visit us. We beg them not to speak Yiddish in the presence of our friends. . . .
Respectfully,
    A Worried Reader
    I thank you in advance,
    Unhappy
    Respectfully,
    The Unhappy Fool
    A Shopgirl
    Skeptic from Philadelphia
    The Discontented Wife
    A Perplexed Mother
    The Greenhorn . . .

1906, 1908, 1910 . . . The queries fill the letterbox of the *Forward*. Letters from Jews originally from Vilna, from Minsk, from Zhitomir. Denizens now of Orchard and Hester Streets in Manhattan. Or of Philadelphia. Or Boston. Or Chicago. Or sometimes marooned in small villages where they were the only Jews for miles. Jews dangling between two worlds. Jews baffled by America, its ways, its opportunities. These were the people Cahan wanted to write about and, perhaps more importantly for him, to write *for*.

Cahan moved from revolution and speech-making to organizing the Jewish workers in the needle trades and to journalism. By 1903 he was molding the *Forward* into a newspaper that spoke to the immigrants in their own language and out of their own concerns. Vulgar, militantly left-wing, with a masthead that reproduced the *Communist Manifesto*'s thrilling call to the workers of the world to unite; a stew of yellow journal sensationalism, nostalgia, instruction, righteous outrage, four-square unionism, criticism; home of fiction and poetry from the best of the Yiddish writers: it stood like a rock. Its famous "Bintel Brief," the advice column that he at first had edited himself and which began appearing about the time Henry James was touring the New York ghetto, was like a history in miniature of an immigrant community as it was forming before its readers' eyes. Writing in English, Cahan gained the attention of that great editor and mentor of writers William Dean Howells, with whom Cahan, Hamlin Garland, and the wunderkind Stephen Crane would breech the sacred precincts of New York's literati, the Lanthorn Club. In 1913 in a series of installments for *McClure's Magazine* that he would later expand into a novel, Cahan created his most memorable literary figure, his political opposite but on a strange and deeper level his double, the millionaire clothing manufacturer David Levinsky.

A Weekend in the Catskills

America is a strange phenomenon for David Levinsky, the hero of the novel that bears his name. A fiction himself, he awakens in the Babylon of his own desires, a place both seductive and forbidding, where identity hangs from the past by a thread that could be snipped at any moment. A millionaire bachelor of forty, a Talmud student turned capitalist, an immigrant Jew who now dines with Gentile textile manufacturers and department store owners, handsome, confident, a freethinker engaged to the wealthy, beautiful, self-satisfied, and quite stupid daughter of an Orthodox father, Levinsky is perpetually on the margins of the new world, a world he can only view as something not quite real.

On his way to visit his fiancée and her family, he has stopped overnight at a Catskills resort. But now eagle-eyed Auntie Yetta, all gold teeth, diamonds, tactlessness, and effusion, a sort of Virgil to this vacationing Dante, drags Levinsky into the domain of the eligible girls of the resort. "And now go for him, young ladies! . . . You know who Mr. Levinsky is, don't you? It isn't some kike. It's David Levinsky, the cloak-manufacturer. Don't miss your chance. Try to catch him."[7] They flutter around the newcomer, chattering, sly and lovely, the young girls of the Catskills. But exile has given Levinsky a kind of second sight. Watching the Saturday dinner procession of the women at the Rigi Kulm, Levinsky is reminded of so many chorus girls parading before a theater audience, or a procession of models in a big department store.

It is a cakewalk without irony and without partners (husbands and fathers being either absent in the sweltering city or completely unimportant to the show), a parade for an audience of other women relentlessly keeping tabs on one another's dresses, shirt-waists, shoes, ribbons, and jewelry. But behind the audience of women is another audience, the invisible audience of the Gentile world. Thus the parade is a cakewalk within a cakewalk. It is as if the immigrants and their daughters are condemned to a perpetual round of imitation, as no one knows better than Levinsky himself, whose fortune was made by his ability to reproduce the cloak designs of the earlier-come German Jews—whose own designs in turn were copied from American tailors who imitated the cloaks of London, as London had imitated those of Paris. Imitation must be an imitation of something, yet that something may be an imitation of something else, and where the chain stops, who can know? (Somewhere in the Goncourt Journals a Parisian society woman excitedly explains that she has got hold of a piece of valuable information: she has learned who dresses the courtesans!)[8] So the Rigi Kulm House, named for a famous Swiss hotel, is an immigrant imitation of Newport, and Newport with its palatial "cottages" an imitation of Europe, and nineteenth-century Europe an imitation of another Europe, a Europe that was only imagined. Like the cloaks his factory turns out by the thousands, those imitations of imitations of imitations, money itself is sterile for Levinsky. It schemes and breeds and reproduces itself—to what end? "Who are you working for?" This is the question that has been posed to him. Bereft of a posterity, a family, a real home, Levinsky has long been consigned to the realm of shades.

My Country

In a land without princes, whom should we envy? Celebrities, surely, boxers and divas and baseball players and the rich. But isn't envy, even with its hint of scorn, a form of worship, and doesn't worship imply abasement? There must not be abasement in a land of free men and women. Thus, in this country without rigid castes, without ancient family lineages or the lineages of great scholars and rabbis, one worships, first and foremost, oneself.

But the self is not stable. Cast adrift from its ancient associations of family, village, and occupation, it rises and falls on the drift of history. Where can it anchor? So one worships what one might become, one worships a second self, mirrored in the newspapers, in the biographies of poor boys like Franklin and Lincoln and the immigrant Carnegie; mirrored too in the fantastic heroes of Horatio Alger Junior's tales, those orphaned, homeless, thrifty, industrious, and finally lucky lads who populated the imaginations of generations of youths in full view of the ranks of starved newsboys and hawkers and kohl-eyed boy prostitutes such as the one who accosted Stephen Crane one night and about whom he vowed to write a story. One might worship, if one were a woman and spent her summers at the Rigi Kulm, the parade of society women who populated the Sunday supplements, with their automobiles and servants and their gowns. Thorstein Veblen, who had watched such parades of gowns and jewels, had seen them as primitive expressions of power and social status, but he had not seen the Rigi Kulm. He had not seen the special anxiety of these newly arrived Americans.

In the dining room at the Rigi Kulm everyone is talking over everyone else. The band plays desperately above the noise. Innocently unaware of the watching Levinsky, the immigrant women flash their diamonds and their gowns, these wives of former pushcart hagglers, coal and ice cellar keepers. Their very language is a sign of the violence of their assimilation, "a hubbub of broken English, the gibberish being mostly spoken with self-confidence and ease. Indeed," Levinsky says snidely, "many of these people had some difficulty in speaking their native tongue. Bad English replete with literal translations from untranslatable Yiddish idioms had become their natural speech."[9] There is a kind of desperation in this scene. It is the desperation of a people clinging to their newly found personae as if, in an instant, everything that has made them could be wiped away. What goes up can go down: failure, bankruptcy, panic. Just outside the doors of the dining room of the Rigi, unheard under the near-hysterical chatter, a pogrom is waiting to burst in.

In 1905 Cahan wrote a novel he called *The White Terror and the Red*. It was a poorly conceived book, its characters, a Russian prince turned revolutionary and the spirited Jewish girl he loves, never quite taking on independent life. But we might read the book in another way, as Cahan's attempt to create on the page what he had fled in life. For all its flaws as a work of the imagination, one chapter is unforgettable: his description of the pogrom at Miroslav. Cahan builds the chapter by increments: the peasants arriving from the countryside, the beginning of the violence in fits and starts, the terror and the drunkenness as the Jews' casks of vodka are broached, and in one of those details that only witnesses can know, the snow of feathers everywhere. Like first blood at a prize fight, Cahan says, slashed featherbeds were an unmistakable sign of the pogrom. When it was over, with the doors and windows of the ghetto smashed and the rioters dispersed or lying drunk in the streets and gutters, the hooves of the gendarmes' horses were muffled by the feathers.

In the dining room of the Rigi Kulm the pianist and the two violinists are desperately pounding and sawing over the bedlam of conversation. Levinsky shuts his eyes and thinks of the floor of the Stock Exchange. The first violinist, who is the conductor, plays American popular songs, hits from the Yiddish stage, selections from *Aïda*, the favorite opera of the ghetto. As a last resort, he plays the "Star-Spangled Banner." Overcome with emotion and love, Levinsky shouts, "My Country!" and the shout is taken up by the diners.[10]

Learning to Dance

In his loneliness and isolation as a greenhorn, David Levinsky had gazed on the habitués of a dance studio where he was sleeping and doing odd jobs. The couples whirled around, parting and coming together, emphasizing to this virginal yeshiva boy how far from home he had come and how far from making a home in this new country he was as well. "Why don't you learn to dance," says his flashy friend, Maximum Max, the "customer peddler" whose wife Levinsky will eventually seduce. But for the time Levinsky is frozen in immobile gazing. At last he is driven away from his gloomy staring as a killjoy. Dancing, he says later on, is not in his line.

Yet all are summoned to the dance. In some way, consciously or not, the yeshiva boys with their earlocks and dark frock coats, the Americanized pushcart vendors with their suave voices, their straw boaters and their diamonds, the girls from the sweatshops—heard or unheard, or reached out for with longing, all know the call of that seductive new tune. "Von, two, tree! Leeft you' feet! Don' so kvick—sloy, sloy! Von, two, tree!"[11] All are summoned to dance, whether with close embrace or tentative, to dance clumsily or gracefully, with resistance or with joy.

Shivering on his bench in the old-country yeshiva, Levinsky, the orphaned boy, had felt himself no stranger to God. That closeness called up its opposite, for he could feel, too, in his sinfulness no stranger to the Devil. It is only in retrospect that we see Levinsky moving farther and farther from this specular pair, until, in America, he becomes a stranger to them both, an atheist whose last remaining temple—City College of New York—he himself destroys by his entry into the world of business and the business of money.

Levinsky's rise is punctuated by love affairs. The first of them, while he was still in Russia, offered a life beyond the narrow confines of Talmud study—a life of sexual liberation and Western education. In America there are other erotic experiences. He learns about Tammany corruption from a Jewish prostitute. He almost succeeds in convincing himself of his attraction to an illiterate factory girl who had wasted herself and her chances at matrimony by obsessively hoarding for a dowry. Most tragically, and the emotional center of the book, is his affair with Dora Margolis, the wife of the friend with whom he boards. Dora is in a sense his female double, burning to acquire education but as a woman able to live only through her Americanized daughter, who she imagines will have everything for which she has sacrificed: an education and a man of her own choosing. All of these women—Dora Margolis may be the great exception—are loved by Levinsky for what they represent, a Western education, money to start his business, comfort and stability. And in the end all reject him. Finally, at the Rigi Kulm, is Anna Tevkin. In Antomir, in the old country, Levinsky had heard from a fellow Talmud student a wonderful story. It was the tale of a poet who wooed the wealthy and beautiful daughter with his passionate and eloquent letters—not to the woman, in fact, but to her father. Now before him stands the beautiful daughter of that poet. There is no more thought, for Levinsky, of the Orthodox girl and her imperturbable mediocrity. Once more Levinsky is blinded by love. But we are not blinded, and what we see is Miss Tevkin, a pretty girl, bright but quite ordinary, really, a stenographer for an attorney. Her brisk opinions of literature are borrowed. She will marry a high school teacher. For Levinsky there is, in the language of the shop girls reading the "Bintel Brief," no Predestined One—or perhaps his Predestined One is the empty embrace of the Bitch Goddess Success.

Night is falling at the Rigi Kulm. Levinsky watches the young people moving along the walk or crossing the lawn and converging on the dancing pavilion. They come singly, in twos or threes or in larger groups, some sauntering, others hurrying, their forms receding through the thickening gloom, then emerging from the darkness into the slanting shaft of light that falls from the pavilion as they vanish into its blazing doorway. Levinsky stands in the shadows, fascinated. The pavilion with its brightly illuminated windows seems to him to be an immense magic lamp, and the young people flocking to it, "so many huge moths of a supernatural species." As Levinsky watches them disappearing into the glare of the doorway he pictures them being burned up and is tempted to join in the unearthly procession, to be burned up like the others. The image passes, and he imagines men and women of ordinary flesh and blood dancing, and is seized by the desire to see the sexes in mutual embrace. So Levinsky enters the pavilion.

The Unsmiling Smile

Success! Success! Success! It was the almighty goddess of the hour.
                                        —*The Rise of David Levinsky*

When Levinsky stepped ashore at Castle Garden in 1885, he had unknowingly stepped into the realm of American fairy tale: the fairy tale of success. Levinsky found in the new world no pogroms, no Black Hundreds, no anti-Semite thugs such as those who killed his mother. There were no princes in America, no czars. The police, by Russian standards, were mild. Yet always there was a loss, a loss and a sacrifice.

From the beginning, peddling from a basket or a pushcart, Levinsky has learned to practice the art of deception, rumpling or dampening new underwear to sell them as used, claiming his customers were getting bargains where there were none. But his more practiced deceptions are tied to his very face. He learns he has a "credit face." Behind this façade he erects one leg of his business empire. The other leg is cheap labor.

Once a reluctant union member himself, he learns how to evade the watchful eye of both the union and the manufacturers association and thus undercut his rivals' prices. He exploits his old-country connection, filling his shop with tailors from his town Antomir, men used to working fourteen hours a day, docile and pious. He plays on his own nostalgia for Antomir and that of his employees, creating an "Antomir feeling" in his shop. He sets up an Antomir society and contributes generously to it. His paternalism is not without profit to him, for he is able through the closed little world of Antomirniks to keep the union at bay and also, during a great strike, swindle the other members of the manufacturers association by keeping men working under the table. Instead of the Gemara he reads Darwin and Spencer now. They coarsen his view of life. He sees it as a vile struggle for existence. The unionized workers are lazy loafers. The socialists, dreamers and frauds. He takes an odd pleasure in finding himself excoriated in a socialist paper along with the Vanderbilts, the Goulds, and the Rothschilds. He is, in the first English phrase his author mastered, which he heard constantly rising out of the ghetto Yiddish, "all right."

Early on in his American education, David Levinsky discovered the unsmiling smile. He saw it on his English teacher Bender, who had been born in the United States, and on the principal of the school. In Russia, at least among the people he had known, one smiled or not. "Here I found a peculiar kind of smile that was not a smile."

> It would flash up into a lifeless flame and forthwith go out again, leaving the face cold and stiff. "They laugh with their teeth only," I would say to myself.[12]

Levinsky discovered real smiles, too, among the Americans and he learned to discern the cold, polite smile that was not a smile from those other smiles from the heart. The smile without a smile can be an emblem of what Levinsky learns in the world of business.

For something is taken out of Levinsky at every step. He is willing to accept it, as he is willing to accept the counterfeit passion of the prostitutes he frequents. Honesty itself becomes a kind of deception. He uses it as a business tool, confessing to a Gentile buyer his lack of knowledge of proper table manners, asking for his help and thus insinuating himself into the buyer's patronage.

Riding with drummers on a train, Levinsky submits to their smutty stories and their boasting with a certain strange eagerness. And when he makes an apt political comment and is invited to dine with Gentile businessmen, he experiences a sense of elation; yet as the dinner progresses he notices that they have probably grown bored with him. One remembers a comment attributed to Bernard Baruch: "a kike is a Jewish man who has just left the room." Even the help he is given by friendly Gentiles—and now and then it is decisive—is tainted. He has lunch with the head of a large woolen mill in the private dining room of a well-known hotel. The mill owner has the look of a college professor or successful physician rather than a businessman, and he addresses Levinsky as "Dave."

> There was a note of condescension as well as of admiration in this "Dave" of his. It implied that I was a shrewd fellow and an excellent customer, singularly successful and reliable, but that I was his inferior all the same—a Jew, a social pariah.[13]

The double consciousness W.E.B. Du Bois saw as burdening the African American's struggle for internal freedom is, for Levinsky, a source of useful information. At the bottom of his heart Levinsky considers himself the man's superior, and finds "an amusing discrepancy between his professorial face and the crudity of his intellectual interests." But the mill owner is a Gentile, Levinsky says, and an American, and a much wealthier man than he, and so he looks up to him.

Levinsky is becoming hollowed out, an empty smile that answers an empty smile.

Yet *The Rise of David Levinsky* is that marvel of writing: a business novel that really *is* about business, that doesn't brush by it as it passes but immerses itself in it. For the rise of David Levinsky on ten dollars of borrowed money to millionaire and philanthropist has a kind of grandeur. This sense of grandeur, and our own emotional investment in Levinsky's rise, create a remarkable psychological texture to the book and make it particularly American. The odds against Levinsky, after all, are very great. So the shifts and desperate stratagems he employs in order to see the buyer of a Midwest department store—as remote, it seems, as an official in Kafka—are part of our own excitement; the lies he tells are seen as strategic coups rather than degrading shifts and dodges. He is climbing a ladder propped up by nothing but his own desire, climbing with all his skill and intellect, a kind of artist of the absurd, since neither Levinsky nor his author nor, perhaps, his audience believes in the soundness of the footing, or can see any goal at the end. And we admire him. Like some performer in a tawdry circus, his peril is worth something; his conquest of vertigo—both ours and his—earns the relief of our applause.

Beyond this, too, a larger story is being told. One that earns Cahan's admiration as well as our own: the story of the wresting of control of clothing manufacturing from the German Jews who had preceded them by impoverished Russian and Polish Jews engaged in creating a great American industry. Toward the end of the novel Levinsky looks out on lower Fifth Avenue, now the center of the cloak-and-suit trade, with its skyscrapers and up-to-date factories swarming with Jewish workers on their lunch hour or going home after a day's work. It marked for him the triumph of the Russian Jews in Americanizing the needle trades with their genius for mechanization and commercial skill.[14] The reproduction of a hundred-dollar gown in a ten-dollar model is for Levinsky no mere apish copying. "We make it our business to know how the American woman wants to look, what sort of lines she would like her figure to have."

> Many a time when I saw a well-dressed American woman in the street I followed her for blocks, scanning the make-up of her cloak, jacket, or suit.[15]

If Levinsky is to be disappointed in his pursuit of individual women, now comes a pursuit of an ideal of a woman in an ideal cloak, comic perhaps, especially when we remember the gimlet-eyed appreciation of each other's gowns by the women of the Rigi Kulm, but also laudable. "The average American woman is the best-dressed average woman in the world," Levinsky goes on to say, "and the Russian Jew has had a good deal to do with making her one."[16] It would be difficult to imagine a European author, French, say, or Russian, writing such a line, a tribute to immigrant industry and at the same time a love letter to all of those sewing-machine girls and stenographers pouring out of the new factories and skyscrapers around Twenty-third and Broadway.[17]

Forgetting

> One cup of Lethe and it's always too late.
> Where are you, *O liebe brayt?*[18]
>
> —Irving Feldman

It is an interesting psychological artifact that Henry Adams, who became obsessed by an ever more virulent anti-Semitism in his old age, compared himself in his *Education* to a Jew, as embedded in the ancient codes of his family and its traditions as if he had been circumcised in the temple in Jerusalem by his uncle the high priest. The point of Adams's *Education* is, of course, ironic; that his education was no education at all for a century that had no use for the virtues of the New England tradition into which he had been born. David Levinsky, in spite of his handicap of being a real Jew, and as much embedded in tradition as Adams's imagined Israel Cohen, and impoverished and orphaned as well, turns out to be supremely qualified for what his century offers in the way of material opportunity. Yet like Adams's, Levinsky's education leaves a great hollow. He finds himself, for all his millions, a failure, but unlike the patrician Henry Adams a failure without the ability to position failure in a philistine era as a species of success, the mark of the superior man.

Often Levinsky passes the old City College on Lexington Avenue and Twenty-third Street. Levinsky, like Cahan, had fled a land that promised only spiritual or even literal death to him, but before him in America was the dream of education. Like the ruined temple of an imagined Jerusalem, City College has become for Levinsky an interior site of longing. No pile of bricks can take the place of such a center, nor even the ideas furiously basted and sewn together and peddled as next season's big sellers, neither the Spencer Levinsky reads nor the dialectic begetting dialectic of the Jewish intellectuals arguing in the Café Royale. Levinsky may only mourn a self he might have been, but it is a self whose possibility he has thrown off carelessly, like a secondhand suit of clothes on some Orchard Street pushcart.

To ask what is the meaning of success for Levinsky, and for his creator, Abraham Cahan, as well, is to ask what is the meaning of failure. *The Rise of David Levinsky* is full of failure, of men who have somehow failed to thrive in the new land, of famous rabbis whose words fall weak and flat on the ears of their American congregations, of great wedding bards who find themselves running hole-in-the-wall printing shops, of heroes of romance, like Anna Tevkin's father, who end getting caught in the real estate game, flapping higher and higher like kites born up by nothing but momentary gusts of air. So success and failure in this book circle around and find themselves in the same place, a kind of hollowness, a deflation. On the other side of the gilded pleasures of the Rigi Kulm are the tenements of the Lower East Side. Cahan knew them both. His "Bintel Brief" was full of letters asking the meaning of success. What did it mean that in their home towns in Russia the "alright-niks" of America didn't have enough bread to satisfy their hunger? What did it mean that the men who were rich back home, who stood with their silver-trimmed prayer shawls by the eastern wall of the *shul*, alas, were poor here?[19] The old country and the new, America and the *shtetl*, confused and devalued each other.

The Old Country itself becomes a different thing as it fades and disappears from memory. Cahan wrote an early story about a Jew who goes back to his native village in triumph after a long stay in America. The closer he gets to the village, the more he sees it as it was, and as it remains. Yet the more familiarly it rises up to greet him, the farther away it is.

> Hello! The same market place, the same church with the bailiff's office by its side! The sparse row of huts on the river bank, the raft bridge, the tannery—everything was the same as he had left it; and yet it all had an odd, mysterious, far-away air—like things seen in a cyclorama. It was Pravly and at the same time it was not.[20]

But the view in *The Rise of David Levinsky* is often reversed; it is not the past that is seen through the wrong end of the telescope but the present, for to Levinsky, and it seems to Cahan as well, the American present, in spite of its incessant opportunity and conflict, is never quite real. Another thing happens too: bereft of its native soil, the old-country past can lose its hold. The tale of Tevkin, the poet, whose letters to his adored one's father won that beautiful and aristocratic girl—the romantic story Levinsky had first heard in the Old Country *shul*—fades out like an old photograph. Ritual becomes a kind of terrible pantomime. We see Tevkin, his prayer shawl over his head, reading the Haggadah—a butt of his children, freethinkers of one variety or another, as he himself had once been—trying to retain something from a past that exists for him only as a series of remembered gestures.

The Tragedy of Success

> Most of the people at my hotel are German-American Jews. I know
> other Jews of this class. I contribute to their charity institutions.
> Though an atheist, I belong to one of their synagogues. . . . I often
> convict myself of currying favor with the German Jews. But then
> German-American Jews curry favor with Portuguese-American Jews,
> just as we all curry favor with Gentiles and as American Gentiles
> curry favor with the aristocracy of Europe.[21]
>
> —*The Rise of David Levinsky*

"There are cases when success is a tragedy," Levinsky thinks, reflecting on
his life. His very success stands in the way of renewing old friendships with
the people from his birthplace or from his early days in America, for they
are mostly poor and his few reunions have led only to the embarrassment of
both parties. In the end, Levinsky triumphs, yet he cannot get accustomed
to his luxurious existence. Social life presents only another ladder with rung
on rung of difference. His love of music leads him into the realm of Jewish
musicians who have become successes in the new world, but he has the sense
that they regard him as a rich boor whose patronage is only for social pres-
tige. He rejects a Gentile woman from his hotel whose company he enjoys
because, as he tells her, "there is a chasm of race between us." "That's an interesting point of view," she replies, a noncommittal smile on her lips. History has moved through him and around him yet Levinsky lives at a static
center. Wifeless, childless, homeless, he remains perpetually an orphan and
his chief pleasure seems to be to brood on the past. He retains a lurking fear
of restaurant waiters.

To use the articulation of Cahan's Marxism, it must be so: Levinsky has
achieved the pinnacle of success in a capitalist world, so he must be the unsmiling beneficiary of its ultimate product, alienation. The spilled milk that
began his career is the spilling of something greater than his blood; it is the
spilling of his purity, the white substance of his soul that had connected him
to the spiritual world of the Antomir Jews.

Cahan too was a success. He had made of the *Forward* a "living novel"
of the immigrants of the Lower East Side, filled it with their stories, their
interests, their politics. A difficult man in a place where difficult men were
not in short supply, for years he had engaged in ceaseless battles with capi-

talists, anarchists, and his fellow socialists. He had gone to meetings and demonstrations, spoken to great crowds and to handfuls of workers in union halls and tenement kitchens. He had fought with Daniel De Leon over the course of American socialism and feuded with the playwright Jacob Gordin for what seems, at this distance, no reason at all. But always there was this sense of distance, of not quite being rooted in a land that, rough and difficult as it might be, was still a dream.

If Levinsky could walk through the halls of his new offices, with its secretaries and showrooms, so in 1910 Cahan could look up at the ten-story *Forward* office building that dominated the Lower East Side. Like his creation, David Levinsky, he had given up a career of intellectual pursuit for a life of action, the Temple of Learning for Broadway. Turning away from the sectarian and the parochial, he had cut his newspaper after the fashion of Hearst and Pulitzer, and in so doing he had created not only a journal but an institution. It was not without its detractors. "Come, come, Karl," the university-trained intellectual Hayim Zhitlovsky imagined Cahan saying to Karl Marx in 1912, "your style is too 'Talmudic.' In its present form it can only be understood by a handful of spiritual aristocrats. Let me fix it up for you."[22] A year earlier a caricature was published showing Karl Marx leaning on the *Forward* building in deep despair. "There is a reason for my tears," he says. "The socialist movement of New York is buried under this ten-story capitalist building." A rooftop banner announces "The *Forverts* Workers Corporation, with Each Floor Housing Special Department": "Deserting Husbands Department"; "*shund* [pulp] Literature Department"; "Black List Department"; "A Place To Pray Day And Night Department"; "Ritual Bath For Kosher Women Department"; "Job-Holders Hall"; "Cursing Department"—the list goes on.[23]

For many years Cahan had ceased to live among the immigrants of the Lower East Side. On and off he lived apart from his wife. Like Levinsky he would spend his last years—he would die in 1951—not in a home, but in a hotel; in Cahan's case, appropriately, that temple of literature, the Algonquin. For all his earned celebrity, he seems to have been, like Levinsky with his millions, a man apart, haunting the fields with binoculars, trying to learn the unfamiliar songs of the American birds. During the First World War, much as his hero Levinsky cut under-the-table deals with his unionized workers, Cahan would make a secret pact to allow the jurist Louis Marshall to privately censor the *Forward* so that it could keep publishing during the

Red Scare that shut down other immigrant and left-wing papers.[24] By 1923, the *Forward* had a circulation of three-quarters of a million copies. It was a major paper. The revolution Cahan had risked his life for and initially welcomed, and whose brutalities he had at first defended,[25] would produce Stalin and a pogrom by other means; moved by the realities of a world that seemed less fluid, less utopian, his labor militancy would become more measured. After the Second World War, his long battle against Zionism would end in a kind of draw.

Two years after Cahan watched the cakewalk contest in Madison Square Garden, he attended a dance of the girls of the cigar makers' union. It was the sixteenth week of the New York cigar makers' strike of 1900. There were two hundred women in the shabby hall, and the girls danced with each other since most of the striking men had found union jobs and were rolling cigars to support the strike. "Girls, it's nearly four months since the present strike began," a forty-five-year-old Bohemian woman said from the rostrum.

> "Four months is a third of a year [wild applause] which means we have been striking a third part of a year [cheers]. . . . It's the will of heaven that we win, and that's why the shops are so busy; why everybody is earning good wages; why we get enough strike benefit to fight our employers until they are compelled to give in. [Cheers.] Will you be true to your union?"
>
> "Yes!" shouted the girls.
>
> "All right. And now let's dance."[26]

It was the kind of luminous moment of worker solidarity that Cahan had witnessed again and again, yet for all his commitment he was never quite able to feel such closeness, was never able to dance at the cigar makers' ball. America had gotten to him, as it had gotten to his hero David Levinsky. The towns they had left in the old country, with their rituals, their poverty, their envies, their walls of constraint, had nevertheless created the sense of a communal world extending both backwards and forwards in time, backwards to the prophets, the exodus from Egypt, the first creation, forwards to that perpetually postponed but always present Next Year and the advent of the Messiah. For the real Americans, the Cahans and Levinskys among them, there could be no such community in a land of individual effort and grinding competition no matter what its pleasures and compensations. The future was not the dream of the present, infusing the daily rituals of work or prayer, justifying the pain of history and proscription, but the ticking of the time clock extending into tomorrow, tomorrow's worry, tomorrow's paycheck, tomorrow's opportunity, tomorrow's cut of a woman's suit. This is the final secret of Cahan's novel: that the paths of its writer and its protagonist that had diverged in the new world had become united in a psychological identity. Whether they knew it or not, it was Emerson's *Self-Reliance*, bloodless, bodiless, and horrible as it might be, more than the Pentateuch or *Capital* that was the sacred text.

In Manski's Alley

When he was ten or eleven years old, in Vilna, in Manski's alley, Abraham Cahan heard from another boy a story he never forgot.

> In that story a treasure is being sought. The man digs deeper and deeper. Suddenly, from deep in the earth, a human voice is heard. Someone is singing. It is a sleeping child. The deeper the digging, the louder and more beautiful becomes the singing voice. The digger is bewitched. Now he no longer seeks the treasure. Instead, he must find the child. But the more frantically he digs, the more beautiful and the more distant is the melodious voice.[27]

Cahan never remembered how the story ended, and indeed it was in a sense his own story, as well as that of his creation and shadow David Levinsky. Through the struggles of his life in the new land, Cahan could faintly hear that child, who was somehow himself as he might have been, singing and compelling him. Thorstein Veblen saw secular Jewish intellectuals like Cahan and his fictional Levinsky, those men with restless feet, as free men, beholden neither to the Jewish world nor to the Gentile, and at liberty therefore to challenge the orthodoxies of both. Happy—if he was happy—in his own silence and alienation, Veblen couldn't imagine the cost of this freedom. Cahan could imagine it. It became his great subject. Levinsky, his fiction, lived it. Bound together in solitude and in the pages of a book, childless shadows of each other, both David Levinsky and Abraham Cahan remained, finally, spectators of the dance to America's tune. On the margins of a country he could admire and condemn but could not love, Cahan wrote a novel about his alter self, a book neither fancy nor burlesque but *straight* in the tradition of the great Russian realists he admired. Whether he recognized his achievement, whether it sufficed, we will never know. But the very act of writing must have drawn him closer to the doomed and endless longing of his creation, the millionaire David Levinsky. It was Levinsky's tragedy that he found a treasure, more than he ever imagined, on the tables of his factory, yet against the whirr of the sewing machines and the thud of the pressing irons he had only a memory of the abandoned boy within him, singing.

Chapter 9
Beyond Syncopation

Behind the Screen

Ferdinand LaMothe, who was not yet Jelly Roll Morton, or even the Winin' Boy, but was certainly carrying the .38 special he had begun to pack soon after he first came to the District as a piano player in the sporting houses at the age of fourteen, remembered Emma Johnson's Circus House in New Orleans.

> They did a lot of uncultured things there that probably couldn't be mentioned, and the irony part of it, they always picked the youngest and most beautiful girls to do them right before the eyes of everybody. . . . People are cruel, aren't they?[1]

Sixteen, seventeen, already he had acquired the Stetson hat, the box-back suit, the Saint Louis flats whose toes turned up to the cuffs of his pants, and always there was that .38 and learning just how cruel people could be. Ferd cut a slit in the curtain they put in front of him. He wanted to see what everyone else was seeing. He wanted to be a sport too.

But the screen in front of the young mulatto virtuoso at the piano was there not so much to prevent him from seeing the whores leapfrogging each other in Emma Johnson's back parlor as to keep the white clientele from seeing him seeing. In 1894 Louisiana amended its Black Laws. Creoles like Ferd LaMothe and Homère Adolphe Plessy—Homer Plessy—lost the racial privilege they had borne for generations as a middle caste between black and white. They were now simply black, thrown back into the same swarm as the Uptown laborers and stevedores. Two years later the United States Supreme Court would rule that Homer Plessy would have to ride in the Jim Crow car. Sophisticated Creole musicians who cut their teeth on old-country quadrilles and the arias from the French Opera House were forbidden to play in the homes of whites and march in their military parades.[2] As it had with Bert Williams, the world had tossed away the complexities of history and the layers of social distinction and simply decided that Ferd LaMothe was black. It didn't really want to see him, just as it didn't want to see Sidney Bechet or an illegitimate child born Back O' Town in 1901 named Louis Armstrong, who would learn to play cornet in the Colored Waifs Home. It might want to hear them.

Traveling on the black vaudeville circuit, playing tent shows in the days when Ma Rainey and Bessie Smith were still advertised as Coon Shouters, hustling pool and hustling women on his way to becoming Jelly Roll Morton, Ferd LaMothe had a good look at what crossing the lines of racial fiction could mean in the South. Propped up in the windows of barbershops and drugstores were photographs of black bodies strung from trees and telephone poles, sometimes burned or horribly mutilated. In 1908 and 1909 Morton himself saw lynchings. He was in New Orleans in 1900 when the city erupted in four days of deadly race riot. He claimed that more than once he had to run from white mobs because some white woman paid a little too much attention to him. The penalty for cutting the curtain at Emma Johnson's was to enter that world of peril. Better to turn that obscene sight inside out, to project your own image on the fictions of the world. For Ferd LaMothe there would be no hiding behind a screen; he would be the screen itself.

On the Colored Tent Show Circuit he blacked up, his light skin and Indian nose absurdly darkened by burnt cork and paint into the grotesque mask of a black caricature of a white caricature of something that may once have been a human being. Reb Spikes said Jelly thought he was funny but never did make anybody laugh. But somewhere on the Benbow Circuit Morton ran into a performer named Butler May. May played blues piano and did an act with his wife under the stage names of Stringbeans and Sweetie May. Stringbeans played the lanky Black Dandy, shabby but piss-elegant, a diamond sparkling in one front tooth. Sweetie May flirted with the audience and jived Stringbeans right back. The laughter skated on the edge of everyone's knowledge of just how close the Sporting Man was, after all, to the Monkey Man, that poor piece of business hanging on to his woman for dear life. The padlock Stringbeans sometimes wore dangling over his crotch could go either way. By 1915 Stringbeans and Sweetie May were laying them in the aisles with their Titanic Routine. Standing over the piano, Stringbeans sang,

> Listen no-good womens
> Stop kickin' us men aroun'
> Cause us men gonna be your iceberg
> And send you sinkin' down. . . .
> White folks got all the money
> Colored folks got all the signs
> Signs won't buy you nothin'
> Folks, you better change your mind.[3]

White folks had all the money for sure and it didn't matter how much sexual magic or art or sheer skill was hidden in the miraculous pool-hustling, card-sharping, piano-playing hands of a mulatto like Ferd LaMothe. You could read the signs better than Marie Laveau and have a High John the Conqueror root in your pocket, wear a Stetson hat and pack a .38, but the white world was nothing to fool with. Better be some grinning cork-blackened Coon, or a pimp with a diamond in your front tooth and a couple of whores on either arm; better be Sweet Poppa Jelly Roll, with stovepipes in your hips and all the girls just begging to turn your damper down. "He's so tall and chancy," Jelly Roll sang,

> He's the ladies' fancy.
> Everybody know him,
> Certainly do adore him.
> When you see him strolling, everybody opens up,
> He's red hot stuff,
> Friends, you can't get enough.
> Play it soft—don't abuse.
> Play them Jelly Roll Blues.

In 1911 Jelly Roll Morton was in St. Louis, hustling the locals by pretending to sight-read whatever they threw at him from the "Poet and Peasant Overture" to every tune Scott Joplin ever wrote (of course he could play them all by heart). Bert Williams was in town and admired a jaunty little ragtime tune that Jelly had just composed, and Jelly renamed it in Bert's honor. It was fitting that they should meet. Both Jelly Roll Morton and Bert Williams wanted to be seen, yet hid themselves as well; the one behind the ostentatious screen that he called "Jelly Roll," the other behind a film of burnt cork.

By 1923, Jelly Roll was still packing the .38, but had acquired a twelve-cylinder touring car, a mouth full of gold teeth, and an odd, wry twist to his lips as if, people said, he were thinking of something or sizing you up. In the "cutting" duels of his early days, he found he was not the fastest player of the ragtime tunes. He did something else. He loosened the rhythmic strictures of rag, and the music came out of its corsets. By slowing the ragtime beat down he opened up the music to a whole new realm of ornamentation and invention. Where once ragtime had skipped, now it began to swing. Morton took a ragtime classic like "Maple Leaf Rag" and made it his own, as Henry Louis Gates Jr. and Martin Williams have described, improvising on its tropes and extending its possibilities, just as the ragtimers themselves had signified on the popular music of their own day and as jazz musicians have signified on each other's compositions and what the hit parade might bring them ever since.[4] Jettisoning the duple time of rag, Jelly laid down a four-beat pulse which would become the basic rhythm of jazz as well as of a music still gestating in the belly of the beast—rock and roll—thus creating a music that didn't even have a name yet, strolling through the melody with an easy, casual lope like a pimp's walk, louche and elegant at the same time, or blazing hot and open now to the brilliance of his invention. He wedded this music to the blues that came from the docks and the turpentine camps and the immense farms of the delta, studded it with fermatas and "blue notes"—flatted sevenths, fifths, and thirds—and grounded it in the rhythms and counter-rhythms that were resonances of the polyrhythm of Africa.

There had been ragtime tangos and habaneras, but in Jelly Roll's hands they reached musical possibilities not available to rag. He called it the Spanish tinge, and it could summon up Cuba and Brazil and Argentina and beyond these deep minor keys, the sonorities of Moorish Spain, resonances that would be exploited for their full emotional range by a young Louis Armstrong in masterpieces like "Tight like This" of 1928 and later on by Miles Davis and Charles Mingus in some of their most moving work. Under Jelly's command the piano became an orchestra. "The Pearls" lays out whole layers of rhythmic texture and variation. Gunther Schuller, in his important book on early jazz, calls Jelly Roll Morton jazz's first composer, its first theorist, and its first intellectual.[5] He was the first jazz musician to write and score his music and he demanded a discipline of his bands—they played it the way Jelly Roll intended, or else—and he made the point by taking out his six-gun and laying it on top of the piano. He claimed to have invented jazz.

You see him in the days of his glory fronting his bands with ostentatious displays of diamonds and sharp suits. He had taken on equally ostentatious sporting-world nicknames. He called himself the Winin' Boy (from the winding and grinding of sex) and sang the filthiest of whorehouse lyrics over the miraculous syncopated arpeggios of that angelic right hand, as if he could hide whatever injuries of race and sexual shame he had experienced behind a glaring persona.[6] He reveled in his gambler-hustler image and that big gun he carried. He sported up and down the West Coast, ran a Black and Tan club in San Francisco until the cops shut it down, chased after his paramour Bessie Johnson, and cut a terrific series of records for Victor in Chicago in 1926. In Los Angeles he told Bricktop he didn't know whether to be a pimp or a piano player. Bricktop had the answer for him: why not be both?[7]

Jelly Roll Morton/Ferdinand LaMothe/the Winin' Boy never made it to Europe like Bricktop or Josephine Baker or Sidney Bechet.[8] Too proud or too dark or too famous or too notorious to slip into the white world, as his lover Bessie Johnson who would become Anita Gonzales and then Anita Ford had, he refused to be hidden behind anybody's screen except his own. He imagined himself free, an aristocrat of music.

> In foreign lands across the sea,
> They knight a man for bravery,
> Make him a duke or a count, you see,
> Must be a member of the royalty.

Sitting in the temple by the king and queen, he strikes up a harmonic chord and the king says "if we can't make Jelly a duke let's make him a lord."[9] He never did get to foreign lands across the sea. Nobody ennobled him but himself. He was troubled with voodoo spells and spent a small fortune to lift imagined curses. Jelly's sense of his Creole superiority might have remained, but he was just another black man to the rest of America. It didn't matter how much his diamond sparkled, as Louis Armstrong put it; he still had to eat in the kitchen.[10] In 1927, recording with a white band called the New Orleans Rhythm Kings in Richmond, Indiana, he let himself be passed off as a Cuban to get a room in a hotel.[11] His ostentatiously paraded virility may have been a pose as well. His fear of being lumped with the reputation piano players had of being girly, like his idol Tony Jackson with his sweet falsetto voice and his swish ways, may have told us more about who he was than he imagined.[12]

Jelly Roll Morton died broke in Los Angeles in 1941. The diamonds had all gone long before: the glittering sleeve bands, the rings, and finally the diamond that winked out from the one front tooth. Just making his way onto the scene in the jazz clubs of L.A. and Oakland and San Francisco was a nineteen-year-old Angelino bass player Jelly wouldn't have known, but who knew Jelly. His name was Charles Mingus.

Myself When I Am Real

I'm Charles Mingus. Half black man, yellow man, half yellow, not even yellow, not even white enough to pass for nothing but black, and not too light to be called white. I claim that I am a Negro. Charles Mingus is a musician, mongrel musician who plays beautiful, who plays ugly, who plays lovely, who plays masculine, who plays feminine, who plays music, who plays off sounds, sounds, solid sounds, sounds, sounds, sounds . . . a musician who loves to play with sound.[13]

—Charles Mingus

He wanted to call his autobiography "Half Yaller Schitt-Colored Nigger." He carried the manuscript around with him until it filled two suitcases. He carried it from studio to studio, carried it from dump to dump, even in the days when he was crazy and evicted and possibly dangerous, until finally an editor dived into it and made of it a small book called *Beneath the Underdog*, divested of most of the rage about a gangsterized music business, heavy on the sexual fantasy—the near pornography that Mingus put in it, he claims, in order to make it sell—but finally, in its truth and in its fiction, a kind of portrait of the artist as a multiracial man in the craziness of postwar, Cold War America. The book, or some version of it, made from scraps of his sessions with his shrink, his memories, his fantasies of sexual prowess, his rants against white America, his rants against the music business, against exploitation, for all its shapelessness and its slovenliness is one of the most honest books on race an American has ever produced. But rage turns into art:

"In other words," Charles Mingus begins, "I am three.

One man stands forever in the middle, unconcerned, unmoved, watching, waiting to be allowed to express what he sees to the other two. The second man is like a frightened animal that attacks for fear of being attacked. Then there's an over-loving, gentle person who lets people into the uttermost sacred temple of his being and he'll take insults and be trusting and sign contracts without reading them and get talked down to working cheap or for nothing, and when he realizes what's been done to him he feels like killing and destroying everything around him including himself for being so stupid. But he can't – he goes back inside himself.[14]

Which one is real? His answer is that they are all real. They and the other Minguses that, like the contents of the many-pocketed coats and trousers he wore, he often kept hidden yet ready to pull out and display and contemplate, but most important, for he was one of America's most original artists, to turn into the stuff of his soaring, spiritual, angry, hoarse, and tender music, a music that could be ferociously satirical and tender at the same time, a music made like him out of a world that resisted him and was ready to worship him and to use him and to betray him, and that in those capacities was like himself.

Nineteen years before Charles Mingus was born, W.E.B. Du Bois penetrated the psychology of the American Negro, burdened with a double consciousness that forced him to measure himself with the tape of a white world. This luminous passage, which I have quoted in Chapter 6, cited or uncited, still haunts American studies of race and culture. But to emphasize only the strange negativity of this double consciousness is to miss the full significance of Du Bois's idea, for the very two-ness and irresolution of this consciousness makes possible a second sight. The veil that hides the African American from himself and from the world becomes the birth caul, both separating the man who has been born with it from other men as if through some primal sin which condemns him to a life of pain and homeless wandering like the blind Tiresias or the blind Oedipus, and at the same time gives him insight, the ability to see the world and its suffering and perhaps to see even beyond.

"If you don't live it, it won't come out of your horn," Charlie Parker told him.[15] And it seemed when Mingus played he had lived all of it: the days in Watts sitting with his stepmother in her Holiness Church with the trombones, the clapping hands, and the ecstasy, listening on his father's forbidden crystal set to the Ellington band blowing through the "East St. Louis Toodle-Oo," listening to Stravinsky and Armstrong and Debussy and Bartok and the Beethoven Quartets and Art Tatum—he was living a whole history of jazz in his music, recapitulating and reinventing the blues and the shouts and the moaning, reinventing Jelly Roll Morton, reinventing everything, often with an ironic twist, with love and irony both. He was recapitulating the things he lived, the castanet-clacking strippers table-dancing in the dives of Tijuana, and the women he loved and all his craziness and rage, the drugs and the alcohol and the lies he told, too; for the music could swell and expand in a kind of controlled bombast that had beneath it a self-mocking, ironic edge which was a constant in his work, yet that same music could warm to incredible tenderness or touch the edge of something almost mystical.

Like his admiration for Duke Ellington, he had a special affinity—call it affection even—for that other complex mulatto genius who preceded him, Jelly Roll Morton. Where others might have seen in Jelly Roll the hokum and braggadocio of the moldy fig and heard in his piano a jazz that was already antediluvian, Mingus listened deeper and heard the kind of innovator he aspired to be, a perfectionist and creator of a music that began to transcend the limitations of its sources, that found a way of extending its forms through pedal-point composition. He wrote a piece called "My Jelly Roll Soul" that satirized the tropes of that primeval jazz with its strutting rhythms and tailgate trombones, but that at the same time uncovered a part of his own soul—or call it history, for when he reprised the music he knew and loved and that had become part of him, a kind of imitation that was so assimilated and ingested that it came out as Mingus, his anger was transformed into satire, and his love into memory. Anger, he told his psychotherapist, was an emotion that had some hope in it. It was despair that was the final enemy. Perhaps that was what he learned when, sleepless and terrified, he checked himself into Bellevue Hospital.

Like Gertrude Stein, he was the baby of the family, was called baby well into his adolescence, lugging his cello—and then his bass—through Watts, shunned by other kids for his light skin, his mixed-race father so light he could, if he chose, have passed into the white world that he despised. A child who was beaten, and who found his home with other outcasts. He longed for his own colorless island, but he longed for belonging too. His father was the illegitimate son of a black field hand and the white granddaughter of his employer; his mother Anglo-Chinese. When he asked who he was, he could find Native American and African, Asian and Mexican and Caucasian from the southern family his angry and sometimes brutal father both boasted of and abhorred. He learned on the streets of Watts that the dark and light routine was all bunk. If there was any Negro in your ancestry you were a nigger to all the greasers, redneck peckerwoods, and like-minded folks whether you were coal black or yellow as he was himself, or had the hazel eyes and sandy hair and gray complexion of the palest Caucasian like his father. It wasn't blood that made Charles Mingus a nigger, but America.[16]

He wanted to be either white or black, one or the other, he said, but he was "a little of everything, wholly nothing, of no race, country, flag or friend." So finally he gassed his hair straight and ran around with the other mongrels at Jordan High, but all of them, the light-skinned Mexicans who called themselves Spanish, the few Greeks and Japanese, the Chinese who said they were white, spoke other languages and could shut him out when they pleased.

> He became something else. He fell in love with himself. "Fuck all you pathetic prejudiced cocksuckers," he thought. "I dig minds, inside and out. No race, no color, no sex. Don't show me no kind of skin 'cause I can see right through to the hate in your little undeveloped souls."[17]

But of course he couldn't maintain that position. He couldn't secede from the Watts of the nineteen-forties or the South of color lines and the North of sub-rosa racial prejudice if he wanted to. And he couldn't secede from that complex man who was himself, whose honesty and rage and self-pity and grandiosity were the very stuff of his music, a man who played the race card, then threw it away, then played it again. His self—or his selves—were also his history and the history of black experience in the United States. His father claimed he had the blood of Abraham Lincoln in his veins, and before that, he claimed, the blood of Africa—the name Mingus was one of the few African names to have survived in America. But there was also a whole culture. Especially music. There was the church in Watts that his tobacco-chewing stepmother took him to. It was a sect that was founded forty-some years before in a former stable on Azusa Street with blacks and whites, Asians, and Latinos singing and shouting in Pentecostal ecstasy to pounding pianos, cows' ribs, thimbles, anything that could be thumped on or blown. By the time Charles Mingus was sitting in the revival church in Watts the ecstatic blending of races and classes had been broken up into separate churches for whites and blacks, but the music remained, the ecstasy and the idea of release from the mundane world, release into some spiritual space beyond the bare walls of a ghetto church and the streets outside and the country itself.[18] He would write a piece called "Wednesday Night Prayer

Meeting" and the music, he said, was the church music he heard with his mother. "The congregation gives their testimonial before the Lord, they confess their sins and sing and shout and do a little Holy Rolling. Some preachers cast out demons, they call their dialogue talking in tongues or talking [the] unknown tongue (language that the Devil can't understand)."[19] That ecstatic unknown tongue was what Mingus was hearing inside himself too in his own Mingusian way. When he was seventeen, on a gig in San Francisco, he met the bohemian painter Farwell Taylor who introduced him to Eastern mysticism, which would continue to inform his thought and his conception of the highest meaning of his work. But always, and it is maybe this that most strongly attaches him to the long tradition of African American art, there is the signifying and the wild humor.

Haunting *Beneath the Underdog* are two specters, the elegant and cold-blooded pimp Billy Bones and the figure of the great bebop trumpeter Fats Navarro. The book as it stands is in large measure a dialogue mediated between these two literary concoctions by Mingus himself. In Watts he learned what it was almost impossible to explain, he told the "Doctor Wallach" of his book.

> How you feel when you're a kid and the king pimps come back to the
> neighborhood. They pose and twirl their watchchains and sport their new
> Cadillacs and Rollses and expensive tailored clothes. It was like the closest
> thing to one of our kind becoming president of the U. S. A. When a young
> up-and-coming man reaches out to prove himself boss pimp, it's making it.
> That's what it meant where I come from—proving you're a man.[20]

It was a dream of power, elegance, and control. Everything that his cousin William Boness—Billy Bones, boss pimp in San Francisco—possessed.

Billy Bones is a fabulous construction, like Stavin' Chain, the mythical figure of absolute potency in African American lore. Billy Bones (Mister Bones?) has to have a special toilet with a lowered bowl tailored to the anatomy of the black man. It's a kind of minstrel show put-on of black potency. More significantly, he stands as a kind of parody of the successful capitalist. For what money buys is, beyond the cars and the houses, autonomy. He holds out to Mingus the figure of Jelly Roll Morton.

> Jelly Roll Morton had seven girls I know of and that's the way he bought the
> time to write and study and incidentally got diamonds in his teeth and prob-
> ably his asshole. He was saying, "White man, you hate and fight and kill for

riches, I get it from fucking. Who's better?" That's what Jelly talked when we hung out and I want you to do likewise.[21]

Scott Saul insightfully sees in the pimps and prostitutes that take up so much of the published text of *Beneath the Underdog* figures for the artist who must prostitute his talent to a capitalist and racist land, apt symbols for Cold War economics.[22] And in fact Mingus chafed under the exploitation of himself and other black musicians, even the very greatest of them. Again and again he tried half-baked or utopian plans to free himself—a counter-festival to the Newport extravaganza, his own record labels. But he was always, he said, a stone capitalist. He would beat white America at its own game. Yet there is more. Mingus's book is a chronicle of his ferocious needs. The Mingus he creates gorges himself on food, on whores, on fame. For under Billy Bones the boss pimp lies the Monkey Man, the man who is led around by a woman on a leash. The pimp is just a way of warding off the Monkey Man for Mingus, who so needed women and the tenderness and confession they allowed him. Beyond his rages and his cruelties, hyped up on weight-reduction pills and uppers and insomnia and Cold War paranoia (one of Mingus's pieces was "Oh Lord Don't Let Them Drop That Atomic Bomb on Me") and above all the need to make his music his way, was a man who was trying to find a place to save and value his belief and his love. In his imagination he stuffed the money his imaginary whores earned for him under his pillow and didn't touch it. Pimps were usually pretty calm people, he said, cool but lively, full of laughs and jokes, and some were even intellectuals. But to be a pimp he would have to lose all feelings, all sensitivity, all love. To be a pimp he would have to die. Kill himself. Kill all feeling for others in order to live with himself. Not to think. To keep going because you're already going.[23] "Why are you so obsessed with proving you're a man," Doctor Wallach says. "Is it because you cry?"[24]

"Minkus! Hey, Minkus! Dat-chew, baby?"

On San Francisco's Fillmore Street, a postwar haven for black America, with its barbecue joints and hip clothing shops and jazz clubs, Mingus ran into Fats Navarro.

Navarro's suit was three sizes too large; it hung on him in folds. He was no longer Fat Girl. He was dying. He was no longer interested in the women Mingus proffered. He had a different woman on his mind, Mingus said, and you took her inside the veins in your arm at night when you were alone. Navarro was "carrying the stick"—a lonely Jesus figure bowed under the weight of a racist world. But he was a Christ without God, a Christ whose love was thwarted by that world and stands, in Mingus's book, for that lonely figure of despair Mingus fears he might one day become himself. For Fats Navarro sees nothing beyond the world of white rip-offs and cruelty. His tuberculosis, which he says he deliberately contracted, and his heroin habit are forms of slow suicide. In his proud isolation his only weapon is that he no longer fears to die.

Often it seems, in reading *Beneath the Underdog*, that America offered the black man, as imagined by the book's author, only two ultimate possibilities: being a pimp or being a Christ. But there was a third possibility in the book, more difficult it may be than either and partaking sometimes of one or the other or both, or contesting both. That was being that most difficult thing, being Charles Mingus. Shaman and charlatan, artist and clown, Mingus could only be himself—himself as played out through all the Minguses he had inside him.

He called jazz "nigger music," and if he as much as anyone knew where he came from musically, he railed at being called a jazz musician. He was a musician. He would not let himself get stuck in any jail of his own or anyone else's mind.

"I don't want to be caught in one groove," he told Nat Hentoff.

Everything I do is Mingus. That's why I don't like to use the word "jazz" for my work. I write what I think is classical music too . . . I want to get to the point where everyone playing something of mine will be able to think in terms of creating a whole, will be able to improvise compositionally so that it will be hard to tell where the writing ends and the improvisation begins.[25]

Billy Bones the pimp and Fats Navarro the dope addict: both of them were in him, both of them needed to be mastered, not rooted out, but transformed. They were embedded in the music he inherited, too, a music born out of the whorehouse and the dive, a bebop frenzy stoked by the heroin that masked that abyss of the artist, the frenetic need to be *on*, to be in a state of constant, mind-bending improvisation. That was the thing he was after, the liberation, the exultation of improvised music, of the improvised life. On Fillmore Street, Fats Navarro, a walking corpse in his now shapeless, hanging suit, shambles into his destiny.

"Later, Mingus."
"Later, Girl. . . . "

Gargantua

En theos, to have the god within you, to be possessed. Enthusiasm.

In 1963 Mingus sat at a piano in a New York recording studio, working through his own compositions and standards like "Body and Soul" and "I Can't Get Started," playing easily, as if he had invented the instrument, trying to recapture the quiet time alone when he was thinking and improvising. You can hear him musing about it on the recording. "I shouldn't be improvising. It's not like sittin' at home," he says, "I can tell you that. It's not like playing by yourself." And someone in the recording booth—his producer? a technician?—answers, "Well, what can we do for you?" And Mingus chuckles. What can anyone do for him?

Once, making some half-cocked movie for the more than half-cocked Timothy Leary, Mingus was told by Leary just to improvise. You can't improvise on nothing, Mingus answered. Now he was improvising on his biography itself, Watts and New York and the early days in San Francisco where he learned from the beatnik painter Farwell Taylor about Hindu mysticism, and learned, most of all, that there were worlds inside him.

It was a meditative music, a kind of contemplation. The opening notes are like a call to prayer, an evocation of Medina or Moorish Andalusia. It was that primordial well that jazz musicians had dipped into long and deep from the beginning. The improvisation was a serious music, of course, but in some of the transitions there is a hint of musical comedy schmaltz, as if Mingus couldn't quite give away those apprentice years of filling in Hollywood film scores for Dimitri Tiomkin.[26] Mingus called this piece "Myself When I Am Real."[27] You can't improvise on nothing. You could improvise on a show tune or a Jelly Roll Morton stomp or a standard by Monk. You could improvise endlessly on "I Can't Get Started." You could improvise most profoundly, most difficultly, on yourself.

Mingus was working toward a music that went beyond the conventional statement and chorus and improvised solos of jazz, a music that was approaching a kind of perpetual improvisation. A music by turns lovely and ferocious, lyrical and chaotic, full of hyperbole and both wicked and loving satire, full of dissonance and lyricism, abrupt changes of tempo and sometimes two tempi or even three working against each other, with many voices playing off each other, like the singing in the black church or the instrumental voices of early New Orleans jazz. The members of the workshop called him, behind his back, Gargantua. Gargantua, because of his rages, his craziness, his terrible appetites. But he was gargantuan in another sense, in his aspiration to consume everything, and in his music to be everything.

> The grotesque body . . . is a body in the act of becoming. It is never finished, never completed; it is continually built, created, and builds and creates another body. Moreover, the body swallows the world and is itself swallowed by the world.[28]

This is Mikhail Bakhtin, writing in the gulag fear of Stalin's Russia, but we can see in his description of that folk symbol of resistance, the grotesque body, a reflection of Mingus's ambitions. "Hog Callin' Blues"; "Eat That Chicken"; "Oh Lord Don't Let Them Drop That Atomic Bomb on Me"; "Better Git Hit in Your Soul"; "Fables of Faubus"; "My Jelly Roll Soul." These, and others of his compositions, have a kind of ferocious hyperbole to them. They might be read as caricatures of the music of African America, the shouting in the churches, old-time New Orleans, Fats Waller's stride piano, bop—a sort of aural minstrel show, a gigantic satire on postwar America, filled with all of the fear and the greed and the rage and the squeals and grunts of the hogs pushing their way to the trough. But at the same time, this music went beyond satire, as Rabelais did, for Gargantua was the world, the world finally triumphant, where life and death, class and culture, all were absorbed in some endless grotesque paean to nature, to the cycles of dying and renewal. The gargantuan body couldn't be contained; it spilled out of itself, it absorbed everything, as Mingus's compositions absorbed the shouts and hollers of the fields, the jazz spilling out from the whorehouses and dives and the classical European music that was finally, at root, one with it. It was a music full of a ferocious release, with its terrible frenzy turned into passion and joy. Mingus's rages at the musicians of his group were both his attempt to get the best that was in them out of their horns, and a way of discharging the pain that was in him. If they were improvising, they were improvising *his* music.

Talking in Tongues

Time, perfect time, Mingus said, was when water dribbles from a faucet's leaky washer. He remembered as an adolescent registering how long the intervals were between each drip and its collision with a rust-stained enamel sink. Maybe he was that adolescent still, daydreaming, hearing—even when he was not listening for it—that steady drip and crash into a sink whose owner has given up hope that the maintenance man will ever replace that rotten old rubber washer, before, as he put it, "time runs out of time."

He played off his whole art and his life against that drip and its despair. Critics, he thought—for he could be merciless toward them—might be that rotten washer. But who was the faucet? ("Wow! Critics! How did they get here? I know. It's Freudian. Faucets and old washers.")[29] Beyond the critics, who he often imagined were more interested in their own cleverness than in hearing the music—really hearing it (Nat Hentoff was an exception)—there was an internal critic that he was always trying to fix. His idea of time in a piece of music became complex. More than the rhythms and sudden accelerations or decelerations of beat that his music was full of, the beat itself was too predictable, too much the dripping faucet. Like Emily Dickinson before him, he fought against that deadly, relentless drip through personal phrasings and punctuations, tried to hear behind it, around it. If you tried to stay dead center or directly on top or on the bottom of the beat, the beat became too rigid on the outside where it was heard. So you drew a picture away from it, an imaginary circle surrounding each beat, with different notes, different sounds of the drum kit, spiraling out and back so continuously that the core was always there.[30] For Mingus this decentering of the beat was a way of fighting against time running out of time. Time flattening itself out to the steady drip and splash of that faucet that no one would fix: if you ceased to hear it at all, time would run out of time and then your singularity, your resistance, would be dead too.

It was just that sort of resistance he wanted from his musicians. He called his group, with its ever changing personnel—the drummer he trained, Dannie Richmond, was one of the few relatively constant members—the Jazz Workshop, for it was a group always in process, always moving, and his club gigs were like one continuous rehearsal, spiked with harangues to the audience for not listening and theatrical (or not so theatrical) rages at his musicians. He wanted more from them; he wanted everything they had to give. He didn't want them to fall back on the familiar riffs and patterns of their solos after the first eight bars—that wasn't really creating; it was filling time—so he began working on new kinds of lines, "foundations for improvising inside a composition."[31] He stopped giving his musicians even the sketchiest written music, and had Dannie Richmond hum his tunes to the group. He was looking for something very deep, something with the emotion of the black church, with its polyphony of voices singing the music, coming in and leaving when the spirit moved them, yet all somehow contained by the spirit itself. The work itself would aspire to a kind of talking in tongues, talking in a language beyond the ordinary meaning of words, of music itself, and Robert Palmer has rightfully found that in the amazing tongue-talking solos of Eric Dolphy and Booker Ervin in the Mingus *Antibes '60* album, where those folk forms from the Sanctified Church that Mingus first recorded in 1959 expanded beyond their original conceptions to incredible open-ended improvisations. It was messy and unbounded sometimes, ragged. If he said jazz was nigger music, what he meant by that was not some narrow view of a segregated world, for in his groups he looked for the best musicians he could find at the moment, without regard to color: he meant that it was a music that came out of the emotional understanding of a history that expressed itself in a performance that was itself a history, and if he borrowed and learned from Bartok and Beethoven and Richard Strauss, he wanted that to be so internalized and embedded in the music itself that it was unrecognizable. In her brief but wonderful memoir, Janet Coleman describes how it went.

> Mingus music is turbulent, lyrical, raucous, funny, witty, unpredictable and oceanic. It unfolds through constantly transforming rhythms: Africa, Latin, Indian, waltz, blues. The arrangements are embroidered lavishly with threads from a vast musical memory: chanting, singing, clapping, moaning, Wagnerian motifs, a phrase from Mozart's "Horn Concerto" (played backward), a snatch of "Tea for Two."[32]

Coleman tells of how the arranger and pianist Sy Johnson learned that some of this pyrotechnical razzle-dazzle was a device for concealing or, as Mingus imagined, "patenting" the classical bedrock informing the music. "I don't want anyone findin' out my shit, man," he said.

His ambition was terrible. As the world poised on the edge of nuclear destruction during the Cuban missile crisis in the fall of 1962, he was planning a massive concert at New York's Town Hall. He would go where perhaps only Duke Ellington had ventured before, into the creation of an extended work for jazz orchestra. There were to be over thirty musicians playing Mingus music new and old, for it became clear Mingus had been working on his idea of a full program for many years. The project was impossibly difficult, both complexly scored and at the same time improvised, a kind of open recording session with an audience. During the performance itself copyists were working frantically, passing out the charts while the orchestra was playing. Technicians were interrupting the musicians, calling out to Mingus. At midnight the union stagehands shut down the set. Someone—it was Clark Terry—was noodling Ellington's "In a Mellow Tone." The project ended in lawsuits (in his anxiety Mingus had smashed trombonist Jimmy Knepper in the mouth, almost destroying Knepper's career), an unsalvageable recording, disaster. Mingus called the work *Epitaph*, and said he meant it for his tombstone.

In 1985 the manuscript of the score of the Town Hall concert was discovered. The scholar and conductor Gunther Schuller—who in 1975 conducted the first fully professional performance of Joplin's *Treemonisha* for the Houston Grand Opera[33]—began to patiently reassemble the score, filling in lacunae and literally cutting and rearranging some sections in preparation for a concert that was ultimately given in 1989. By then Mingus had been dead for ten years. Many of the musicians of his era were gone, too; men he'd worked with, fought with, learned from. Charlie Parker was dead, and Lester Young ("Goodbye Pork Pie Hat" Mingus had written in tribute). Fats Navarro was dead at twenty-six in 1950. Eric Dolphy, of all the men Mingus worked with, save perhaps only Dannie Richmond, the closest to him, was dead from a sudden, undiagnosed diabetic coma in 1964. Duke Ellington, the man who had most inspired Mingus, died in 1974. Thelonious Monk in 1982. The Town Hall concert score, as Schuller assembled it, was not only an autobiography of Mingus, with the breadth of his musical learning, everything from Indian court music to the avant-garde symphonic works he grew up with, but contained within it a history of jazz. There is a reworking of the swinging church anthem "Better Get It in Your Soul"; a joyous Jelly Roll Morton piece, Jelly's "Wolverine Blues," revisited; and a piece Mingus came to call "Monk, Bunk and Vice Versa (Osmotin')"— *osmotin'*, from *osmosis*, being a word of his coinage that indicated his method of absorbing, borrowing, signifying on jazz history, from Thelonious Monk to New Orleans trumpeter Bunk Johnson. But Schuller's reconstruction of *Epitaph* is, finally, a conjecture. *Epitaph* could never be finished, never exist in one final, authentic version, just as for its composer the music he heard in his mind could never be finished.

Mingus succumbed to ALS in Mexico in 1979 and his ashes were strewn on the Ganges. Jelly Roll too is gone with his flashy suits and his diamond tooth. But beyond the recordings Jelly made with his bands, his wonderful piano, with its complex rhythms and its consummate style; beyond those remarkable tapes he made for Alan Lomax toward the end of his life, singing those whorehouse lyrics of the days when he began to play in the bordellos and saloons of New Orleans in a voice wispy, almost tender; beyond his memories of Buddy Bolden and Tony Jackson and Mamie Desdunes with her three-finger blues, and the sports with their box-back coats and Stetsons that sat like crowns on their heads, Jelly lives in the tradition of an art of which he was one of the founders, lives still in his music, so lovely, so full of joy—"Wolverine Blues," "The Pearls," "King Porter Stomp," "Milneburg Joys," and all those beautiful rag tangos and habaneras. For all his boasting, much of what he claimed he first discovered for jazz might well be true. As, for all his gargantuan ambition, much of what Charles Mingus discovered for music was true.

Shadow Dancing

> Here they come, look at 'em, syncopatin'. Goin' some, ain't they demonstratin'? . . . The only way to win is to cheat them. You may tie them but you'll never beat them. . . . They're in a class of their own. . . . Cake walking babies from home.
> —Clarence Williams, C. Smith, and H. Troy,
> "Cake Walking Babies from Home"

About the time Charles Mingus was hitting his stride, the then-adolescent writer Mel Watkins, sitting in the rundown black movie theater in Youngstown, Ohio, that its patrons referred to as "The Rat Show," saw what he called a fantastic charade of black performers acting out scenarios that came from a white world. The situations were wrong, the emotional rhythms were askew, the priorities were off-key, the motivations alien. It was, he said, a harmless, less demeaning kind of minstrelsy, and the response from the working-class audience was more often than not catcalls, as well as heedless, often caustic, but always riotous laughter.[34] Later on, as he investigated the underground tradition of African American humor,

Watkins found a world of shadows. He wrote of Daddy Rice, the white minstrel, who danced Jim Crow all over America, and of a special moment in his act when he would open the pack on his back to reveal a black child, who would mimic his moves across the stage, a shadow of a shadow. But then we are all somehow shadows of who we imagine ourselves to be. And shadows of the world that tries to capture us as we strut and posture in its momentary gaze.

We accept the pattern set by the simulacra of that imaginary ideal world, in order that, in the words of Scott Joplin's and Scott Hayden's cakewalk, there will be Something Doing—Something Doing instead of Nothing Doing. In a world without originals it is not in the simulacrum of race, which is the imitation of an imaginary Nothing, that we find our Something, or in the cultural model that is handed us, the New England Renaissance, or the davening in an Old World synagogue, or the Grand March at the cotillion, but in our inspired improvisation on the theme of contingency. Either we are instruments of a symbolic register that our cultures embed in us, an unvarying code that we are constrained to apply to the wilderness of signs and metaphors that we find ourselves negotiating, or we are given as our birthright, as the anthropologist Dan Sperber says, only a set of general instructions and a strategy for learning. Lacking some innate inner schema or explicit instruction, only such a method can make possible some shared orientation, if only a partial one, of all the members of a single society, can make of the diversity of their beliefs, their rituals, their ceremonies, and the ceaseless repetition of these something that is neither contingent nor absurd. Yet the symbolic evocation is never completely determined. "There always remains to the individual a considerable degree of freedom."

> Cultural symbolism creates a community of interest but not of opinions, which—be it said in passing—has always troubled churchmen and politicians, manufacturers of ideology, obstinate misappropriators of symbolism.[35]

It is in precisely this degree of freedom between the terms of the social code, in this negotiable space of individual invention, which the writers and thinkers and artists I have chosen to study in this book chose to live. They found the meaning of their lives and works—in the words of William James's friend Paul Blood recalling the spiraling out of the engraver's lathe—"ever not quite," and like those inspired breaks Louis Armstrong and Sidney Bechet trade to the tune of "Cakewalking Babies from Home,"[36] those soaring improvisations that just can't wait, the cakewalkers are beyond mockery, beyond imitation. In this luminous moment their histories cling to them like rags, as they shine and improvise, strutting their sorrows and triumphs and our own, in beauty and in joy.

Notes

Introduction

1. Thomas Jefferson, *Notes on the State of Virginia*, in *Thomas Jefferson, Writings*, ed. Merrill D. Peterson (New York, Literary Classics of the United States, Library of America–17, 1984), pp. 290–291.

2. Bakhtin gives the most complete statement to his theory in his "Discourse in the Novel," in *The Dialogic Imagination: Four Essays by M. M. Bakhtin*, ed. Michael Holquist, trans. Caryl Emerson and Michael Holquist (Austin, University of Texas Press, 1981).

3. Mark Twain, *In Defense of Harriet Shelley* (New York, Harper and Brothers, 1897), pp. 2–3.

4. Henry James, *Henry James: Letters to A. C. Benson and Auguste Monod; now first published and edited with an introduction by E. F. Benson* (London, Elkin Mathews and Marrott; New York, Charles Scribner's Sons, 1930), p. vi.

Chapter 1: Ghost Dance

1. *The Varieties of Religious Experience: A Study in Human Nature* (1902), in William James, *Writings 1902–1910*, ed. Bruce Kuklick (New York, Literary Classics of the United States, Library of America–38, 1987), pp. 149–150.

2.

This fabulation of a reality unknown in itself—a fabulation consisting of procedures and representations—is founded on a threefold experience: first, that of the shaman himself, who, if his calling is a true one (and even if it is not, simply by virtue of his practicing it), undergoes specific states of a psychosomatic nature; second, that of the sick person, who may or may not experience an improvement of his condition; and finally, that of a public, who also participate in the cure, experiencing an enthusiasm and an intellectual and emotionally satisfaction which produce collective support, which in turn inaugurates a new cycle.

Claude Lévi-Strauss, *Structural Anthropology*, trans. Claire Jacobson and Brooke Grundfest Schoepf (New York, Basic Books, 1963), p. 179.

3. James, *Varieties of Religious Experience*, p. 133.

4. Michael Hittman, *Wovoka and the Ghost Dance* (expanded edition), ed. Don Lynch (Lincoln and London, University of Nebraska Press, 1990), p. 17.

5. Hittman, *Wovoka and the Ghost Dance,* p. 173.

6. Christina Klein, "'Everything of Interest in the Late Pine Ridge War Are Held by Us for Sale': Popular Culture and Wounded Knee," *Western Historical Quarterly,* 30, no. 1, Spring 1994, pp. 55–58; Robert M. Utley, *The Last Days of the Sioux Nation* (New Haven, Conn., and London, Yale University Press, 1963), pp. 1–4; Richard E. Jensen, R. Eli Paul, and John E. Carter, *Eyewitness at Wounded Knee* (Lincoln, University of Nebraska Press, 1991), pp. 105–113.

7. This event is the subject of Frank Bergon's moving historical novel, *Shoshone Mike.*

8. Gerald Vizenor, *Fugitive Poses: Native American Indian Scenes of Absence and Presence* (Lincoln and London, University of Nebraska Press, Bison Books, 2000), p. 15.

9. The conclusion of Frederick Jackson Turner's celebrated essay "The Significance of the Frontier in American History," stimulated by the supervisor of the federal census's 1890 comment, has in retrospect an ominous ring: "He would be a rash prophet who should assert that the expansive character of American life has now entirely ceased. Movement has been its dominant fact, and, unless this training has no effect upon a people, the American energy will continually demand a wider field for exercise." Richard W. Etulain, ed., *Does the Frontier Experience Make America Exceptional?* (Boston and New York, Bedford/St. Martin's, 1999), p. 40.

10. Eugenia Kaledin, *The Education of Mrs. Henry Adams* (Philadelphia, Temple University Press, 1981), p. 6.

Chapter 2: Valentines

1. George Wilson Pierson, *Tocqueville in America* (1938; Baltimore and London, Johns Hopkins University Press, 1996), pp. 55–56.

2. Alexis de Tocqueville, *Democracy in America,* vol. 2, the Henry Reeve Text as revised by Francis Bowen, now further corrected and edited with introduction, editorial notes, and bibliographies by Phillips Bradley (1945; New York, Vintage Books, 1990), p. 59.

3. Ralph Waldo Emerson, "The American Scholar: An Oration Delivered Before the Phi Beta Kappa Society, at Cambridge, August 31, 1837," in *Essays and Lectures,* ed. Joel Porte (New York, Literary Classics of the United States, Library of America–15, 1983), p. 70.

4. Emerson, "American Scholar," pp. 68–69.

5. Henry James, who had written a damning review of *Drum Taps* as a young man, but who as an old man could read lines from Whitman with a powerful effect, shrewdly summed up the "scandal" of Whitman's works against the bourgeois platitude of impropriety that was imposed on "improper" works: "It was to be true

indeed that Walt Whitman achieved an impropriety of the first magnitude; that success, however, but showed us the platitude returning in a genial rage upon itself and getting out of control by generic excess." Henry James, *Autobiography: A Small Boy and Others*, edited and with an introduction by Frederick W. Dupee (New York, Criterion Books, 1956), p. 46.

6. Another of these smart New England girls was the definitely uncloistered Elizabeth Stoddard, whose remarkable 1862 novel *The Morgesons* eviscerates the same stultifying Massachusetts towns and their constraints on the mind and the passions (especially those of women) that her contemporary Emily Dickinson did.

7. Quoted in the introduction to Julia A. Moore, *The Sweet Singer of Michigan: Poems by Mrs. Julia A. Moore*, edited and with an introduction by Walter Blair (Chicago, Pascal Covici, Publisher, 1928), p. xxii.

8. Francis Otto Matthiessen, *American Renaissance* (New York, Oxford University Press, 1941), pp. 11–12.

9. Richard B. Sewall, *The Life of Emily Dickinson* (1974; Cambridge, Mass., Harvard University Press, 1994), p. 622.

10. Edward Emerson, *Emerson in Concord: A Memoir Written for the "Social Circle" in Concord, Massachusetts* (Boston and New York, Houghton Mifflin; Cambridge, Mass., Riverside Press, 1888), p. 14.

11. Sewall, *Life of Emily Dickinson*, p. 128.

12. Sewall, *Life of Emily Dickinson*, p. 156.

13. Sidney Lanier, *The Science of English Verse* (New York, Charles Scribner's Sons, 1914) pp. 186–189, 246–248.

14. Sewall, *Life of Emily Dickinson*, p. 248. The whole of the description is drawn from Susan Dickinson.

15. Emily Dickinson, *Selected Letters*, ed. Thomas H. Johnson (Cambridge, Mass., Belknap Press of Harvard University Press, 1958), p. 174.

16. "The 'I think' which Kant said must be able to accompany all my objects, is the 'I breathe' which actually does accompany them. . . . Breath, which was ever the original of 'spirit,' breath moving outwards, between the glottis and the nostrils, is, I am persuaded, the essence out of which philosophers have constructed the entity known to them as consciousness." William James, "Does 'Consciousness' Exist?" in William James, *Essays in Radical Empiricism* (1912; Lincoln, University of Nebraska Press, 1996), p. 37.

17. John Shoptaw, "Listening to Dickinson," *Representations*, no. 86, Spring 2004, pp. 37–38.

As the rest of the lyric confirms, there are three beats per verse. . . . To give the opening trochaic rhythm its due, we must wait out the first upbeat by pausing slightly and dwelling on 'Come.' We will also hover over and imbibe both long-voweled, alliterating syllables of 'slowly –'; and if we are not to slur our words, we must pause between the two long *e*'s in 'slowly Eden!' the final short syllable of the seductive address. (Eden is where you are) being the first true upbeat. Three words: three kinds of pauses.

18. "Mine – by the Right of the White Election!" she had written, perhaps of her poetic "crown"; white being her preferred mode of dress and a reference to famous lines from her favorite book in the Bible, Revelation: "and they shall walk with me in white: for they are worthy. *He that overcometh* the same shall be clothed in white raiment; and I will not blot out his name out of the book of Life." See Sewall, *Life of Emily Dickinson*, p. 138.

19. Sewall, *Life of Emily Dickinson*, pp. 536–538.

20. Emily Dickinson, *Selected Letters*, ed. Thomas H. Johnson (Cambridge, Mass., and London, Belknap Press of Harvard University Press, 1958), pp. 207–209.

21. Dickinson, *Selected Letters*, p. 208.

22. Dickinson, *Selected Letters*, p. 210.

Chapter 3: Cakewalk

1. George Washington Cable, "The Dance in Place Congo," *Century Magazine*, February 1866. This African American *insolence* trespassed on some northern white sensibilities as well. The usually sensitive observer Thomas Wentworth Higginson compares the courteous demeanor of the men of his black regiment to the "upstart conceit which is sometimes offensive among free Negroes at the North, the dandy – barber strut." Thomas Wentworth Higginson, *Army Life in a Black Regiment* (Boston, Fields, Osgood, & Co., 1870), p. 29.

2. Cable, "Dance in Place Congo."

3. Philip D. Morgan, *Slave Counterpoint: Black Culture in the Eighteenth-Century Chesapeake and Lowcountry* (Chapel Hill and London, University of North Carolina Press, 1998), p. 596.

4. Morgan, *Slave Counterpoint*, p. 584.

5. Cable, "Dance in Place Congo," p. 528.

6. Katrina Hazzard-Gordon, *Jookin': The Rise of Social Dance Formations in African-American Culture* (Philadelphia, Temple University Press, 1990), p. 55.

7. Frederick Douglass, *Narrative of the Life of Frederick Douglass, An American Slave, Written by Himself* (1845), in William L. Andrews and Henry Louis Gates Jr., eds., *Slave Narratives* (New York, Literary Classics of the United States, Library of America–114, 2000), pp. 289–290. It must have been later that Douglass began to understand that there were messages encoded in the sorrow songs. He learned that Canaan could stand for the North, and wrote in another version of his autobiography that it was the song "Run to Jesus" that first suggested to him the thought of escaping from slavery. See Lawrence W. Levine, *Black Culture and Black Consciousness: Afro-American Folk Thought from Slavery to Freedom* (New York, Oxford University Press, 1977, 2007), p. 51.

8. Henry Louis Gates Jr., *The Signifying Monkey* (New York and Oxford, Oxford University Press, 1988).

9. Marshall and Jean Stearns, *Jazz Dance: The Story of American Vernacular*

Dance (1968; New York and Cambridge, Mass., Da Capo Press, 1994), p. 22. The basic cakewalk steps were embellished by variations such as "pitchin' hay," "corn shuckin'," and "cuttin' wheat" that betray the country and African origins of the dance, according to Hazzard-Gordon, *Jookin'*, pp. 19–20.

10. Stearns and Stearns, *Jazz Dance*, pp. 22–23.

11. Peter Wood, "'Gimme de Kneebone Bent': African Body Language and the Evolution of American Dance Forms," in *The Black Tradition in American Modern Dance*, ed. Gerald E. Myers (Durham, North Carolina, American Dance Festival, 1988), p. 8.

12. "Brought to the Americas in the motor-muscle memory of the various West African ethnic groups, the dance was characterized by segmentation and delineation of various body parts, including hips, torso, head, arms, hands, and legs; the use of multiple meter as polyrhythmic sensitivity; angularity; multiple centers of movement; asymmetry as balance; percussive performance; mimetic performance; improvisation; and derision. These esthetic and technical commonalities continued to be governing principles as dance moved from its sacred context to the numerous secular uses it acquired under slavery." Hazzard-Gordon, *Jookin'*, p. 18.

13. LeRoi Jones (aka Amiri Baraka), *Blues People: Negro Music in White America* (1963; New York, Harper Perennial, HarperCollins, 2002), p. 86. The pagination in this edition is the same as in the original 1963 edition.

14. Brooke Baldwin, "The Cakewalk: A Study in Stereotype and Reality," *Journal of Social History* 15, no. 2 (Winter 1981), p. 212.

15. An interesting piece in an important African American newspaper sees the cakewalk coming out of the plantation slaves' attempts to dignify their wooing and unofficial marriages. See *Freeman* [Indianapolis], November 27, 1897.

16. Amy Charters, *Nobody: The Story of Bert Williams* (New York, Macmillan, 1970), p. 35.

17. Sidney Finkelstein, *Jazz: A People's Music* (New York, Citadel Press, 1948), pp. 67–69.

18. Gunther Schuller, *Early Jazz: Its Roots and Musical Development* (New York and Oxford, Oxford University Press, 1968), pp. 15–17.

19. Wood, "'Gimme de Kneebone Bent,'" p. 4.

20. Hans Nathan, *Dan Emmett and the Rise of Early Negro Minstrelsy* (Norman, University of Oklahoma Press, 1962), pp. 200–203, where other examples of this early minstrel syncopation are given. "Doctor Hekok Jig" and another of Nathan's examples, "Pea-Patch Jig," can be heard on *The Early Minstrel Show* compact disk, New World Records, Recorded Anthology of American Music, 80338-2/DIDX #034774, 1985.

21. Edward A. Berlin, *Ragtime: A Musical and Cultural History* (Berkeley, Los Angeles, and London, University of California Press, 1980), p. 67.

22. Traveling through the South in the 1930s, Gertrude Stein talked to the editor of a southern newspaper who recalled that one rainy Sunday someone had mentioned Robert E. Lee, and his father-in-law had said, "yes he was a great man a great

man and we all love him and I sometimes think that if he had been here of a rainy Sunday well yes I would not want him here all day of a rainy Sunday." Gertrude Stein, *Everybody's Autobiography* (1937; London, Virago Press, 1985), p. 214.

23. The social world of African American Sedalia at the turn of the nineteenth century, and much of the information on Scott Joplin, is found in Edward A. Berlin, *The King of Ragtime: Scott Joplin and His Era* (New York and Oxford, Oxford University Press, 1994).

24. See Cecil Brown, *Stagolee Shot Billy* (Cambridge, Mass., and London, Harvard University Press, 2003); and Cecil Brown, "We Did Them Wrong: The Ballad of Frankie and Albert," in *The Rose and the Briar: Death, Love and Liberty in the American Ballad*, ed. Sean Wilentz and Greil Marcus (New York and London, W. W. Norton, 2005).

25. Scott Joplin, *Complete Piano Works*, ed. Vera Brodsky Lawrence, with an introduction by Rudi Blesh (1972; New York, New York Public Library, 1981), p. xxx.

26. James Weldon Johnson, *The Autobiography of an Ex-Colored Man* (1912, 1927; New York, Vintage, 1989, with introductions by Carl Van Vechten and Henry Louis Gates Jr.), pp. 98–101.

27. The examples of ragtime's baleful effects are all found in Berlin, *Ragtime*, pp. 38–44, 101.

28. Berlin, *Ragtime*, p. 42.

29. Berlin, *Ragtime*, p. 51.

30. See also the cakewalk witnessed by the guests of a swank Jacksonville hotel, in Johnson, *Autobiography of an Ex-Colored Man*, pp. 85–87. Johnson claims this genteel stroll was the original cakewalk.

31. This dream is shared by the narrator of *The Autobiography of an Ex-Colored Man*, when after delighting an audience of Berlin musicians with his virtuoso performance of a ragtime piece, one of the men takes over the piano bench and develops it "through every musical form." "I sat amazed. I had been turning classic music into rag-time, a comparatively easy task; and this man had taken rag-time and made it classic," p. 142. By 1903 one European composer, Debussy, at least, had done just this with his "Golliwog's Cakewalk." The narrator of *The Autobiography's* dream of turning ragtime and the black folk music of the South into classical music parallels Johnson's own ambition to turn black vernacular speech into literature; pp. 142–143.

32. Scott Joplin, *Complete Piano Music*, p. xxxix.

33. Henry Lewis Gates Jr. and Cornel West, *The African-American Century: How Black Americans Have Shaped Our Country* (New York, Simon & Schuster, 2000), p. 40.

34. Alex Ross, *Listen to This* (New York, Farrar, Straus and Giroux, 2010), pp. 39–40. Of course I only imagine that Louis XIV's performance at Versailles as a Moor in Lully's ballet took place in the Hall of Mirrors.

35. Ann Charters, *Nobody: The Story of Bert Williams* (New York, Macmillan, 1970), pp. 8–9.

36. Charters, *Nobody*, p. 28.

37. Charters, *Nobody*, p. 105.

38. Louis Chude-Sokei, *The Last "Darky": Bert Williams, Black-on–Black Minstrelsy, and the African Diaspora* (Durham, North Carolina, Duke University Press, 2006).

39. Marva Griffin Carter, "Removing the 'Minstrel Mask,'" *Musical Quarterly* 84, no. 2 (Summer 2000), p. 210.

40. Charters, *Nobody*, p. 7.

41. Quoted in David Krasner, *Resistance, Parody, and Double Consciousness in African American Theatre, 1895–1910* (New York, St. Martin's Press, 1997), p. 10.

42. Charters, *Nobody*, p. 138.

43. Charters, *Nobody*, p. 133.

44. Charters, *Nobody*, p. 132.

45. Charters, *Nobody*, p. 107.

46. See Levine, *Black Culture and Black Consciousness*, p. 405, for a song popular among African Americans in the 1920s:

They put the coon on the gallows

An' told him he would die;

He crossed his legs an' winked his eye

And sailed up in the sky.

47. Ralph Ellison, *Shadow and Act* (New York, Random House, 1964), pp. 53, 55.

Chapter 4: Monsters

1. Joseph Brent, *Charles Sanders Peirce: A Life*, revised and enlarged edition (Bloomington and Indianapolis, Indiana University Press, 1993), p. 103.

2. Brent, *Charles Sanders Peirce*, p. 69.

3. Brent, *Charles Sanders Peirce*, p. 70.

4. Charles Sanders Peirce, *Collected Papers of Charles Sanders Peirce*, vol. 2, ed. Charles Hartshorne and Paul Weiss (1931–1958; Cambridge, Mass., Belknap Press of Harvard University Press, 1960), p. 135.

5. Ralph Ellison, *Shadow and Act* (New York, Random House, 1964), p. 66.

6. Charles Sanders Peirce, *Writings of Charles Sanders Peirce: A Chronological Edition*, vol. 1, ed. Max S. Fisch (Bloomington, Indiana University Press, 1982), p. 444.

7. "The real, then, is that which, sooner or later, information and reasoning would finally result in, and which is therefore independent of the vagaries of me and you. Thus, the very origin of the conception of reality shows that this conception essentially involves the notion of a COMMUNITY, without definite limits, and capable of an indefinite increase of knowledge." And thus, "the social principle is rooted intrinsically in logic." Charles Sanders Peirce, quoted in Brent, *Charles Sanders Peirce*, p. 73.

8. Stephen Crane, *The Monster*, in Stephen Crane, *Prose and Poetry*, ed. J. C. Levenson (New York, Literary Classics of the United States, and Library of America–18, 1984), p. 396.

9. Crane, *Monster*, p. 395.

10. Crane, *Monster*, p. 402.

11. Charles Sanders Peirce, "Some Consequences of Four Incapacities," in *Essential Writings*, ed. Edward C. Moore, with a preface by Richard Robin (Amherst, New York, Prometheus Books, 1998), p. 118.

12. *Measure for Measure*, II, ii, 117.

13. Stephen Crane, "The Open Boat," in *Prose and Poetry*, p. 890.

14. Christopher Benfey, *The Double Life of Stephen Crane: A Biography* (New York, Knopf, 1992), p. 104. The pagination in the 1994 Vintage edition is the same as the Knopf 1992 edition I cite.

15. Frank Bergon, *Stephen Crane's Artistry* (New York and London, Columbia University Press, 1975), p. 35.

16. Bergon, *Stephen Crane's Artistry*, p. x.

17. R. W. Stallman, *Stephen Crane: A Biography* (New York, George Braziller, 1968), pp. 192, 201.

18. Stephen Crane, "The Red Badge of Courage Was His Wig-Wag Flag," in *The University of Virginia Edition of the Works of Stephen Crane*, vol. 9: *Reports of War*, ed. Fredson Bowers, with an introduction by James B. Colvert (Charlottesville, University of Virginia Press, 1971), p. 138.

19. Stallman, *Stephen Crane*, p. 387.

20. King's theory anticipated, in its own way, the "punctuated equilibrium" of Stephen Jay Gould (but without King's sense of a divine program emerging from the geological cataclysms forcing biological change).

21. The story of this marriage and its significance in a racialized America is told in Martha A. Sandweiss, *Passing Strange: A Gilded Age Tale of Love and Deception Across the Color Line* (New York, Penguin Press, 2009).

22. Max H. Fisch, *Peirce, Semeiotic, and Pragmatism*, ed. Kenneth Laine Ketner and Christan J.W. Kloesel (Bloomington, Indiana University Press, 1986), p. 238.

Chapter 5: The Soul Shepherd

1. Ralph Waldo Emerson, "Experience," in *Essays and Lectures* (New York, Literary Classics of the United States, Library of America–15, 1983), p. 471.

2. Alfred Habegger, *The Father: A Life of Henry James, Sr.* (New York, Farrar, Straus and Giroux, 1994), p. 3.

3. Habegger, *Father*, p. 305.

4. Erik H. Erikson, *Identity, Youth and Crisis* (New York, W. W. Norton, 1968), p. 151.

5. Robert D. Richardson, *William James: In the Maelstrom of American Modernism* (Boston and New York, Houghton Mifflin, 2006), pp. 120–122.

6. William James, *Varieties of Religious Experience*, in *Writings 1902–1910* (New York, Literary Classics of the United States, Library of America–38, 1987), pp. 149–151.

7. William James, "A Pluralistic Mystic," in *Writings 1902–1910*, p. 1295.

8. James, "Pluralistic Mystic," p. 1309.

9. William James, "On Some Hegelisms," in *Writings 1878–1899*, ed. Gerald E. Myers (New York, Literary Classics of the United States, Library of America–58, 1992), pp. 677–679.

10. William James, *The Principles of Psychology*, vol. 1 (1890; New York, Dover, 1950), pp. 288–289.

11. James, *Principles of Psychology*, vol. 1, p. 255.

12. James, *Principles of Psychology*, vol. 1, p. 289.

13. James, *Principles of Psychology*, vol. 1, p. 291.

14. James, *Principles of Psychology*, vol. 1, p. 401.

15. Richardson, *William James*, p. 303.

16. From James's preface to *The Will to Believe*, quoted in William James, *Essays in Radical Empiricism*, ed. Ralph Barton Perry, with an introduction by Ellen Kappy Suckiel (1912; Lincoln and London, University of Nebraska Press, Bison Books, 1996), p. xix.

17. James, *Varieties of Religious Experience*, p. 399.

18. Louis Menand, *The Metaphysical Club* (New York, Farrar, Straus and Giroux, 2001). The other members of the Metaphysical Club were Nicholas St. John Green, Joseph Bangs Warner, John Fiske, Francis Ellingwood Abbot, and Chauncey Wright.

19. To distance himself from such applications, Peirce renamed his theory *pragmaticism*, a name, he said, ugly enough to be safe from kidnappers.

20. Bertrand Russell, *A History of Western Philosophy* (1945; New York, Simon and Schuster, 1972), p. 818.

21. William James, "Answer to a Questionnaire [1904]," in *Writings 1902–1910*, pp. 1183–1185.

22. Gardner Murphy and Robert O. Ballou, *William James on Psychical Research* (New York, Viking Press, 1960), pp. 263–264.

23. James, *Varieties of Religious Experience*, pp. 128–129.

24. James, *Varieties of Religious Experience*, p. 151.

25. David Levering Lewis, *W. E. B. Du Bois: A Biography* (New York, Henry Holt, 2009), p. 75.

26. James, *Varieties of Religious Experience*, pp. 433–434.

27. James's dream is recounted in Erickson, *Identity, Youth and Crisis*, pp. 205–206.

28. Printed as number three in Freud's published account.

29. Saul Rosenzweig, *The Historic Expedition to America (1909): Freud, Jung and Hall the King-maker* (St. Louis, Rana House, 1994), p. 418.

30. C. G. Jung, *Memories, Dreams, Reflections*, Recorded and edited by Aniela Jaffé, trans. Richard and Clara Winston (New York, Pantheon/Random House, 1973), p. 150.

31. James, *Principles of Psychology*, vol. 2, p. 336.

32. James, "Pluralistic Mystic," p. 1312.

33. James, "Pluralistic Mystic," p. 1313.

Chapter 6: The Return of the Novelist

1. Henry James, *The American Scene* (1907), in *Collected Travel Writing: Great Britain and America*, ed. Richard Howard (New York, Literary Classics of the United States, Library of America–64, 1993), p. 411.

2. Henry James, *The Complete Notebooks of Henry James*, edited and with introductions and notes by Leon Edel and Lyall H. Powers (New York, Oxford University Press, 1987), p. 238.

3. James, *American Scene*, p. 412.

4. James, *Complete Notebooks of Henry James*, p. 240.

5. James quotes inexactly. The *lines*, from *Paradiso* X, 128–129, as translated by Mark Musa, reads, "to this peace / he came from exile and from martyrdom."

6. James, *Complete Notebooks of Henry James*, p. 240.

7. Leon Edel, preface to the one-volume edition of *Henry James: A Life* (New York, HarperCollins, 1987).

8. Quoted in Edel, *Henry James*, p. 87.

9. Edel, *Henry James*, p. 498.

10. James, *American Scene*, pp. 426–427.

11. Theodore Roosevelt, "What 'Americanism' Means," *The Forum* 17 (March–August 1894), p. 201.

12. Henry James, *Literary Criticism*, vol. 1, ed. Leon Edel with Mark Wilson (New York, Literary Classics of the United States, Library of America–22, 1984), p. 665.

13. James's essay "The Question of Our Speech" was originally delivered to the graduating class at Bryn Mawr on June 8, 1905.

14. James, *American Scene*, p. 464.

15. James, *American Scene*, p. 465.

16. Henry James, *Letters*, vol. 4, ed. Leon Edel (Cambridge, Mass., and London, Belknap Press of Harvard University Press, 1984), p. 354.

17. James, *American Scene*, p. 688.

18. James, *American Scene*, p. 658.

19. James, *American Scene*, p. 659.

20. James, *American Scene*, p. 660.

21. James's amanuensis, Theodora Bosanquet, makes an important observation about James's method: "He went so much further than anyone else has ever been along his own line just *because* he spent all his time at the one business of receiving and analyzing and appraising and transmitting the impressions life showered on him. It's ridiculous to blame him for not appreciating the lessons of history and the rights of women." Theodora Bosanquet, *Henry James at Work, with Excerpts from Her Diary and an Account of Her Professional Career*, edited and with notes and introductions by Lyall H. Powers (Ann Arbor, University of Michigan Press, 2006), p. 26.

22. James, *American Scene*, p. 662.

23. James, *American Scene*, p. 681.

24. James, *American Scene*, p. 654.

25. W.E.B. Du Bois, *The Souls of Black Folk* (1903), in *Writings*, ed. Nathan Huggins, New York, Literary Classics of the United States, Library of America, 1986), p. 364.

26. Edel, *Henry James*, p. 615.

27. Henry James, *Letters*, vol. 4, *1895–1916*, ed. Leon Edel (Cambridge, Mass., and London, Belknap Press of Harvard University Press, 1984), p. 355.

28. James, *Complete Notebooks of Henry James*, p. 237.

29. Bosanquet, *Henry James at Work*, p. 32.

30. James, *Principles of Psychology*, vol. 1, p. 255.

31. Henry James, *Autobiography: A Small Boy and Others, Notes of a Son and Brother, The Middle Years*, edited and with an introduction by F. W. Dupee (1913, 1914, 1917; New York, Criterion Books, 1956), pp. 51–52.

32. Edel, *Henry James*, p. 680.

33. James, *Autobiography*, p. 54.

34. James, *Autobiography*, p. 55.

35. For James's thoughts on the centrality of fairy tales, see Henry James, *Literary Criticism*, vol. 2 (New York, Literary Classics of the United States, Library of America–23, 1984), pp. 1183–1184.

36. James, *Autobiography*, p. 95.

37. James, *Autobiography*, pp. 16–17. Dupee, in his introduction, p. xii, stresses the importance of this gaping for a small, powerless boy.

38. James, *American Scene*, pp. 429–430.

39. James, *Small Boy and Others*, p. 164.

40. James, *Small Boy and Others*, pp. 231–232.

41. From James's short story, "The Middle Years," in Henry James, *Complete Stories*, vol. 4, *1892–1898* (New York, Literary Classics of the United States, Library of America–82, 1996), p. 354.

42. From his letter of July 10, 1915, to H. G. Wells. Henry James, *Letters*, vol. 4, ed. Leon Edel (Cambridge, Mass., Belknap Press of Harvard University Press, 1984), p. 770.

43. Leon Edel, *The Life of Henry James*, vol. 5: *The Master (1901–1916)* (Philadelphia and New York, J. B. Lippincott, 1972), p. 242.

44. Edel, *Henry James*, p. 690.

45. Henry James, *The Letters of Henry James*, vol. 1, selected and edited by Percy Lubbock (New York, Charles Scribner's Sons, 1920), p. 88. Leon Edel believed Gosse's picture was colored by Gosse's memories of the older James.

46. Edel, *Henry James*, p. 511. Theodora Bosanquet, his perceptive typist, wrote,

He was obliged to create impassable barriers between himself and the rest of mankind before he could stretch out his eager hands over safe walls to beckon and bless. He loved his friends, but he was condemned by the law of his being to keep clear of any really entangling net of human affection and exaction. His contacts had to be subordinate, or indeed ancillary, to the vocation he had followed with a single passion from the time when, as a small boy, he obtained a report from his tutor showing no great aptitude for anything but a felicitous rendering of La Fontaine's fables into English.

Henry James at Work, pp. 48–49.

Chapter 7: An Innocent at Cedro

1. Max Lerner, introduction to *The Portable Veblen* (New York, Viking Press, 1948), pp. 48–49.

2. Thorstein Veblen, *The Theory of the Leisure Class: An Economic Study of Institutions* (New York and London, Macmillan Company, 1899), pp. 264–265.

3. John P. Diggins, *The Bard of Savagery: Thorstein Veblen and Modern Social Theory* (New York, Seabury Press, 1978), pp. 101, 103–104.

4. Thorstein Veblen, "An Early Experiment in Trusts" (1904), collected in *Thorstein Veblen: The Place of Science in Modern Civilisation and Other Essays* (New York, Russell & Russell, 1961), p. 504.

5. Joseph Dorfman, *Thorstein Veblen and His America* (1934; New York, Viking Press, 1940), p. 425.

6. Robert L. Duffus, *The Innocents at Cedro: A Memoir of Thorstein Veblen and Some Others* (New York, Macmillan, 1944), p. 58.

7. Duffus, *Innocents at Cedro*, p. 64.

8. Duffus, *Innocents at Cedro*, p. 120.

9. David Riesman, *Thorstein Veblen: A Critical Interpretation* (New York, Seabury Press, 1960), p. 107.

10. There had been no one to name Ishi, and in any case he would not have cared to reveal his real name to anyone other than his closest family.

11. Herbert Luthin and Leanne Hinton, "The Story of Lizard," in *Ishi in Three Centuries*, ed. Karl Kroeber and Clifton Kroeber (Lincoln and London, University of Nebraska Press, 2003), pp. 293–317.

12. Thorstein Veblen, "The Instinct of Workmanship" (1898), collected in Thorstein Veblen, *Essays in Our Changing Order*, ed. Leon Ardzrooni (1934; New York, Augustus M. Kelley, 1964), pp. 81–82. "All men have this quasi-aesthetic sense of economic or industrial merit, and to this sense of economic merit futility and inefficiency are distasteful. . . . It is needless to point out in detail the close relation between this norm of economic merit and the ethical norm of conduct, on the one hand, and the aesthetic norm of taste, on the other. It is very closely related to both of these, both as regards its biological ground and as regards the scope and method of its award."

13. Dorfman, *Thorstein Veblen and His America*, p. 295.

14. Alex Beam, "The Naughty Professor," *Stanford Magazine*, September–October 1997.

15. Testimony of Mr. Frederick W. Taylor, April 13, 1914, United States Congress, Senate. *Industrial Relations: Final Report and Testimony Submitted to Congress*

by the Commission on Industrial Relations, Created by the Act of August 23, 1912, 64th Congress, 1st Session, 1916, vol. 1 (Washington, D.C., U.S. Government Printing Office, 1916), pp. 778–779.

16. "The 'common laborer' is, in fact, a highly trained and widely proficient workman when contrasted with the conceivable human blank supposed to have drawn on the community for nothing but his physique." Veblen, quoted in a note in Riesman, *Thorstein Veblen*, p. 120.

17. Working briefly in Washington during the First World War, Veblen wrote a paper saying that the best way to meet wartime wheat production was to give the Wobbly harvest stiffs what they wanted.

18. Thorstein Veblen, "Bolshevism Is a Menace—to Whom?" (1919), in *Essays in Our Changing Order*, p. 411.

19. Dorfman, *Thorstein Veblen and His America*, pp. 436–437.

20. Thorstein Veblen, *The Instinct of Workmanship and the State of the Industrial Arts*, ed. Murray G. Murphey (1914; New Brunswick, N.J., and London, Transaction, 1990), pp. xl–xlii.

21. Dorfman, *Thorstein Veblen and His America*, p. 497.

22. Dorfman, *Thorstein Veblen and His America*, pp. 497–498.

Chapter 8: The Rise of Abraham Cahan

1. I am indebted for this idea, and for others in the chapter, to Irving Feldman. The frontier was not only figurative but for some Jews literal, with agricultural colonies—almost all of them failures—set up in Texas, Oregon, and Utah among other places. I would give much to read the Yiddish of such works of Jewish wandering in the New World as I. J. Schwartz's poem "Kentucky," cited in Irving Howe's *World of Our Fathers*.

2. Jacob Gordin, *The Jewish King Lear*, trans. Ruth Gay, with notes and essays by Ruth Gay and Sophie Glazer (New Haven, Conn., and London, Yale University Press, 2007), p. 22.

3. Abraham Cahan, *The Education of Abraham Cahan* (vols. 1 and 2 of *Bleter Fun Mein Leben*), trans. Leon Stein, Abraham P. Conan, and Lynn Davison, introduction by Leon Stein (Philadelphia, Jewish Publication Society of America, 1969), pp. 240–241.

4. Cahan, *Education of Abraham Cahan*, p. 399.

5. Abraham Cahan, *Grandma Never Lived in America*, edited with an introduction by Moses Rishin (Bloomington, Indiana University Press, 1985), pp. 419–420.

6. The late Michael Rogin has written of the complex meaning for Jews and Americans of this blackface masquerade. Michael Rogin, *Blackface, White Noise: Jewish Immigrants in the Hollywood Melting Pot* (Berkeley, Los Angeles, and London, University of California Press, 1996). Other immigrant Jews, like Israel Baline (Irving Berlin), celebrator of the "Easter Parade" and "White Christmas," and Jean

Schwartz, who did not stop with his cakewalk "Dusky Dudes" but extended himself even farther with "Chinatown My Chinatown" and "The Hat My Father Wore upon St. Patrick's Day," provided the words and the music for similar rituals of assimilation. I would like to see that hat.

7. Abraham Cahan, *The Rise of David Levinsky* (1917; New York, Random House/Modern Library Paperback, 2001), p. 397.

8. To be exact, the reference may be found in Edmond and Jules de Goncourt, *Pages from the Goncourt Journals*, edited, translated, and with an introduction by Robert Baldick (New York, New York Review Books, 2006), p. 140.

9. Cahan, *Rise of David Levinsky*, p. 415.

10. In 1911 Irving Berlin emitted just such a patriotic effusion, the perennially popular anthem "God Bless America."

11. Cahan gives a wonderful description of Professor Peltner's dancing school in his fine early novella *Yekl*. Abraham Cahan, *Yekl and the Imported Bridegroom and Other Stories of Yiddish New York* (1896, 1898; New York, Dover, 1970), pp. 15–23.

12. Cahan, *Rise of David Levinsky*, p. 126.

13. Cahan, *Rise of David Levinsky*, p. 490.

14. Cahan, *Rise of David Levinsky*, p. 432.

15. Cahan, *Rise of David Levinsky*, p. 433.

16. Cahan, *Rise of David Levinsky*, p. 433.

17. One Russian writer who was Levinsky's contemporary would certainly not have been capable of it. The great American settlement-house founder Jane Addams remembered visiting Tolstoy at Yasnaya Polyana in 1896. He frowned at her leg-o'-mutton sleeves and commented that there was enough stuff on one arm to make a frock for a little girl. Then he asked his visitor if she did not find such a dress "a barrier to the people." Addams was able to reply that exaggerated as the sleeves were, they did not compare in size to those of the working girls of Chicago, and that nothing would more effectively separate her from "the people" than simpler dress; and then that even if she had wished to imitate him and dress as a peasant—he was wearing his peasant blouse—it would be hard to choose *which* peasant among the thirty-six nationalities she and her colleagues had recently counted in her ward. Jane Addams knew those working girls, and well. Jane Addams, *Twenty Years at Hull House* (New York, Macmillan, 1911), pp. 267–268.

18. *O liebe brayt*, Yiddish for "O beloved bread." From "The Lost Language" in Irving Feldman, *Collected Poems: 1954–2004* (New York, Schocken Books, 2004), pp. 9–10.

19. "Bintel Brief," p. 140.

20. Abraham Cahan, "The Imported Bridegroom," in *Yekl*, p. 103.

21. Cahan, *Rise of David Levinsky*, p. 516.

22. From Irving Howe's masterful *World of Our Fathers: The Journey of the East European Jews to America and the Life They Found and Made* (New York, Simon & Schuster, 1976), p. 507.

23. Zvi Hirsch Margoshes, *Der Forvertsisn*, in Ehud Manor, *Forward: The Jewish*

Daily Forward (Forverts) Newspaper. Immigrants, Socialism and Jewish Politics in New York, 1890–1917 (Brighton and Portland, England, Sussex Academic Press, 2009), p. 109.

24. Manor, *Forward*, p. 11

25. For Cahan's initial enthusiasm for the Bolshevik Revolution and his startling defense of its dictatorial suppression of competing parties, see Howe, *World of Our Fathers*, pp. 540–541. Howe quotes the Menshevik leader Raphael Abramovitch, who met Cahan in Berlin in 1920. Cahan embraced him, but when Abramovitch attempted to tell him of the Bolshevik repressions, Cahan put his hands over his ears and cried, "Don't destroy my illusions, I don't want to hear." Cahan would later become a staunch opponent of both American and Russian Communism. Paul Buhle, scholar of the American Left, terms Cahan's later position McCarthyism.

26. Cahan, *Grandma Never Lived in America*, pp. 397–398.

27. Cahan, *Education of Abraham Cahan*, p. 51.

Chapter 9: Beyond Syncopation

1. Alan Lomax, *Mister Jelly Roll: The Fortunes of Jelly Roll Morton, New Orleans Creole and "Inventor of Jazz"* (1950; Berkeley, Los Angeles, and London, University of California Press, 2001), p. 127.

2. LeRoi Jones (Amiri Baraka), *Blues People: Negro Music in White America* (1963; New York, Harper Perennial, 1999), pp. 75–76.

3. Marshall and Jean Stearns, "Frontiers of Humor: American Vernacular Dance," *Southern Folklore Quarterly* 30, no. 3 (September 1966), pp. 228–230. For more on Butler May, see Doug Seroff and Lynn Abbott, "The Life and Death of Pioneer Bluesman Butler 'String Beans' May: Been Here, Made His Quick Duck, and Got Away," *Tributaries: Journal of the Alabama Folklife Association* (2002), pp. 9–48.

4. Henry Louis Gates Jr., *The Signifying Monkey: A Theory of African-American Literary Criticism* (New York and Oxford, Oxford University Press, 1988), p. 63.

5. Gunther Schuller, *Early Jazz: Its Roots and Musical Development* (New York and Oxford, Oxford University Press, 1968), pp. 135, 143. I have largely relied on Schuller for my account of Jelly Roll Morton's innovations.

6. Phil Pastras has speculated with insight on Morton's sexual persona. Phil Pastras, *Dead Man Blues: Jelly Roll Morton Way Out West* (Berkeley, Los Angeles, and London, University of California Press; Chicago, Columbia College, Center for Black Music Research, 2001), pp. 16–17, 108–109.

7. Pastras, *Dead Man Blues*, p. 87.

8. In her biography of Josephine Baker, Phyllis Rose quotes black expatriates such as James Weldon Johnson, Richard Wright, and the journalist Joel Augustus Rogers on the sense of freedom black Americans felt in Paris. Phyllis Rose, *Jazz Cleopatra: Josephine Baker in Her Time* (New York, Doubleday, 1989), pp. 74–75. For the irascible Sidney Bechet, Europe was, to say the least, a mixed blessing. He was deported from England for attempted rape and imprisoned for eleven months in France for a shooting in Montmartre.

9. Lomax, *Mister Jelly Roll*, p. xvii. I have interpolated Jelly Roll's lyrics from Alan Lomax's Library of Congress recordings of 1938.

10. Terry Teachout, *Pops: A Life of Louis Armstrong* (Boston and New York, Houghton Mifflin Harcourt, 2009), p. 25.

11. Howard Reich and William Gaines, *Jelly's Blues: The Life, Music and Redemption of Jelly Roll Morton* (Cambridge, Mass., Da Capo Press, 2003), p. 86.

12. His wife, Mabel Bertrand, told Alan Lomax that Jelly might be described as undersexed.

13. Gene Santoro, *Myself When I Am Real: The Life and Music of Charles Mingus* (New York, Oxford University Press, 2000), p. 263.

14. Charles Mingus, *Beneath the Underdog: His World as Composed by Mingus*, ed. Nel King (New York, Alfred A. Knopf, 1971), p. 3.

15. Santoro, *Myself When I Am Real*, p. 78. See also Sidney Bechet, *Treat It Gentle: An Autobiography* (1960; Cambridge, Mass., Da Capo Press, with a new preface by Rudi Blesh, 1978):

> Most people, they think they make themselves. Well, in a way they do. But they don't give enough credit to all the things around them, the things they take from somebody else when they're doing something and creating it . . . things like what it is you remember, or how you feel, or what you're going to do. Things like being a kid and waiting in a field for the late afternoon to be night, like standing by a river, like remembering the first time you heard the music, who it was was playing it. Things like that, they're just life. (p. 139)

Bechet's great theme in this and other passages in his autobiography is the centrality of memory in jazz.

16. Mingus, *Beneath the Underdog*, p. 30.

17. Mingus, *Beneath the Underdog*, p. 66.

18. The account of William Joseph Seymour's church is taken from Mark Zwonitzer, with Charles Hirshberg, *Will You Miss Me When I'm Gone?: The Carter Family and Their Legacy in American Music* (New York, Simon & Schuster, 2002), pp. 133–136.

19. Charles Mingus, quoted by Robert Palmer in his album notes to *Mingus Antibes '60* (1960, 1986; Rhino, 1994).

20. Mingus, *Beneath the Underdog*, p. 6.

21. Mingus, *Beneath the Underdog*, pp. 267–268.

22. Scott Saul, "Outrageous Freedom: Charles Mingus and the Invention of the Jazz Workshop," *American Quarterly* 53, no. 3 (September 2001), p. 397.

23. Mingus, *Beneath the Underdog*, p. 212.

24. Mingus, *Beneath the Underdog*, p. 4.

25. Quoted in Santoro, *Myself When I Am Real*, pp. 301–302.

26. Santoro, *Myself When I Am Real*, p. 56.

27. Like a number of Mingus pieces, it underwent changes in name and is called "Adagio ma non Troppo" in a version scored for orchestra by Alan Raph.

28. Mikhail Bakhtin, *Rabelais and His World*, trans. Hélène Iswolsky (1968; Bloomington, Indiana University Press, 1984), p. 317.

29. From Mingus's liner notes to his 1963 album, *The Black Saint and the Sinner Lady* (1963; Impulse!, 1986).

30. Mingus, *Beneath the Underdog*, pp. 350–351; and Santoro, *Myself When I Am Real*, pp. 177–178.

31. Santoro, *Myself When I Am Real*, p. 301.

32. Janet Coleman and Al Young, *Mingus/Mingus* (New York, Limelight Editions, 1994), p. 17.

33. There had been two earlier performances in 1972 by the Music Department at Morehouse College and the Atlanta Symphony.

34. Mel Watkins, *On the Real Side: Laughing, Lying and Signifying—The Underground Tradition of African-American Humor That Transformed American Culture, from Slavery to Richard Pryor* (New York, Touchstone / Simon & Schuster, 1994), pp. 353–354.

35. Dan Sperber, *Rethinking Symbolism*, trans. Alice L. Morton (Cambridge and London, Cambridge University Press, 1975), pp. 136–137.

36. Clarence Williams, C. Smith, and H. Troy, "Cake Walking Babies From Home," as recorded in New York, January 1925, by Clarence Williams's Blue Five, Okeh 73083-A, and found on the Timeless Records compilation *The Young Sidney Bechet 1923–1925*, 1998.

Acknowledgments

For blessed is he who has dropped even the smallest coin into the little iron box that contains the precious savings of mankind.

—Henry James, *The Tragic Muse*

As I worked on this book I found many other explorers of this realm of satire and improvisation, especially in African American culture, most notably Henry Louis Gates Jr. in his now-classic *The Signifying Monkey*, and most prophetically Ralph Ellison. I have tried to indicate my debts to these and other writers and scholars in my notes and in these acknowledgments.

I would like to thank Kristin Hanson, Irving Feldman, Frank Bergon, Bill Issel, Tony Papanikolas, Jeff Wyneken, and Rodger Birt for taking the time to discuss the issues in this work. John Dizikes suggested I include William James in my list of intellectual cakewalkers, and in so doing added six months to the writing of the book, but also, I think, strengthened it. The anonymous readers who reported on my manuscript made important suggestions, which, mostly, I took. The book is dedicated to my wife Ruth Fallenbaum for her years of reading this and other of my manuscripts, for unflagging support, good suggestions, and for nitpicking over issues best left to copy editors. Finally, I want to thank my long-suffering piano teacher and music consultant LaDene Otsuki for her help and patience. Like the indiscretions in my performances of "Wall Street Rag" and "Swipesy," the help was hers and the mistakes—and this is true for all the other named and unnamed helpers in this book—all mine.

Racial satire remains a powerful force in African American life and art, and extends from comedians such as Richard Pryor and others whose names everyone knows to Jimi Hendrix's "Star-Spangled Banner" at Woodstock and to visual artists such as Robert Colescott, Kara Walker, Glenn Ligon, and Kerry James Marshall. Spike Lee's wonderful film *Bamboozled* takes the minstrel show into the present and turns it inside out, while Bill T. Jones's "Last Supper at Uncle Tom's Cabin" and Ishmael Reed's *Mumbo Jumbo* brilliantly continue African American critiques of race throughout American history and culture in dance and literature. In the mid-nineteen-sixties, the San Francisco Mime Troupe performed an outrageous blackface farce on American racism and racial attitudes, skewering black and white, the hip and the straight, as described in detail in Peter Coyote's 1998 memoir *Sleeping Where I Fall*. More recently the stage play *The Scottsboro Boys* plays off minstrel show tropes against racial injustice in the 1930s American South. The French too have made contributions to this strain of satire, notably Jean Genet's savage *The Blacks: A Clown Show*, and an interesting seventeen minutes of a lost silent film of 1927 by Jean Renoir have been recently reissued in a collection of Renoir films as "Charleston Parade" (Sur un air de Charleston), clips of which can be seen on YouTube.

Perhaps the cakewalk, that central piece of my work, did not in fact finally die out. You can see it on YouTube as teenagers dance the stroll in the mid-fifties, and well into the twenty-first century as couples on *Soul Train* do their thing with style and panache and even a bit of satire between two lines of dancers waiting their turn. The Cakewalk's energies also survived into the 1980s in the spectacles of New York's drag balls, documented in Jennie Livingston's justly famous movie *Paris Is Burning*. It was a world in which a doubly marginalized minority—marginalized by race and by their homosexuality—performed for each other in just such a competition as the cakewalkers had engaged in a hundred years earlier. The contestants walked alone, in imitation of a fashion-show runway stroll, mugging and voguing in a style that combines their envy and their rage at the models of elegance they caricature and wish to become, a world they well know is made up only of appearance. If they achieved some moment of freedom and grace in this competition of cruelty and imitation, they had, after all, achieved what the figures of this book have aspired to.

Source Acknowledgments

The Amherst College Archives and Special Collections, the Emily Dickinson Collection; and the Library of Congress Farm Security Administration / Office of War Information collections have generously allowed the public to download their digitized holdings without restriction or charge. The author thanks the former for Emily Dickinson's "Tell all the truth" and the latter for the Walker Evans Minstrel Show Posters. Random House of Canada (Tundra Books) has kindly transmitted a digitized image of Arlene Alda's photograph of Nathalie Gumpertz's front room from 97 Orchard Street, New York: Stories of Immigrant Life.

The author gratefully acknowledges the following for permission to reprint materials in their possession:

Arlene Alda and the Lower East Side Tenement Museum for the photograph of Nathalie Gumpertz's front room.

CAKEWWALK INTO TOWN, written by Taj Mahal © 1972 EMI Blackwood Music Inc. & Big Toots Tunes. All rights administered by Sony/ATV Music Publishing LLC, 424 Church Street, Nashville, TN 37219. All rights reserved. Used by permission.

"I breathed enough to take the trick," "There's a certain slant of light," "The first day's night had come," "They shut me up in prose," "I cannot live with you," by Emily Dickinson reprinted by permission of the publishers and the Trustees of Amherst College from THE POEMS OF EMILY DICKINSON: READING EDITION, edited by Ralph W. Franklin, Cambridge, Mass.: The Belknap Press of Harvard University Press, Copyright © 1998, 1999 by the President and Fellows of Harvard College. Copyright © 1951, 1955 by the President and Fellows of Harvard College. Copyright © renewed 1979, 1983 by the President and Fellows of Harvard College. Copyright © 1914, 1918, 1919, 1924, 1929, 1930, 1932, 1935, 1937, 1942 by Martha Dickinson Bianchi. Copyright © 1952, 1957, 1958, 1963, 1965 by Mary L. Hampson.

"Cake Walking Babies From Home": Words and Music by Henry Troy, Chris Smith and Clarence Williams. Copyright © 1929 Universal Music Corp., Christie-Max Music and Great Standards Music Publishing Co. Copyright Renewed. All Rights for Christie-Max Music and Great Standards Music Publishing Co. admin-

Notes for Further Reading

Chapter 1: Ghost Dance

The principal source for the Ghost Dance still remains James Mooney's *The Ghost-Dance Religion and the Sioux Outbreak of 1890*, originally published as part 2 of the Fourteenth Annual Report of the Bureau of Ethnology by the Government Printing Office, Washington, D.C., in 1896, republished in a centennial edition with a brief but valuable introduction by Raymond J. DeMallie in a Bison Books edition by the University of Nebraska Press in 1991. For more information on Wovoka, or Jack Wilson, the Ghost Dance Prophet, see Michael Hittman, *Wovoka and the Ghost Dance*, expanded edition, edited by Don Lynch (Lincoln and London, University of Nebraska Press, 1997). Much has been written on shamanism and the North American trickster figure, of course, but Claude Lévi-Strauss, *Structural Anthropology*, trans. Claire Jacobson and Brooke Grunfest Schoepf (New York, Basic Books, 1963). Chapter 9, "The Sorcerer and His Magic," is especially illuminating. The most trenchant critic of the tendency to look at Native Americans as tragic victims rather than as ingenious and creative refashioners of the terms of their history is novelist and critic Gerald Vizenor. Readers willing to brave his neologisms and repetitive exposition will find his *Fugitive Poses* exceptionally stimulating and refreshing. Gerald Vizenor, *Fugitive Poses: Native American Indian Scenes of Absence and Presence* (Lincoln and London, University of Nebraska Press, 1998).

Chapter 2: Valentines

Richard B. Sewall's *The Life of Emily Dickinson* (1974; Cambridge, Mass., Harvard University Press, 1994) is an excellent biography that gives a very full picture of Dickinson's life and milieu. His discussions of her family life and her poetic development are sensitive and thoughtful. Readers interested in interpretations of individual Dickinson poems might do well to start with Helen Vendler's *Dickinson: Selected Poems and Commentaries* (Cambridge, Mass., and London, Belknap Press of Harvard University Press, 2010). The sheer physical presence of Dickinson's work, often written on scraps of paper and old envelopes in her unique hand, is interesting in itself and gives an intimate sense of her presence. See Amherst's digitized archive at https://acdc.amherst.edu/#explore/asc:17712/asc:17714.

Chapter 3: Cakewalk

Henry Louis Gates Jr., *The Signifying Monkey: A Theory of African-American Literary Criticism* (Oxford and New York, Oxford University Press, 1988). This important book grounds African American literary composition in the many-sided folklore of signifying—the creative response to a given text through satire, improvisation, and extension which Gates ultimately sees originating in the West African mythology of divination.

Marshall and Jean Stearns, *Jazz Dance: The Story of American Vernacular Dance* (1968; New York, Da Capo Press, 1994), is a comprehensive account of African American dance. Eric Lott, *Love and Theft: Blackface Minstrelsy and the American Working Class* (New York and Oxford, Oxford University Press, 1993)—lovely title!—is one of a number of excellent recent books to examine the social and psychological complexities of minstrelsy. Edward A. Berlin's *King of Ragtime: Scott Joplin and His Era* (New York and Oxford, Oxford University Press, 1994) and his *Ragtime: A Musical and Cultural History* (Berkeley, Los Angeles, London, University of California Press, 1980) are good places to start an investigation of ragtime music and its origins. Gunther Schuller, *Early Jazz: Its Roots and Musical Development* (New York and London, Oxford University Press, 1968), is essential for the student of jazz. Schuller is also important in reviving Joplin's opera *Treemonisha* as well as his orchestral scores through his work as a conductor. Listen to Scott Joplin, *Treemonisha* (Deutsche Grammophon 435709-2, 1976). The Joplin works conducted by Schuller and the New England Chamber Orchestra on *Scott Joplin: The Red Black Book* (Angel EMI CDC-7 47193 2, 1985) are especially zestful. There are, of course, many solo piano recordings of Joplin pieces, including a few re-recordings of Joplin's own piano roll performances.

Ann Charters, *Nobody: The Story of Bert Williams* (New York, Macmillan, 1970), is a solid biography with reproductions of songs sung by Bert Williams and George Walker. Clips of the unfortunately few films Bert Williams made are easily found on YouTube, while his recordings, with their subtlety and humor and (by contemporary standards) shocking racial caricature, are also available. See, for example, *Bert Williams: The Early Years, 1901–1909* (Archeophone Records, Pioneers series 5004, 2004). The most useful overview of African American culture remains Lawrence W. Levine's *Black Culture and Black Consciousness: Afro-American Folk Thought from Slavery to Freedom* (Oxford and New York, Oxford University Press, 2007).

Chapter 4: Monsters

Joseph Brent, *Charles Sanders Peirce: A Life*, revised and enlarged edition (Bloomington and Indianapolis, Indiana University Press, 1993, 1998), is an excellent account of Peirce and his work. Louis Menand, *Pragmatism: A Reader* (New York, Random House Vintage, 1997), has a representative selection from Peirce's papers on pragmatism, as well as those of his colleagues William James and Oliver Wendell Holmes Jr. The selection continues with later pragmatists such as John Dewey and with essays showing this philosophy's continuing influence. Peirce's writing on semeiotics is more difficult to come by in an inexpensive edition but a compilation of his important essays titled "Logic as Semiotic: The Theory of Signs" can be found in Justus Buchler, ed., *Philosophical Writing of Peirce* (1940; New York, Dover, 1955). Charles S. Peirce, *The Essential Writings*, ed. Edward C. Moore with a preface by Richard Robin (Amherst, New York, Prometheus Books, 1998), is exactly what it says. I have used R. W. Stallman, *Stephen Crane: A Biography* (New York, George Braziller, 1968), and to some extent Stanley Wertheim and Paul Sorrentino, *The Crane Log: A Documentary Life of Stephen Crane, 1871–1900* (New York, G. K. Hall / Simon & Schuster Macmillan, 1994), for information on Crane's life. Paul Sorrentino's recent biography of Crane, *Stephen Crane: A Life of Fire* (Cambridge, Mass., and London, Belknap Press of Harvard University Press, 2014), should also be consulted. And since this is a book on style, Frank Bergon, *Stephen Crane's Artistry* (New York and London, Columbia University Press, 1975), has taught me much and has much to teach.

Chapter 5: The Soul Shepherd

Robert D. Richardson, *William James: In the Maelstrom of American Modernism* (Boston and New York, Houghton Mifflin, 2006), is a serviceable recent biography, especially useful in showing James's role as a socially committed intellectual and in giving an account of his scientific and philosophic discoveries. Louis Menand, *The Metaphysical Club* (New York, Farrar, Straus and Giroux, 2001), gives an important view of William James and his circle of friends, including Charles S. Peirce and Oliver Wendell Holmes Jr., at an important point in his career, and of the philosophy of pragmatism and its ramifications for American life. James's own books are quite readable, written in a direct and often even conversational style. *The Varieties of Religious Experience* (New York, Random House Vintage paperback, 1990) is surely his most read, for its literary qualities and apt illustrations. But his *Essays in Radical Empiricism* is well worth examining for the nonspecialist as well as the historian and student of philosophy. Originally published in 1912, it is available in paperback: William James, *Essays in Radical Empiricism* (Lincoln and London, University of Nebraska Press, Bison Books, 1996).

Chapter 6: The Return of the Novelist

Leon Edel, *Henry James: A Life* (London, Flamingo (HarperCollins, 1985), is a polished, one-volume condensation of Edel's five-volume *The Life of Henry James*. For an intimate view of the elderly James and his method of composition, Theodora Bosanquet, *Henry James at Work*, edited and with notes and introduction by Lyall H. Powers (1924; Ann Arbor, University of Michigan Press, 2006), is excellent. Bosanquet was James's amanuensis at the close of his life, and this edition, which also includes excerpts from her diary and an account of her professional career, shows her to be an insightful critic and skillful writer. The critical literature on Henry James is of course vast, but John F. Sears's introduction to the Penguin edition of James's *The American*

Scene, the work I focus on in this chapter, is both readily available and excellent. Henry James, *The American Scene* (1907; New York, Penguin Books USA, 1994).

Chapter 7: An Innocent at Cedro

Joseph Dorfman, *Thorstein Veblen and His America* (New York, Viking Press, 1934), is a solid biography. John P. Diggins, *The Bard of Savagery: Thorstein Veblen and Modern Social Theory* (New York, Seabury Press, 1978), gives a better and more lively account of Veblen and his place in economic and social theory; while a good selection from Veblen's writings, with an excellent introduction by Max Lerner, can be found in *The Portable Veblen* (New York, Viking Press, 1948). For a warm and touching view of Veblen, recommended for readers wishing a sense of this strange and difficult person, see Robert L. Duffus, *The Innocents at Cedro: A Memoir of Thorstein Veblen and Some Others* (1944; Clifton, N.J., Augustus M. Kelley, 1972).

Chapter 8: The Rise of Abraham Cahan

Ronald Sanders, *The Downtown Jews: Portrait of an Immigrant Generation* (New York, Harper & Row, 1969), is in large part a biography of Abraham Cahan, but readers may also wish to consult Cahan's own autobiography, the first two volumes of which have been translated from the Yiddish and published as *The Education of Abraham Cahan*, trans. Leon Stein, Abraham P. Conan, and Lynn Davison (Philadelphia, Jewish Publication Society of America, 1969). Irving Howe, with the assistance of Kenneth Libo, *World of Our Fathers* (New York, Simon & Schuster Touchstone, 1976), is an indispensable book on the immigrant Jews of New York's Lower East Side, their theater, politics, art, and daily life. Readers can hear the voices of some of these immigrants in Isaac Metzker, ed., *A Bintel Brief: Sixty Years of Letters from the Lower East Side to the Jewish Daily Forward*, with a foreword and notes by Harry Golden, trans. Diana Shalet Levy (New York, Schocken Books, 1971).

Chapter 9: Beyond Syncopation

The best account of Jelly Roll Morton's place in jazz history and technical innovations is to be found in Gunther Schuller, *Early Jazz: Its Roots and Musical Development* (New York and London, Oxford University Press, 1968). Jelly Roll's story, drawn from tape-recorded interviews in Washington, D.C. in 1938, is found in Alan Lomax's *Mister Jelly Roll: The Fortunes of Jelly Roll Morton, New Orleans Creole and "Inventor of Jazz,"* updated with a new afterword by Lawrence Gushee (1950; Berkeley, Los Angeles, London, University of California Press, 2001). Phil Pastras, *Dead Man Blues: Jelly Roll Morton Way Out West* (Berkeley, Los Angeles, London, University of California Press; Chicago, Columbia College, Center for Black Music Research, 2001), gives valuable insights into Morton's psychology and his days in California. Rounder Records has issued the Lomax interviews for the Library of Congress in a wonderful eight-volume set, which includes Lomax's *Mister Jelly Roll* (Rounder 11661-1888-2 DG01 and 11661-1888-2 DG02, 2005). A one-disk compilation of highlights from the series is also available.

Gene Santoro, *Myself When I Am Real: The Life and Music of Charles Mingus* (New York and Oxford, Oxford University Press, 2000), is a comprehensive biography of Charles Mingus. Janet Coleman and Al Young, *Mingus/Mingus* (New York, Limelight Editions, 1994), give warm and intimate views of this difficult master. And of course Mingus's own *Beneath the Underdog: His World as Composed by Mingus*, ed. Nel King (1971; New York, Vintage Books, 1991), his fictionalized autobiography, is a powerful work on race and the music world in the United States. The side of Mingus's work I have emphasized, his outrageous satire of race and Cold War American culture, is best heard on his albums *Blues and Roots* (1960; Atlantic R2 75205, 1998) and *Mingus Oh Yeah* (1962; Atlantic 90667-2, 1987, 1988). To hear his inspired, improvisational approach in full cry before a live audience listen to *Mingus Antibes '60* (1976, 1985; Rhino Records, 1994).

Name Index

Note: Page references in *italics* refer to illustrations.